MAKING AN ATLANTIC WORLD

Making an Atlantic World

Circles, Paths, and Stories from the Colonial South

James Taylor Carson

The University of Tennessee Press / Knoxville

Copyright © 2007 by The University of Tennessee Press / Knoxville.
All Rights Reserved. Manufactured in the United States of America.
Cloth: First printing, 2007.
Paper: First printing, 2015.

Portions of this book previously appeared as "Sacred Circles and Dangerous People: Native American Cosmology and the French Settlement" in *French Colonial Louisiana and the Atlantic World*, edited by Bradley G. Bond. Reprinted by permission of Louisiana State University Press. Copyright 2005 by Louisiana State University Press.

Portions of this book previously appeared as "American Historians and Indians" in *The Historical Journal* 49 (2006): 1–13. Reprinted by permission of Cambridge University Press and the editors of *The Historical Journal*.

Portions of this book previously appeared as "When Is an Ocean Not an Ocean? Geographies of the Atlantic World" in *Southern Quarterly* 43, no. 4 (Summer 2006): 16–45. Copyright 2006 by The University of Southern Mississippi. Reproduced by permission.

Carson, James Taylor, 1968-
  Making an Atlantic world : circles, paths, and stories from the colonial South / James Taylor Carson. – 1st ed.
    p. cm.
    Includes bibliographical references and index.
    ISBN-13: 978-1-62190-061-0

1. Southern States–History–Colonial period, ca. 1600–1775. 2. Southern States–History–Colonial period, ca. 1600–1775–Historiography. 3.Southern States–Race relations. 4. Southern States–Race relations–Historiography.
5. Acculturation–Southern States–History. 6. Europeans–Southern States–History. 7. Colonists–Southern States–History. 8. Africans–Southern States–History. 9. Slaves–Southern States–History. 10. Indians of North America–Southern States–History. I. Title.

F212.C28 2007
305.800975'09032–dc22   2007013792

Dedicated to

James Russell Carson

And the memory of
Basil Taylor Bennett II

Contents

Acknowledgments   ix

Introduction   xi

Chapter 1. Founding Peoples   1

Chapter 2. Invasions   45

Chapter 3. Paths   77

Chapter 4. Creoles   99

Notes   123

Index   161

Acknowledgments

This book was born of my emigrant experience. I moved to Canada ten years ago and, in the process of studying for my citizenship test, came across the concept of "founding peoples," part of the Liberal government's mission to construct the Canadian state as a multicultural parliamentary democracy to which all citizens belonged. By hook and by crook, and in citizenship classes across the country, the concept of founding peoples has usurped a place formerly reserved for the august and, to me anyway, obscure "Fathers of Confederation." After reading my citizenship materials it became clear to me in ways I had often felt but had never quite been able to articulate that a concept like "founding peoples" had interesting critical potential, especially when set against the United States' notion of "founding fathers." The Canadian concept repositions the ways in which we are able to imagine the colonial past and the multicultural present, to see that nations are never made but are rather always in the making.

The citizenship test was easy. Writing this book was not. Namely because I have tried to traverse different disciplines, reconfigure the ways in which we think about time, space, and narrative, and redress a number of scholarly imbalances that characterize the realms of native, colonial, and African historiography. Rendering the founding peoples as commensurate peoples raised a number of authorial challenges as did the bedeviling question of maps. Odd as it may seem, there are no maps in this study of landscape and cosmology. Even though the cartography of the colonial South is vast and rich, to my mind the only way to get at the land was through stories, and so I have relied on narrative rather than illustrations. I might add that, since I was raised a Baptist, a fear of images comes naturally to me.

A number of institutions and individuals have helped me along the way. Funding from the Social Sciences and Humanities Research Council of Canada and the Chancellor's Research Award at Queen's University made possible a number of archival trips and the hiring of research assistants. I also owe a special debt of gratitude to Prof. Bernard Bailyn. When I attended the Atlantic World workshop at Harvard University in late summer 2002, Professor Bailyn asked the class during a discussion of Frank Tannenbaum's *Slave and Citizen* why scholars had forsaken the suggestive essay for the ponderous monograph. Taken by his query, I resolved to transform my seminar paper about imagining past landscapes into the essay you now hold in your hands. The seminar participants, particularly Christer Petley, David Preston, Jean Russo, and Bradford Wood, provided important support and citations. Other friends and colleagues—Ian Chambers, Bethany Chaney, Robbie Ethridge, Anne Godlewska, Elsbeth Heaman, Mary Rita Holland, Karen Landman, Greg O'Brien, Jamie Paxton, Bob Shenton, Norman Shields, and Uyilawa Usuanlele in particular—have offered, among other things, interesting challenges, useful sources, and beneficial editorial directions. Similarly, the anonymous referees shaped the manuscript in important ways, and I am grateful for the challenges they raised while my editor, Scot Danforth, showed great faith in the project. And last, thanks to Catherine Dhavernas for her grace and generosity.

Portions of this work have appeared previously and are reprinted here with the publishers' permission: "Sacred Circles and Dangerous People: Native American Cosmology and the French Settlement" in *French Colonial Louisiana and the Atlantic World*, edited by Bradley G. Bond, is reprinted by permission of Louisiana State University Press and copyright 2005 by Louisiana State University Press. "American Historians and Indians" in *The Historical Journal* 49 (2006): 1–13 is reprinted by permission of Cambridge University Press and the editors of *The Historical Journal*. "When Is an Ocean Not an Ocean? Geographies of the Atlantic World" in *Southern Quarterly* 43, no. 4 (Summer 2006): 16-45, is copyright 2006 by The University of Southern Mississippi and reproduced by permission.

The book is dedicated to my grandfathers, Basil Taylor "Zoo" Bennett and James Russell Carson, for it was they who taught me about the land and how to sucker tomatoes, scare squirrels, worm corn, gig frogs, pinch catalpa worms, divine water, gather hickory nuts, and feel at ease among the trees. Living so far north now I sure do miss those trees.

Introduction

He was the chief of the Taensas, or rather that was how a Capuchin father stationed in New Orleans described the man who had told him a story about the creation of the world. The man in question and the people on whose behalf he spoke, however, had long thought of themselves not so much as Taensas but as the real and true people, a kind of self-identification that bespoke a degree of self-importance and great pride of place in the land. What made them real and true was their central place in the greater scheme of things. In some ways their world appeared to be constituted of fundamental oppositions. The sun's rays, for example, brought warmth, life, and order to the sacred circle upon which it shone while earth's disruptive yet life-giving powers gestated in deep pools of water, welling to the surface to receive the sun's light to yield the maize, beans, and children that made their lives possible. The great birds of the sky wheeled in the air to keep at bay the powerful serpents that inhabited the underground pools. And water doused fire while fire put an end to the damp. It fell to the real and true people who inhabited this world to make their own living in-between birds and snakes, fire and water, and sun and earth.[1]

When he was young the so-called Taensa chief's elders took him down to the river to show him what made him real and true. Passing the clatter of waking families, smoldering fires, and well-swept courtyards, he and his family would have exited the town through the log palisade that set their homes off from the surrounding world's dangers. Any number of meandering trails would have led them through green fields of maize in summer, or brown stretches of broken stalks and stubble in the fall and winter, to the shore of the river that returned new life to their land every spring. When the adults splashed the young ones with earth's water and then held them up to dry in sun's warmth, they taught them that it took water and light to make them real and true.[2]

Other people who might have seen the same river and the same sun would not necessarily have seen the same landscape as the real and true people, and they would have told different stories about what happened between the sky and the earth and what it all meant. An *intendant* in New Orleans, for example, might have wondered how many more concessions could be backed up to the river while the *habitants* who toiled on the land knew that the stands of oak that dotted the low-lying countryside signaled the presence of fertile soil. A Bamara man who had escaped servitude on one of the *habitations* might have wondered about the snake that dwelled at the bottom of the river and murmured a hopeful prayer before he plunged in to escape his pursuers and their baying hounds. Each story would have made the place in a particular way, one that reflected the needs, practices, and beliefs of the particular person or people who made it. Such stories would have situated the place, what we too often take to be an objective physical setting, in reference to any number of historical trajectories. "Places," philosopher Edward S. Casey reminds us, "not only *are*, they *happen*."[3]

This book is an attempt to reconstruct the landscapes of a handful of places some would know as colonies—Virginia, South Carolina, Georgia, and Louisiana—and others would know as either the sacred circles they and their people inhabited or as places of death, destruction, and servitude; and to reconstruct the cosmologies that explained them through the recovery of stories like the one the so-called Taensa chief told the Capuchin in 1725. Past peoples' testimonies, recollections, and observations about land transformed collections of trees, rocks, soil, and water into narratives that rooted them in the particular places they inhabited, and it is in these narratives, these stories, where we find the first chapters of the autobiography of the South.[4] To be sure, documents drawn up by the invaders and colonial promoters attributed all sorts of wonderful properties to the land they either imagined or beheld. But the trees with astounding girths, the fields that needed no tilling, the fish that choked the rivers, and the fowl that eclipsed the sun all read today, and perhaps did then as well, like futile gestures to at once attract newcomers and deny the hard work of planting oneself in someone else's place, often with someone else's labor. The colonial contacts, confrontations, and accommodations that remade this place from a world dominated by fields of maize, imposing mounds, and red paths of war and white ones of peace into one transgressed by imperial enterprises, epidemic diseases, and enslaved laborers brought into the open the landscapes and the cosmologies that had sustained peoples' visions of land in places as far flung as the greenswards of medieval England, the gardens of al-Andalus, the market stalls of West Africa, and the hamlets of Coosa. At the points of first contact conversations arose as each of the colonial South's three founding peoples—the first people, the invading people, and the enslaved people—sought to adapt themselves to the presence of the others while all the time striving to maintain the integrity of their worlds as they imagined them. Their conversations offer us glimpses of the actions, decisions, and ideas that made the places and spaces of the colonial South part of a broader Atlantic world.

If the reconstruction of past landscapes from archived documents and cataloged artifacts teaches one thing, it is that undertaking such a task is difficult but important. Historians of the colonial Americas have begun to consider land as an object every bit as socially constructed as the people who inhabited it. William Cronon's striking interpretation of the landscape and ecology of colonial New England demonstrated the degree to which cultural constructions of landscape were as implicated as the people in the settlement of the region. Jean O'Brien's juxtaposition of New English and Natick notions of place and personhood underscored the invaders' rapaciousness and the first peoples' loss. Thomas Hatley's use of Cherokee color concepts, Matthew Dennis's reconstruction of Haudenosaunee landscapes of peace and power, Robbie Ethridge's reconstruction of Creek ecology, April Lee Hatfield's interest in the plural geographies of colonial Virginia, and Philip Arnold's foray into the hermeneutics of occupation that drove the Spanish conquest of the Valley of Mexico have all brought to life vivid worlds that a term like "land," when used to describe the object of settlement, effaces completely. Still, such works are exceptions to a general rule. All too often, geographers John Paul Jones and Wolfgang Natter have noted, historians relegate space "to an inert horizontality" which has the effect of substituting a seemingly neutral and altogether barren understanding of space for the multiple constructions that tied past people to past places and, in terms of the colonization of the South, enjoined each founding people in the construction of the other's world.[5]

To track the history of places involves treading a fine line between recognizing the land's raw materials—trees, rocks, rivers, and mountains—and acknowledging cultural constructions of such things in landscapes. Parking lots, subdivisions, and the fast-food sprawl that has enveloped so many of the South's towns and cities have all but obliterated the material forms of past landscapes. Streams that today run muddy with the run-off of commercial agriculture and suburban development once startled visitors with their sparkling clarity and healthful properties. Massive canebrakes once followed the banks of meandering streams and rivers to provide shelter and forage for bears and other animals as well as hiding places for people in peril. Overgrazing by hogs and cattle, as well as the invaders' deliberate clearing efforts, removed from the land what had once been its signal green standards.⁶ And, of course, land that was once possessed in common is now divided, bought, and sold as regularly as the seasons change. To compensate for such changes, any reconstruction of early landscapes leans on a reconstruction of the values that underpinned the landscapes. In other words, on cosmology. In the colonial South the cosmologies that came into contact in the sixteenth and seventeenth centuries afforded different readings of the land but, at the same time, made space for the existence of outsiders. The conjunctures that came from contact, however, occurred in particular places which had the double effect of unsettling the ground between cosmology and landscape and of dissolving the boundaries that had defined one people as real and true and another as Castilians, or long knives, or Negroes. By the eighteenth century, however, new cosmologies had arisen to enable the founding peoples to speak to one another in a shared vernacular of paths, places, and skin colors that each understood.

The study of human landscapes has moved well beyond the environmental determinism that characterized geographies of the nineteenth and early twentieth centuries as scholars turned their attention towards questions concerning the relationship between the universality of nature and the particularity of culture. While some have proposed a third way that places unique cultural constructions in dialogue with apparent universal material realities like "nature," other scholars have contended that culturally constructed landscapes do not hover like mirages above some kind of real nature.⁷ What was the Australian outback to the English and the Irish was to the Pintupi an enduring landscape that, like all life, had been born in the Dreaming. What was the Pacific Ocean to European navigators was, for the inhabitants of the island of Tanna, a road to other islands and nearby peoples. What agents of the colonial office in West Africa took to be trees were to other people the repositories of spirits, sacred charters to the land. And what we take today to be the Atlantic Ocean has been to other people in other times the salty seed of life, the river of the world, and the abode of the Leviathan.⁸ The past then did not play out in a natural landscape, the inert horizontality that Jones and Natter identified, wholly unconnected to the historical people and places that comprised it. Nature, in the end, was not the setting for the founding peoples' various struggles but rather the basis of the differences between them. "It is only through culture," anthropologist Bernard Cohn has suggested, "that we construct nature, not the other way around."⁹

But is culture the solution to the problem of nature? Based on any number of critical readings of academic disciplines, postcolonialists have concluded that the concept of culture has facilitated the rise of capitalist modes of production and modern nation states out of the miseries of colonization while at the same time it has obscured the complex contradictions of daily life. Other problems remain unresolved. How and why do cultures change? If cultures are always in the process of becoming, how can they ever be said to exist? And on what terms can they be compared?[10] Such problems are troubling, but, as anthropologist Robert Brightman has suggested, they may overstate the case. What is at stake in any history of contact, however, is an exploration of how, anthropologist Irene Silverblatt has argued, "contests over social selves, over potential ways of being human, lay at the heart of the colonial enterprise." To articulate the richness and complexity of how the founding peoples of the colonial South made the land that made them who they were involves recovering their understanding of how the world worked and where they fit within it. It requires reconstructing, as historical ethnogeography, their conceptions of place, landscape, and cosmology as well as their ecologies—the practices that enacted the existence of the world as they imagined and lived in it—and how those practices and the beliefs they sustained endured over time. And it demands an approach that foregoes the linear track of progress and embodies instead ways of storytelling that capture the elliptical and often overlapping contours of this multicultural past. The performance of the map by the real and true people when they went to water, for example, changed over time as did the landscape and the cosmology that explained it. Indeed, when placed in an historical context a ritual like going to water shifts from a specific practice that invoked a particular place to one of several segments in an ongoing dialogue with the world, a poetics of place and space, that responded to changes in the land. In the absence of pristine places and original acts, the poetics of place and space offer an entry point, for the first people at least, to the notion of living in-between and of being real and true.[11]

The real and true people never exercised complete control over either their surroundings or their persons, but their ability to create landscapes through practices that substantiated their beliefs, like going to water, and that contested the landscapes of others, like building a palisade around their town, afforded them a measure of power and agency in the construction of the world they inhabited and experienced. Outsiders had always pressed on their world and played an important part in its making. Colonization, however, introduced outsiders of a different magnitude to the places and spaces that the real and true people occupied. What made them distinct were their belief systems, their technologies, their forms of social organization, including slavery, and their possession of endemic diseases that, when landed in the Americas, cut wide swaths through the people who met them.[12]

To be sure, disparities in power marked relations between each of the founding peoples, but what was the nature of this power? Archaeologists like Tina L. Thurston and Timothy Earle have depicted power as the deployment of material resources to sustain unequal relationships predicated upon the imposition of a dominant group's will, a definition in keeping with the general theme of colonial historiography. In such formulations ideas are important to power but only in so far as they facilitate hegemony, induce foes to become allies, and forestall either competition over resources or resistance to those in power. In such moments those in power deploy force to preserve their power.[13] Land was one of the most important material resources in the contest of colonization, but to follow materialist notions of power too closely privileges an ostensibly objective reality—nature again—against the different cosmologies and landscapes that unspatialized histories—Natter and Jones again—obscure. As far as power goes, then, it would be a mistake to assess the collision of worlds that followed contact solely in terms of conquest and dominance over life and land. To do so would be to miss the dynamism of colonization and the various inflections of power that contact created. Indeed, power marks more than an ability to prevail in a contest; it signifies as well a person's or people's ability to establish and to contest meaning.[14]

Tracing meaning through the practices that sustained it offers a way around the totalizing tendencies of culture models and can unsettle the utility of the broad socio-cultural terms that tend to structure histories of colonial America. The basic division of people into categories like white, black, and Indian looms over the terrain of the past, pointing us towards the conflicts that emerged between people of different skin colors and statuses of freedom. But, at the same time, past and present interest in skin color precludes us from considering the first people, the invading people, and the enslaved people as, on some level, one people—a colonial people. Theda Perdue's recent deconstruction of the concept of mixed-bloodedness, for example, has shown how racial language casts anything that is neither purely European nor innately Indian as somehow partial and, by implication, incomplete, unnatural, and, therefore, marginal. Our inability to move beyond such racial terms to frame our understanding of past societies has had the unfortunate effect of coding colonial history as natural history in which it makes sense that "Indians" lost, "whites" prevailed, and "blacks" endured. History, though, is a moral discourse, not a natural one, and, in the case of colonization, the scholar's task is to recover past peoples' humanity and historicity from the oblivion to which a term like *Indian* or a concept like *wilderness* can consign them. The notion of oblivion probably overstates the power of European colonization, but as literary scholar George B. Handley has noted, it nonetheless alerts us to the risk of, as he saw it, "perceiving existing memories of conquest, enslavement, and colonization as naturally born from history itself, not as selected recollections that have emerged in the context of a struggle among competing powers of representation."[15]

Landscapes afford ideal sites for witnessing the engagements between competing powers of representation because, as artifacts of practice and thought, such places embody the historical and ecological consciousnesses that created them in the first place. "All history becomes clear," Édouard Glissant has written, "if the changes in the land's appearance are followed over time." Where the practices and the ideas that informed changes in the land can be recovered, they invariably overlap and contest one another, and while such overlappings can get lost in the binary assumptions to which terms like *black and white* or *frontier and metropole* give rise, they point nonetheless toward a conception of the past at odds with more linear and hierarchical forms of history.[16]

Historian and poet Edward Kamau Brathwaite began the interpretive quest for a different kind of American past when he set aside the black/white model of the history of Jamaica in the hopes of locating the historical roots of a new kind of identity, a creole one, that might look more to the possibilities of the future than to the perils of the past. "The process of creolization," he wrote " . . . is a way of seeing the society, not in terms of white and black, master and slave, in separate nuclear units, but as contributory parts of a whole."[17] The conditions under which such contacts, exchanges, and contributions occurred varied from place to place and from time to time, as did the degree to which first people, invaders, and enslaved people resisted one another, borrowed from one another, or simply found common ground between one another. The creole people who emerged from such contact, however, did so not necessarily as mixed-bloods, mulattos, or mustees, or even Euroamericans, Native Americans, or African Americans—characters who were half this and half that. Rather, they emerged from contact together as whole people who carried within them, albeit to differing degrees, the contact situations into which they had been born, in which they lived, and which they made and remade their places as part of the day-to-day business of life. And they projected their *créolité* onto the world around them in their thoughts and deeds first as founding peoples and then as emerging Southerners.

Historians of the colonial South have tended to recognize the cosmopolitan composition of colonial societies from Virginia to South Carolina to Florida to Louisiana. Peter Wood and Judith Carney, for example, have explored how South Carolina's rice economy reflected both African and

European antecedents that came together in the low country to create a uniquely Carolinian way of life and work. Daniel H. Usner Jr. has tracked the connections that people like the Taensas forged with invaders and enslaved people as all of the inhabitants of the lower Mississippi valley struggled to stay alive through the first half of the eighteenth century. The tensions that brought Virginia into a war of independence against the Crown, according to Woody Holton, related as much to Shawnee and Cherokee opposition to land speculation and plantation owners' fears of the people they owned as they did to Viscount Bolingbroke's diagnoses of corruption in the English constitution. Such recent work has given modern heft to the story that the so-called Taensa chief told the Capuchin, and to which I will return in due course, about the importance of the founding peoples' relationships to one another and to the constitution of colonial society, all of which highlights the desirability of transversal points of view for the region's broader historical interpretation.[18]

At present, however, the ways in which scholars tend either to explain or to represent the South as a place often reflect not a multiplicity of possible perspectives but rather particular political and historical assertions about its objective existence. In Timothy Silver's study of the environment in the colonial and early national South, for example, he described the region in the abstractions of science—geology, hydrology, zoology and botany—but in the process left unasked what a person from the Gold Coast or what a Cherokee might have thought about the land, the plants, and the animals. Resorting to scientific language to depict the South as a place may not seem overtly political, but when Silver argued that the climate of North America, not the people, provided colonists with maize, or that, in contrast to the invaders who thought far in advance, first people lived a more hand-to-mouth existence he moved from a seemingly neutral assumption about the inherent fertility of the land to a denial of the vital knowledge, practice, and belief that the first people had used for millennia to create the environment into which the invaders stumbled and, after looking around, lauded as a paradise on earth. Similar assumptions informed the maps that introduced volume 1 of William J. Cooper's and Thomas E. Terrill's *The American South: A History*. Their depictions of physical, geographical, and political features locate both enslaved people and first people in reference to their places within larger colonial and national spaces without addressing other competing perceptions of the same space.[19]

Such environmental, geological, and cartographical representations embody normative conventions about land, space, and place that, while not necessarily historical in the broadest sense, neither are they "inert horizontalities." They are loaded with assumptions and expectations. What such conceptual and cartographical conventions perpetuate is a deep-seated American belief that the land was empty and ripe for remaking as a New Jerusalem, a City on the Hill, or a Garden; or, taking two steps back, that the settlers had even come to a New World. Such sentiments were common in the colonial period and remain so today. The consideration of the land mass we know today as the Americas as a "New World," Walter Mignolo has suggested, "brings to the foreground the larger issue of the arrogance and ethnocentrism of observers for whom what is unknown does not exist," and influences our ability to imagine other possible pasts for the South.[20]

Historians have successfully revised longstanding notions of the colonial South as a place of conquest where civilization triumphed over savagery by laying bare the multiple roots of the region's various colonial societies. But the spaces that the people inhabited and imagined and the places they made for themselves still remain fairly unknown. To begin to piece together the multiple constructions of the colonial South as a particular place, we need to start at the beginning, to go back to the relationships between place and landscape that defined the founding peoples before contact and that, after first contact, provided the spatial context in which the invading people, first people, and the enslaved people made their own places.

Opening the construction of the colonial South to the competing notions of landscape that made it a real place on the ground is then the first task of this book. It is what a colleague of mine likes to refer to as the view from thirty thousand feet—a reconnaissance of how a region came into being out of contact between peoples from three distinct places and how through the processes of encounter, invasion, and colonization they came to see each other as inhabitants of a world they all shared. Such an approach should bring the multiple landscapes and cosmologies of the colonial South, and of the broader Atlantic world to which it belonged, to the forefront while at the same time exposing the concealed convergences of history that lie beneath the land. Indians, whites, and blacks were not the only people who made the South. There were others whom we can only begin to see once we figure out how to name them—the creoles.[21]

For the elders who had taken the so-called Taensa chief to water, their own sense of the world, their poetics of in-between, altered to accommodate the invaders and the enslaved, but their basic assumptions about their own pride of place in the land persisted well into the colonial period. Such persistence and change in practice and belief reflected the dynamic relationship between space and place, for neither the invading peoples nor the enslaved people remained fixed in the land. As they moved through space and exercised their own kinds of power, they too shaped the centrality of who the real and true people were as well as their struggle to live in-between. To remain in place as the real and true people when those around them insisted on calling them Cherokees, Creeks, Taensas, Chickasaws, savages, and Indians stood as one of their greatest challenges in the colonial era. This is what the chief explained in the story he told the Capuchin, but before turning to his tale we must situate his life and his lesson more broadly. Just as his story began with a time of creation, so too must this one.

Chapter 1

FOUNDING PEOPLES

Poetry is a nice place to start a journey toward the ever-receding horizons of the past that we so often turn from in silence.[1] "The stone had skidded arc'd and bloomed into islands," E. K. Brathwaite wrote more than thirty years ago. And where the stone touched the water only to resume its flight again he saw whole worlds rising to the surface: Cuba, Jamaica, Grenada, and Guadeloupe. Islands. Plantations. Masters. Slaves. Sugarcane. Blood. Each the spawn of the Atlantic world. It is easy and almost intuitive to hear the words *Cuba* or *Grenada* and to imagine them as places on a map: jagged little configurations of shades of brown and green and yellow that darken with the rising elevations they depict, surrounded by counterpoint shades of blue reaching out away from the pale Caribbean basin, past the continental shelf, and into the azure of the open Atlantic. But if places have objective knowable qualities they also have their deeply subjective sides, and these tend to be easy to forget. We often take geography to be an immutable fact when, in both its physical and cultural forms, it is in fact a bloom of sorts, a momentary product of life's dialogues, contests, and compromises.[2]

While this book focuses on telling the story of a place that people from three different continents created, sight of its broader connections to the Atlantic world should not be lost. The Atlantic world wound its way into many places. The ports of England bustled with cargoes from far away. Coffle trails snaked along the Senegal and Gambia Rivers to the sea. Men burrowed holes to seek the silver of Potosí. And the cowboys of Chota, Coweta, and Tallassee tended cattle in ways not dissimilar to the ways they had hunted deer once upon a time. Such places began in an ocean that afforded opportunities for the peoples of Europe, Africa, and what came to be called the Americas to become involved in one another's lives. Indeed, this book fits well into what historian David Armitage has defined as "cis-Atlantic history" which, he has written, "studies particular places as unique locations within an Atlantic world and seeks to define that uniqueness as the result of the interaction between local particularity and a wider web of connections." Armitage, however, names port towns and cities as the most likely sites for such investigations and consigns the first people to those foreign and exotic societies that marked the Atlantic world's peripheries. By the same token he is quite clear in assigning the English the primary place in defining the Atlantic world. Such an assertion rests on an answer to a very basic question that Armitage posed. "Is not an ocean," he asked, "a natural fact?"[3]

The answer, however, is not as straightforward as it would seem. To reply that an ocean is not a natural fact might beggar belief, but it is not. It is a cultural proposition that carries with it any number of assumptions and blind spots and, in effect, substitutes a seemingly natural understanding of space for the multiple cultural constructions that tied past people to past places.[4] To reconstruct the histories and geographies of the Atlantic world, we must set aside the inert horizontality of fact and confront the vastness of the cultural places and spaces that it contained. My intention is not to supplant the concept of the Atlantic world but to make space within it for alternate conceptions of the places that made the creation of this world possible.

But there is more to it than the simple recognition of past perceptions of landscape. J. G. A. Pocock, writing about British history several years ago, argued for the need to find ways to talk about plural or multicultural histories; to divest ourselves of the ethnocentrisms and nationalisms that entailed, as he put it, "a high degree of commitment to a single and uniting point of view." Any attempt to recover the variety of past peoples and their practices must therefore be implicated in the consideration of current debate about multiculturalism. Building on the work of creole theorists like Brathwaite and Glissant, Rex Nettleford has identified the Americas as a space uniquely situated in terms of its human past to challenge notions of exclusive authorship and to unsettle one culture's claim to epistemological pre-eminence over others.[5]

There is another pressing question that also bears some attention. Our knowledge of the Atlantic world's founding peoples is asymmetrical, not just in terms of the abundance or scarcity of sources we have to document their past lives but in the fundamental approaches scholars take to writing about them. For first people, the pre-contact record consists of excellent archaeological work as well as upstreaming from documents written in the early contact period, what some refer to as proto-history. The European side of the story, however, is richly documented. So rich, in fact, that one can speak of individuals and interior lives while with the first people we can offer only bland generalizations about cultural phases or periods that may have no correlation with life as the people knew it. For Africa the archaeological cupboard is relatively bare while protohistoric documents contain the same biases and blind spots as those that describe first contact in the Americas. Moreover, scholars tend to rely on upstreaming from ethnological and anthropological work in Africa that often looks no farther back than the mid-nineteenth century. With such incommensurate literatures and ways of knowing, bringing the three founding peoples together on the printed page is daunting because there is another asymmetry at play as well.

Great asymmetries of power prevailed in the contact and colonial period, and the question about sources is important here because it is the European record which allows us to see the past on an individual scale. By comparison first people and Africans tend to come across as cardboard characters who can seem as timeless as they are empty. I have adopted two deliberate strategies to circumvent the problem. The first is to situate the South's postcontact history in reference not to European history but rather to the millennia of human occupation that preceded the naming of America. My tendency, in later chapters, for example, to jump two centuries from Jamestown to Louisiana without losing my stride might strike some as odd or inappropriate, but two centuries are but an eye-blink in the region's human history. The second is to subject the Europeans, as best I can, to the limitations of the other two great continental literatures. To speak of French Catholics and English Protestants, for example, rather than of Christians would enable the Europeans to spring to life in a level of detail not possible for the other two founding peoples. Working to the finely grained detail that is possible with European sources enables the replication of such asymmetries of knowledge and power when they ought to be muted. Iniquities followed from contact, but they were not necessarily present at the moment of first contact. By adopting such narrative and methodological strategies, it is possible to restore to each of the founding peoples a rough sense of equivalence and possibility.[6]

There are important disagreements over how the first people came to inhabit the place we know today as North America. Archaeologists point to a history of migration from Siberia to North America. The people came on foot, the story goes, thousands of years ago in pursuit of large mammals, in a time that was cooler and drier than what we know today. So much of the oceans' water had frozen into glaciers at either pole that land emerged where the seas had receded, enabling people to go places and to inhabit sites that are today submerged. The exact dates of their arrival will never be known, and even between places as close to one another as the present-day north Georgia piedmont and the Florida panhandle estimates for their arrival can vary by a few thousand years. Whatever the precise date, people had made their way about twelve thousand years ago into what is known today as the Deep South. They entered the tidewater of Virginia somewhat later, perhaps eight thousand years ago. But to the descendents of these first people, their origins are clearer. In the beginning they came out of the ground, dried themselves in the sun, and made their place in the world. "We are among all our own relations," one Cherokee poet saw when she looked at the world around her, "which include the 'standing people'—the vast staunch company of trees who have seen generations of the 'walking people' come and go."[7]

Many things make it hard to know the first generations of the walking people. The stuff they left behind tends to consist of stone tools, knapped flint blades, and the piles of flakes that craftsmen produced wherever they sat down to turn rocks into tools and blades. Whatever they might have made of wood, bone, or plant fiber has crumbled to dust, corroded in acidic soils, or otherwise been lost. And who among us is able to ask the standing people for their side of the story? Extrapolating what the first walking people thought and felt from such remains or from oral traditions that might reach back to these early days is beyond difficult, perhaps even impossible. And other factors compound our inability to fathom the relationships between such objects, the people who made them, and the places where they were found.[8]

Archaeologists call the early walking people "Paleoindians." The prefix "Paleo" situates them in reference to a normative chronology that projects today's modernity backwards in time to our "primitive" forebears. The "Indian" side of the compound term is just as anachronistic. From his grave, wherever his bones may actually lie, Columbus has cast a long shadow. He was the one who set the walking peoples' past in reference to a particular imperial moment, and it was he who first fixed the reading of that past as a beginning of time, a moment of first contact with the people he called "Indios." That powerful and pernicious word has enabled scholars to isolate two continents' worth of people from an ancient tradition of stone tool work that reached around the globe and that is more accurately described as human rather than as Indian.[9]

The implications of "Indian" are compounded by our total inability to know what these people called themselves and the places they inhabited. When archaeologists write about sites like Clovis, the Macon plateau, Windover Pond, or Salts Cave they link the artifacts they have found, and the people who made them, to nearby towns or physiographic features. While such nomenclature affords a useful way to discuss sites and their relationships to each other, modern toponymic references place the walking people in a context so wholly removed from the ones in which they killed mammoths, kindled fires, or knapped blades that they seem invariably out of place in today's world even though their occupations reach back millennia. Locating their sites in reference to places like Georgia, Virginia, Florida, and the South only compounds the distortions of time and place through which we view them.

Such concerns are not idle criticisms. It is important to recognize the degree to which the colonial and national landscapes of the Americas have blotted out the landscapes that preceded them. According to anthropologist Joanne Rappaport, who has devoted her attention to historical memory in the Columbian Andes, scholarly conventions, like physiographic descriptions of Southern soils or terms like *Paleoindian*, can work "as tools for dominating Native Americans by denying them access to a knowledge of their own past."[10] Calling the so-called Paleoindians *first people* or *walking people* may not solve all of the problems, but it at least signals a start in the rehabilitation of the language scholars use to describe and interpret America's ancient past. At the very least such terms situate the people they describe either in a proper chronological or even moral context that acknowledges their temporal and ideological relationship to the region and its history. As well, each term contests ever so subtly the historical and geographical cants of conquest we have at hand to describe, to interpret, and to get to know them. Still, to revise anthropological and archaeological conventions is not to discard them entirely. To convey what the people might have been like, we do have to locate them on a modern map, and we do have to describe the ways they lived in ways that make sense to us. If such terms distort the picture, perhaps reminding ourselves we are concerned with first people or walking people rather than Paleoindians or Archaic Indians and that we are looking for how they saw the world is enough to begin to even things out.

The places the walking people made were drier and cooler than today. While they probably collected any number of grains, berries, grasses, and nuts, clearly they depended on hunting, killing, and processing the bodies of mammoths, sloths, camels, horses, and, to us today, more familiar animals like deer, turkeys, and opossums. The herds of the great mammals needed water, so the first people tended to gather around watering holes. But they moved around either to pursue the herds or to take advantage of seasonal opportunities at other places. River floodplains and coasts provided habitats for the fish, shellfish, and waterfowl they harvested. And while they packed their gear to carry to the next destination, they left behind large piles of shells and bones that, over decades, centuries, and then millennia, whitened in the sun and told their children and their children's children that these were good places to live. Camps in the uplands put them in forests where hardwoods replaced softwoods as the climate warmed, the glaciers melted, and the seas rose. Acorns and other nuts offered a fall bounty for them and the animals they hunted, and the winds and rains of time as well as upheavals in the earth's crust revealed deposits of quartz, chert, and other minerals that they preferred for the manufacture of tools and ornaments.[11]

The warming climate and the efficacy of flint blades hafted to stout hardwood shafts worked together to drive into extinction the large mammals the first people had hunted. Living in groups of perhaps fifty the first people began to turn a closer eye to their local environments to exploit more intensely the plants and animals they could find at hand. Innovations followed their change of focus. Where earlier stone points were lanceolate in shape, tool-makers began to fashion spear points with stems that made them easier to haft to shafts and more sturdy in the kill. While they still frequented watering holes, they now pursued deer, bears, turkeys, and other creatures in the country.[12]

In 1982 a backhoe operator in present-day Brevard County, Florida, turned up human bones along with the sod he was excavating from a pond. What he and his neighbors called Windover Pond had perhaps eight thousand years before been a site of great and somber importance to some first people. For about one thousand years, first people wrapped their dead in cloth made from plant fibers, sank them into the shallow pond, and staked the cloth to the pond's bottom to ensure their loved ones stayed submerged. But no ancient stake could hold against the metal teeth of a Caterpillar. Clearly such ponds were crucial sites for hunting and living. But, in light of later beliefs about origins in mother earth, about the life-giving powers of water, and about the bodies of the dead setting claims to the land for the present and future, it is possible that the first people who had left their dead at the bottom of the pond carried in their heads a belief system that would become more readily apparent in pottery motifs, ornamental designs, and public architectures in later millennia as their descendants learned to temper, to coil, and to fire clay; to hammer cold copper, and to heap the earth in the form of great mounds.[13]

Over a period of several thousand years, people continued to follow the seasonal round of moving from shore camps to upland camps, but, over time, as they watched, thought, and talked, they figured out how to train the plants they gathered to grow near their camps. In developments wholly indigenous to the region, first people, most likely the women, began to save and plant the seeds of squashes, gourds, and sunflowers and to reap harvests that could feed more children than their grandparents would have dared.[14] Such developments may have enabled a group of people in present-day northeastern Louisiana, the inhabitants of a site called Poverty Point, to build the region's first large mound center. They situated their mounds and homes in reference to relationships between the sun, the earth, and the horizon that had probably preoccupied the first people for ages. Six concentric sets of octagonal ridges encircled the village center, and aisles radiated out through the ridges. From the sky it looked like the sun had dropped a pebble in a pond or a spider had woven a great web. A giant mound in the shape of a bird dominated the near skyline, seventy-five feet above the alluvial plain on which the settlement sat. The mounds and layout of the village suggest the broad outlines of a story that posited an opposition of sky and earth and that found expression in the ceremonial and burial mounds that placed the deceased in the earth while bringing the living closer to the sun. Trade tied the site's occupants to other people far and near. Blades and tools of local material were used along with ones made of flints and stones that originated in present-day Tennessee, Illinois, and Georgia. Such social connections attested to the skill of early merchants and to the people's power, making Poverty Point somewhat anomalous in a landscape dominated by small groups of people who spent their lives hunting, collecting, and, with eyes fixed on their neighbors or with ears open to stories from afar, gardening.[15]

Early horticulture fed larger populations. Men began to manage greater expanses of forest to maximize the hardwoods' production of mast, and at various points across the region people sank their hands in the earth, mixed it with water, clay, sand, and shell, and began to fashion pots for cooking and for storage. The pots also afforded surfaces on which they could write their own stories.[16] People still shifted around the landscape, leaving great mounds of sun-bleached shells on the coasts and by the shores of rivers and dumping cracked bones and broken nutshells in the garbage pits that pocked the clearings of their upland camps. But with an increasing reliance on horticulture, villages along the ridges that divided the hardwood forests from the piedmont and river plains grew larger and more populous.[17] For some of these societies, plant food may have accounted for three-quarters of their diet, with the bulk of that coming from the garden crops that their ancestors had first tamed. In other places, such as present-day Florida, riverine or coastal resources proved so plentiful that people may have had neither the interest nor the need for planting gardens.[18]

Outside influences were equally important in enabling the broad transformation of these societies from hunters and collectors to hunters, collectors, and gardeners. Some innovations, the bow and the arrow for example, had an immediate impact on food collection. Through contact with people in the west who made small-stemmed arrow points and people to the north who preferred triangular points, tool-makers from the Tombigbee River Valley to the Georgia uplands began affixing smaller triangular points to the arrows they had learned how to make. The day of the heavy thrusting spear had drawn to a close. Stone blanks for crafting arrowheads on location left the quarries of the mountains and moved down the Potomac River in exchange for the pottery, foodstuffs, or prestigious shell goods that the inhabitants of the Chesapeake sent in return.[19]

The trade in shells, pottery, and foodstuffs for flint blanks or arrowheads was but one small part of broader trade networks that tied villages to people across the continent, but the ties were particularly close to a group of people to the north who lived along what we call the Ohio River Valley. The Hopewellians, as we know them today, built large mounds and developed a complex of ideas and artifacts that had broad appeal. In exchange for marine and freshwater shells and perhaps exotic minerals, the northerners sent southward bundles of mica disks, copper earspools, copper armbands, stone pipes, and similar items crafted from cold-hammered meteoric iron. The impact of such goods was profound. Local leaders who left this world took such items with them to the next stage of their lives, and local craftspeople took inspiration from the exotic items and began to fashion local versions. At the Kolomoki site in Georgia, artisans hammered local copper into sheets that they embossed with snake and bird designs that echoed those from the north, and they knapped flint blades like those obtained from the moundbuilders as well. In Florida, people molded the same clay that made their pots into figurines of naked, barebreasted women, which they then placed in fires for a final finish.[20] The earth that had been a woman in their stories had found her way into their hands and homes. Clay, water, women, and fire offer suggestive clues as to how these people might have understood their world. Women, of course, gave birth, and their fabrication of pots from clay and water, products from under the earth, point to symbolic links between women, the earth, and life.

Water, clay, and fire anchored later generations' universe too, the edges of which expanded at a speed far slower than light. Across present-day Georgia and neighboring portions of Florida, South Carolina, North Carolina, Tennessee, and Alabama, groups of people began manufacturing a pottery that archaeologists call Swift Creek. The pottery provides one of several windows into the imagined spaces of the walking people's world. We may debate whether or not the etchings on the pots constitute writing for they are today almost illegible, but not because of blurred lines or blotted strokes. Swift Creek potters carved intricate designs on wooden paddles that they then used to imprint the outside surfaces of their pottery, and we simply do not know the depths to which they valued the images and associated ideas that they inscribed on their pots. The curving lines of their designs traced a number of stylized images that suggest a particular kind of cosmology. Many designs depict plants and animals typical to the forests and prairies that the people inhabited—flowers, snakes, owls, buzzards, falcons, frogs, and the mosquitoes that must have annoyed them beyond belief. But occasionally someone carved a paddle that mixed a coiled serpent with the crested head of a bird.[21]

Other designs provide an interpretive context in which to read the animals. Potters, for example, often set their serpent designs in counterclockwise spirals representing perhaps water and a direction away from the sun that moved in a clockwise direction through the sky. The placement of bird figures in spirals, perhaps figurative winds, that turned clockwise bolsters the notion that somehow snakes and the earth and birds and the sky constituted the endpoints of a complicated continuum of beliefs about place and space and where the people located themselves. Other paddles marked the pots with crosses signaling the four cardinal directions of the sky and disks surrounded by concentric circles that might have drawn the sun and its radiant fire on to the pots women used to boil water, cook stews, and store berries or acorns. Sun, sky, and birds and their counterweights water, earth, and serpents operated in a world framed by the four directions.[22]

Swift Creek people swapped their pots widely, and the same designs imprinted by the same paddles appear across their sites. The people, like their forebears, tended to locate their major villages in particular places, typically ridges that overlooked creeks or rivers. Ideally, the sites would be positioned between upland hardwood forests where deer lived and nuts were plentiful and lowland plains where periodic flooding and fertile alluvial soils could nourish their gardens. In the transition from upland to lowland, shoals would have formed in the rivers and creeks to provide beds for freshwater mussels, pregnant smallmouth bass, and fiercely territorial bream. In the Oconee River Valley, the Little River site is perched on a ridge overlooking a creek, and the Lingerlonger site too is poised high on a ridge within eyesight of a bend in the river. The Swift Creek site, where archaeologists found the first examples of the pottery, sits by the Ocmulgee River while the nearby Hartford site overlooks an ancient ford. Such sites and other related ones are also close to trails noted in the historic period and that probably had been in use for centuries, if not millennia. The Hartford site, for example, sits on what the invading people called the Uchee trail while the McKeithen site in northern Florida, which was occupied after the Swift Creek period had passed, sat at a crossroads of trails running to the four directions. While the ridge locations maximized access to forest and river resources, the trails tied such communities into networks that reached far and wide.[23]

Trade in pottery, shells, copper and iron ornaments, and various kinds of stones and blades bound people together across the region and expressed in various ways their needs, wants, and beliefs. But it was the mounds they built, perhaps even as tribute to the sky and the earth, that established them as peoples against their neighbors. The mounds transformed villages or clusters of villages into the centers of whole universes. They brought into play the cosmic forces that covered forest floors with acorns, that filled gardens with the drooping heads of sunflowers and the sticky seed clusters and green leaves of chenopodium, and that transformed mounds of discarded seashells into monuments of human effort. Full bellies kept the first people going through the day-to-day routines of home life, through the seasonal rounds of hunting, collecting, and gardening, and through the cycles of birth, growth, and death. But to make such practices and processes meaningful, they, like their ancestors, turned to the earth and to the sky to give themselves meaning, hope, power, and purpose.

What we know today as northern Florida and the Chattahoochee River Valley of Georgia was, in the excited words of one archaeologist, a "hot spot" of mound building activity.[24] The mounds that rose across the woodland landscape served a number of purposes. They provided sites where local and long-distance relationships could be celebrated. Like the Hopewellians to the north who had inspired the mound builders, hunters and gardeners brought deer haunches, baskets of nuts, acorns, and sunflower seeds, and other items to the top of the mounds for their transformation into human food. The cooks, probably women, dug shallow pits and kindled fires into which they placed pots of water. To boil the water they placed heated stones inside of the pots and then added the ingredients for soups and stews. Outsiders and insiders met on the mounds' flat tops to eat, for meals provided a welcome while also binding the parties together in relationships of mutual dependency. When guests were fed they were obliged to reciprocate and may have offered copper ear spools or intricately stamped pottery made by artisans of great renown in return for the welcome they had received.[25]

Mounds drew local people together as well. In addition to feasts atop the platform mounds, dome-shaped burial mounds offered resting places for important individuals. The cluster of mounds known today as Kolomaki, for example, served as a ritual center for villages at either end of the Chattahoochee River Valley. The mounds framed the sky and the sun's path from east to west, and workers covered them in layers of red clay, the color of the earth, and white clay, the color of the sky, to bring the cosmos together in a monument built by the people's collective energy and dedication. Between the mounds stretched a wide plaza that afforded places to gather for feasts as well as funerals. Twelve mounds in West Tennessee, known as the Pinson site, were, in their time, the largest such ceremonial center in the region. They attracted rural folk from all around, who came to celebrate, to mourn, and to bury their dead with goods that denoted their importance—copper ear spools or necklaces of freshwater pearls. To accentuate the power of the deceased and the power of their land, the Pinson mound builders positioned their largest ceremonial mound adjacent to the bluff that overlooked a branch of the Forked Deer River. Anyone approaching the site by canoe would have looked up to see the mound towering over the shore and, in its reflection in the water, it would also appeared to have plunged deep into the earth, leaving those on the water's surface exactly in-between. The great pyramid's four corners invoked the bounds of the world while nearby sat another mound formed in the shape of a bird, a creature of the sky that, in conjunction with the earth of the other mounds, brought all of the forces of the cosmos to bear on this one place.[26]

The Weeden Island people of northern Florida, whose pottery supplanted that of the Swift Creek people between A.D. 200 and 900, built mounds too. At the McKeithen site mourners moved from one platform mound where bodies were dismembered and cleaned for burial and, later, exhumed for removal to another mound for interment in, first, a charnel house and, second and last, in the mound itself. The movement of the dead and the living from one mound to the next across and around the public plaza established a sacred charter to the land they inhabited and mimicked the clockwise passage of the westering sun overhead. The mounds contained generations of dead and offered a blunt reminder of the cycle of life within which they all lived. At the same time, though, death unsettled the certainties of life and identity, so the people covered the ground where the bodies had been prepared with white sand to cleanse the area of the taint of death, and they daubed the bones of their kinfolk with red ochre to prepare them for their return to the earth whence they had come. The passage from life to death invoked a betweenness that was inherently unstable and dangerous. Fires atop the mounds heated pots that bore four animal heads, one for each of the cardinal directions. But rather than shaping falcons, deer, or snakes, animals that belonged to clean and proper categories, the potters formed the heads of transitional and improper animals, dogs that lived on the offal of human habitations, and vultures, birds of the sky that gorged themselves on the dead of the earth. Mourners who drank the ceremonial black drink took it from a spout formed by one vulture's beak in such quantities that they vomited to cleanse themselves of any impurities they may have ingested and to restore to them the balance that people needed to move properly between the sky and the earth.[27]

Societies such as those that gathered at the Pinson or Kolomoki or McKeithen mounds expanded and contracted over time owing to unclear fluctuations in trade and the food supply and the vagaries of political and social life. What is clear, however, is that new kinds of societies emerged out of the growing populations of this woodland world that were qualitatively different from anyone who had come before. The new people drew upon indigenous political models such as those crafted by the Coles Creekers, the Hopewellians, the Swift Creekers, and Weeden Islanders, but the real impetus for their new social formations came from the mound builders and maize growers of Cahokia, a site near present-day St. Louis, Missouri. Maize horticulture, along with the knowledge and organizational practices such cultivation required and enabled, enabled leaders to fashion polities that were hierarchical instead of egalitarian, that relied more on horticulture than hunting and collecting, that required communal pools of labor and storage, and that built even larger and more elaborate mound centers. And the first steps these people took was to move down from the ridge tops and transitional zones that had been home to the first people for millennia into the fertile bottomlands where the region's rivers deposited the soil and nutrients required by maize, the hungriest of plants.[28]

Archaeologists call the new people Mississippians. They typically relied on fields of beans and maize for sustenance and, like their forebears, constructed large ceremonial plazas, mounds, and defensive works. But where the earlier places consisted primarily of small platform mounds and rounded burial mounds, Mississippians built larger ones that recognized particular chiefly or priestly lineages rather than kin groups as a whole. Power remained clustered around access to and control of exotic goods and foodstuffs, but Mississippian icons like circles and crosses and forked eyes joined images of birds, snakes, dogs, and panthers while copper, shell, and clay remained the prized media. What really set the Mississippian societies apart was their size relative to earlier groups. Commoners tended to cluster in small hamlets along the waterways, some of which may have been large enough to warrant the construction of council houses to organize their affairs. But the trails and rivers that cross-hatched the countryside tied them all into networks of space and power that emanated from the great mounds that positioned chiefs and priests over them and in-between the dark of the earth and the light of the sun.[29.]

Political, social, and economic relationships within and between chiefdoms created particular landscapes. Warfare between polities in what is known today as the Tombigbee River Basin, for example, had the effect of creating buffer zones devoid of human habitation between the different chiefdoms. Such zones may have constituted landscapes of wildness and impermanence where hunters and warriors vied to extend the immanent power of the mounds they served beyond the pales that guarded their respective homes. In the present-day lower Mississippi Valley, archaeologists have tracked the movement of boundaries and the shifting nature of power and landscape as the small chiefdoms of the ninth and tenth centuries gave way to larger chiefdoms that possessed both the labor and the coordination to erect defensive works. By the twelfth century fortified towns had spread across the Mississippian world. What archaeologists call hegemonic warfare, in contrast to earlier modes of raiding, enabled large chiefdoms to mobilize perhaps thousands of warriors for concerted attacks on fortified centers. In some respects the rise of hegemonic warfare suggests greater competition for land, people, and places, but at the same time the landscapes of war created a larger space that bound victims and victimizers, and the discrete places they inhabited, to one another. Such social and political connections rooted Mississippians' senses of peoplehood in the monumental structures that endowed their land and their societies with power.[30]

If access to prestige goods or fertile land stood as an important imperative for war, their acquisition shaped internal lines of power and place too. Bones disinterred from the Lake Jackson site in the present-day Florida panhandle, for example, show that the descendants of the Weeden Island people continued to associate power with access to prestige goods, especially those gotten through long-distance trade. Repoussé copper plates, stone and copper axes, pearls, shell beads, and shell gorgets comprised a portion of the goods that chiefs and priests acquired from sites as far away as present-day northern Georgia and eastern Tennessee and beyond in exchange for their own shell and pearl beads, shark teeth, and bundles of ceremonial plants. Exchanges of such goods enabled far-flung leaders to obtain rare items with which they denoted their authority and deployed their power, and the landscape of peace that trade created counterbalanced that of war, giving the Mississippian world a cosmological dynamism that wrote a horizontal plane of human relationships across the vertical axis that linked the sky to the earth. One of the most conspicuous symbols Mississippian leaders used to express their power was an image of an equilateral cross enclosed in a circle that artisans often inscribed on shell ornaments and pottery vessels. The arms of the cross marked the four positions of the sun during the passage of each day, and the circle set off the orderly place of the cross from the disorderly space of the outside world. The two arms that also divided the top half of the circle, the upperworld of the sun, fire, and birds, from the bottom half, the earth that was home to water and serpents, marked the space where the real and true people struggled to live in-between.[31]

Where mounds closed the distance between the sun and the earth, so too did clear paths of peace and broken paths of war bind the ceremonial centers that dotted the region. Most of the centers shared an architecture and site design that found expression through four basic features: ceremonial and burial mounds, public plazas, defensive works, and the passageways that tied all three together as places and that linked these places to the spaces of the outside world.[32] On the banks of the Black Warrior River stand the remains of one of the largest Mississippian sites, Moundville, where one large central mound and fifteen more modest ones surrounded a large central plaza that today is still open to the hot Alabama sun. The King site on the Coosa River in Georgia, one of the constituent towns of the Coosa chiefdom that flourished in the sixteenth century, occupied approximately two thousand acres of alluvial floodplain. A defensive perimeter comprising a ditch and a wooden palisade set off the domestic structures as well as the public plaza and ceremonial mounds from the surrounding fields and forests. A ditch also surrounded the two temple mounds on the Macon plateau that the descendents of the Swift Creek people had built. Travelers on the Ocmulgee River, however, would not have seen the ditch but rather the large primary temple mound soaring above the bluffs that fell to the river, its surface covered with glistening red clay. For perhaps two centuries people toiled to build the seven large mounds that made up the Lake Jackson site, six of which stood in pairs arranged along the path of the sun on either side of a rill of water. Mounds differentiated such places from other less specialized centers of population and held the immediate horizon. Their association with chiefs, priests, ceremonial buildings, and elite burials gave physical expression to the hierarchical lines of kinship and power that held Mississippian societies together between the fiery sun and the damp earth. Broad public plazas, however, gave the people a say in the delicate cosmological balance that the chiefs, priests, and mounds maintained. The grammar of the mounds and plazas and the gateways that joined them supported in this way social conversations that probably involved expressions of consensus as well as dissent over matters crucial to the people's interests. In the practice of such poetics, each polity came to see itself as the seat of the one true people.[33]

The paths and powers of the Mississippian world reached beyond the core group of chiefdoms that constituted the Mississippian South. In the St. Johns Valley of present-day northeast Florida, for example, the people who had once traded in Swift Creek pots, once coiled and stamped their own Weeden Island pottery, or once trafficked in Hopewellian grave goods adopted some Mississippian practices, but they retained many of their old ways too. Like their neighbors, they built platform mounds, valued copper plates inscribed with the unblinking eye of the sun, and sent smoke into the sky through the mouths of pipes carved in the images of birds. But they did not cultivate maize to the same extent, so they simply incorporated kernels into their centuries' old pattern of hunting deer and other mammals and collecting freshwater and saltwater shellfish, berries, nuts, roots, and seeds. Both the size and the reach of their societies remained small relative to their Mississippian neighbors to the north.[34]

Among the sounds, rivers, and estuaries of what is today eastern North Carolina and southeastern Virginia, maize fuelled the growth of palisaded villages that defended riverine soils. Within the palisades, households emerged as the organizational units of the village economy, tended family fields, and stored their surpluses for future use. At the same time, with the communal requirements to defend the fields of maize came the longhouses that sheltered ruling families, the communal granaries that bound the community's work to the leader's authority, and the burial mounds that held the collective memories of families whose ancient ancestors had made their living by hunting and collecting in small family groups. Between the fortified circles stood forestlands where hunters found their game, warriors found their enemies, and boys found their manhood. The land beyond, of course, offered other opportunities as well. Trade in chert and other minerals from the mountains remained important as was the newer traffic in beans, maize, and other horticultural goods. Villages held feasts to bring together prospective trading partners and allies and to share the food that bound them in a common social world.[35]

Such places were, by virtue of ties of trade, communication, and practice, set within a space that, on a very basic level, found its unity in the notion of being in-between, but we can also see another unity born of the need to cultivate, store, and process maize. Before accepting this unity as a function of either climate or nature, however, it must be remembered that people passed knowledge of maize from the Valley of Mexico into the valley of what is today the Mississippi River and, from there, to points east. To be sure maize diminished in importance the farther north one went, but from Moundville to Fort Jackson to Etowah to the Chesapeake tidewater, the walking people used it to build places predicated on social stratification, mastery of sacred power, and control of arable land. The organization of each society around maize, and the intercession of humans between the sky and the ground that made it sprout, imprinted life and landscape in numerous ways, ways that would in time become familiar and crucially important to the invaders who would come to settle on the shores of the walking people's land.[36]

Across the waters that surrounded the first people's world lived another people who also saw the cosmos in terms of circles and crosses, birds and snakes, and true and false people. As the seeds and the knowledge to grow wheat and other cereals moved out of the valleys of the Tigris and the Euphrates Rivers into southern and central Europe, people began to write their impressions of the world on the pottery they used and the fetishes they honored. Incised or painted crosses depicted the four cardinal points of the world, the passage of time, and the rhythms of life while black snakes crawled across the curved surfaces of their bowls and connoted the mysterious powers of life and water. Depictions of birds brought to life the sky world that, in conjunction with the waters of life, brought health and prosperity to the world of humans.[37] Babylonians looked beyond the Bitter Waters that surrounded their world to the quarters of the sun, the houses of the winds, and the ends of the earth. And when they looked to the sky their eyes followed a great staircase that had descended from the gods down to the earth they inhabited. Germanic craftsmen embossed circular sheets of gold to depict their own take on the cosmos while other societies projected vertical dimensions onto the sacred circle. From Mesopotamia to Scandinavia people imagined a great tree of life standing in the middle of the world with its roots sinking to the depths of the earth and its branches reaching toward the heavens. Trees, springs, and rivers crackled with life, and people propitiated them for health, food, aid, and advice. Here and there they carved the rocks that dotted their landscape with images of circles enclosing trees, and they heaped dirt and rocks into mounds that drew the earth and sky closer together and that returned the bodies of the dead to the earth.[38]

Greeks sat astride the great roads that carried the caravans, armies, embassies, and seeds that bound Europe and Asia into a broader world. An astronomer in Asia Minor, Thales of Miletus, pondered many of the same mysteries that had preoccupied the Babylonians, and he burrowed through ancient archives in search of explanations about how the world had come to be. What he learned has been lost to the ages owing to the destruction of manuscripts and the burning of libraries, but buried in a few surviving fragments that mention his pupil, Anaximander of Miletus, later generations of philosophers located in the teachings of Thales the first stirrings of something new, something outside of the circle that had expressed the perfection and divinity of their world for so long and the tree of life that united the sky and the earth. Anaximander proposed that the one-dimensional circle that appeared in Babylonian rock carvings and Germanic dials, when taken together with such structures as the cosmic staircase or the tree of life, may have in fact depicted the earth as a sphere. The cosmographers who followed Thales and Anaximander and who pondered their first findings remembered their names as a beginning for good or for bad.[39]

Aristotle derided Thales and Anaximander for allegedly holding fast to notions of a flat circular earth that somehow floated in a vast pool of water. The Pythagoreans, however, who had mapped onto the world around them the geometric perfection of the sphere they so admired, received no such abuse at the great philosopher's hand. Indeed, Aristotle revised their work to propose a working model of the earth and the cosmos in which a spherical heaven revolved around a spherical earth. The size of the earth, however, was infinitesimal in comparison to the surrounding heavens, according to his calculations, and not even that well known, from his perspective, in spite of its small size. Other continents, beyond the sight of the known world, he surmised, probably shared the watery surface of the earth.[40]

Aristotle described a perfectly balanced universe in which four basic elements gave substance and meaning to the physical world. Earth, air, fire, and water created a harmony of contrary properties as dry and moist, hot and cold, light and heavy, and straight and curved that, while always reducible to their constituent and permanent elements, nonetheless created the conditions on which the change and decay of the universe depended. Hippocratic physicians opened the cosmic story told in each body, parsed the combinations of elements, and found that men were hot because they possessed the fire that lit the seed of life while women were cool and watery, unpredictable and fecund. In the meeting of the two came life as well as death.[41] So long as fire, water, air, and earth mixed in equal portions, they offset decay and ensured the permanence of the earth and the heavens. Behind it all lay a divine plan predicated on the maintenance of balance between elements, humors, and people. The divinity went by many names—Zeus, Zen, the god of lightening, the son of time, the city god, the fruitful god, "him through whom we live." "Under his motionless and harmonious rule," Aristotle revealed, "the whole ordering of heaven and earth is administered, extending over all natural things through the seeds of life in each both to plants and to animals."[42] But even these names give only a partial accounting of Zeus' importance as the ultimate seat of power. The Orphic hymns to which Aristotle and his fellow citizens listened during their sacred services declared that the son of time was also the "breath of all," the sea, the sun, and the moon. "Zeus," the chorus sang, "is male and female of sex."[43] Neither man nor woman but both, Zeus embodied the contrary forces of the universe, made them one, and ensured the balance and order of the sky and of the earth from his high seat on Olympus.

The thinkers of Classical and Hellenistic Greece gave way to the leading lights of Rome in due time, but the Greeks' original works continued to set the parameters of cosmological and geographical thinking. Posidonius, a Syrian, opened an academy in Rhodos where he and his pupils revived and revised Aristotle's work on climatic zones. Just as with the form of the world, Aristotle had followed the early Pythagoreans who had divided the terrestrial globe into five bands according to temperature and habitability. Two barren frigid zones covered the extreme ends of the world, and one equally desolate torrid zone circled the earth at the equator. Between the northern and southern frigid zones and the torrid zone of the equator stretched temperate lands that were home to temperate people like the Greeks and Romans.[44] Pliny the Elder, who was born in Roman Gaul in A.D. 23, too saw the world as a perfect sphere divided in climatic zones, and he conceived of the vault of heaven as a god that, like Zeus, was "eternal, without bounds, neither created, nor subject, at any time, to destruction." The four elements remained the basis of the material world, and their attributes continued to shape the ideal world, but Pliny went farther in locating specific sources of divine power. The sun, for example, contained the life and mind of the universe and burned as the male "God of nature."[45] The female moon balanced the sun, for it was her light that dissolved water into a vapor that the sun's rays could in turn consume. The planet Venus sparked the generative power of the earth, its plants, and its animals while earth satisfied the wants of mortals. Galen further refined Aristotle's basic cosmology by carrying it into both anatomy and physiology. Building on the writings of the Hippocratic physicians of the mid-fifth to mid-third century B.C., he used anatomy and physiology to inquire into the purposefulness of nature's great design.[46]

Mortals differed because of the variability of heat, cold, dryness, and moisture across the globe. To account for such discrepancies, Pliny reiterated Aristotle's zonal categories, but he added to Aristotle's argument by incorporating the greater reach of Roman knowledge of distant lands and peoples. Aristotle's uninhabitable zones, in his hands, transformed into the populated margins of the known world. At either pole, Pliny wrote, stood a polar zone that was so cold, wet, and dark that the inhabitants had "white skins and long light hair." Around the center of the earth ran a torrid zone that was so hot, dry, and bright that its inhabitants suffered from scorched hair and burned skin under the unmediated rays of the sun. Between each pole and the torrid zone, however, lay temperate lands whose denizens reflected the balance of their land and climate. Neither too light nor too dark, they were just right. Perhaps it was these people Pliny had in mind when he ascribed to man the destiny to command all others.[47]

One of the features that made temperate people superior to others was agriculture, the domestication, command even, of plants and animals for the service of men. The farming complex that supported the Classical world had spread from the fertile crescent of Mesopotamia into Europe by way of present-day Greece and Bulgaria. The temperate environment of Europe proved conducive to the Near Eastern agricultural complex of farming and livestock raising, and by about 4000 B.C. had reached western Europe where a world of cleared forests, ploughed fields, and clustered villages spread across the land. The farmers of the Roman empire fused the towns and hamlets of the Mediterranean world into a cohesive political and economic world and inherited the crops, techniques, and landscapes that earlier generations had perfected. And when the Germanic nations overran the empire they too perpetuated millennia-old patterns of land use.[48]

The Muslim invaders from northern Africa who toppled the Visigothic kingdoms in Iberia in the early eighth century, however, revolutionized the landscape. The Umayyad dynasty planted itself in the fertile fields of the old Roman province of Baetica and renamed the place al-Andalus after the Vandals they had vanquished. They carried with them technology and knowledge that they had learned from their contact with India, and Moorish farmers cultivated hardier and more productive crops than their Roman and German counterparts had. While peasants rented communal fields from either the caliph or a landlord, more prosperous freeholders cultivated fruits and vegetables for town markets on plots held in severalty. Tuareg clans took to the mountains where they grazed sheep and cultivated olive orchards while indigenous Hispanics continued to raise the cereal crops typical of the Near East. Muslim land use, however, was far more intensive than the Hispano-Romans' extensive agriculture, and their irrigation technologies employed water wheels and canal designs that were more efficient than the gravity-driven Roman systems. Densely populated villages, clustered around fortified castles that defended the sources of water and towns, unseated the old Roman villas and Visigothic manors as the centers of economic and political power. As the Iberian economy took off, so too did the diet, the health, and the quality of life of the descendants of the original Iberians and the Mozarabs, the people who synthesized the ways of the conquerors with the old faith and ways of the Romans and made for themselves a new way of life.[49]

While the Roman empire crumbled, the dissemination of Classical knowledge did not stop. The Muslims who had founded al-Andalus had preserved Classical texts in the academies of Baghdad, Damascus, and Cordova. Galen's medical writings, for example, survived in Muslim archives until Constantine Africanus's eleventh-century translations in Latin began to filter into the Christian world. The Muslim cosmographer Edrisis, who had been born in Ceuta in 1099, accepted an appointment to the court of Prince Roger of Sicily, and he blended Arabic notions that the great world sea was landlocked with Aristotelian assertions about climatic zones. In the last half of the thirteenth century the Byzantine scholar Maximus Planudes reconstructed a number of ancient maps, and his efforts initiated a number of translations of Claudius Ptolemy from Arabic to Greek that ultimately reached European readers through Latin translations in the early fifteenth century. By 1477 Nicholas Germanus had published a definitive edition of Ptolemy that ran through several printings while Pliny the Elder's *Historiae naturalis* followed a similar course and ran through forty-six editions between 1450 and 1550. The Latin geographer Solinus, who had cribbed Pliny in the third century, found new audiences in fourteenth- and fifteenth-century Europe for his tales of black people who possessed neither mouths nor noses and dog-headed folk who lived at the edges of the world. The English Franciscan Bartholomew Anglicus published an encyclopedia sometime around the mid-thirteenth century that reaffirmed the veracity of Aristotle's elements and recalled Pliny's assertion that the dew of Venus nourished the earth while late-sixteenth-century London physicians popularized Galen's writings on bodies, humors, and temperments.[50]

As leading church figures confronted the most learned minds of the pre- and proto-Christian past, they sought to bring the corpus of Classical learning under the control of the divine spirit of the scriptures. In some respects, a Christian accommodation to Classical explanations about the movement of planets, cycles of the moon, blowing of the winds, and ebb and flow of the tides was not difficult. The problem lay in the ascription of greater meaning within a Christian universe. Isidore, Bishop of Seville in the early seventh century, played a pivotal role in braiding together Augustinian and Classical knowledge. In his book, *De natura rerum*, the bishop drew heavily on Latin sources like Pliny to adapt the Classical natural world to his theology. Winter thus became a season of tribulation not unlike the despair of the fall of man. Easter signaled rebirth and hope in salvation while the dry hot summer tested men's faith. The sun stood for Christ while the moon, stripped of the womanhood ascribed by Pliny, embodied the church that basked in the glory of Jesus' light. The Venerable Bede's *De ratione temporum*, published in 725, harmonized the calculation of the spring equinox so that, in accordance with the Nicene Creed, Christians could celebrate Easter together no matter where they lived. Out of his efforts came the Christian conviction that the winter solstice marked the darkness of the world at Christ's birth while the summer solstice signaled his glorious resurrection.[51]

On other points, clerics could not reconcile Classical knowledge with the teachings of the Bible. Cosmas Indicopleustés, for example, took Aristotle head on and argued that no such thing as ether held the world and the heavens together in one great whole. On the contrary, he argued, the Father had created the heavens and the earth as two distinct bodies that were no more unified than were men and their god. The Egyptians too, like Aristotle, believed that the sky was a sphere, he added, hoping to heap further ridicule on Aristotle's ideas. Nor did the antipodes of Aristotelian and Ptolemaic geography exist. How did Cosmas Indicopleustés know? The scriptures contained no mention of such a place. It was, he proclaimed, impossible to be a true Christian and believe in such fanciful notions.[52]

Outside of the walled monasteries and universities of Christian Europe, people across the continent still held beliefs that had survived the martyrdom of the saints. In the fields rolands—great trees or staffs that stood in memory of the great tree of life—brought the endpoints of the cosmos together and gave farmers a central point of reference around which their own life in-between could revolve. The contentiousness that greeted the Christian constructions of the world that threatened to displace older and more local forms of indigenous belief and knowledge made the landscape of Europe one that was perpetually in the making. The seasonal rhythms of sowing, reaping, and harvesting moved people in a common round of purpose and life, and they located models of their world in the stuff of daily life. A miller in Friuli in what we know today as Italy, for example, found a model for the creation of the cosmos in the curdling and fermentation of cottage cheese. In England rural folk carved figures into the wood frames of their doorways and fireplaces to guard against the fell spirits that threatened their health and livelihoods. Outside, they manipulated spiritual forces to bring rain, to moderate the temperature, and to increase the fertility of the soil, or they turned to their priests who took holy water and crucifixes out into the fields. The abbot of Bry St. Edmunds in England, for example, always kept on hand relics for conjuring rain and for preventing weeds from taking root. In 1543 a terrible thunderstorm that blew over Canterbury so frightened the folk that they ran to the church for holy water to sprinkle on their homes. On the continent in the early ninth century Bishop Agobard of Lyon debated with peasants who held that certain people could conjure hail, lightening, and storms and wreak havoc on the fields of rye and wheat that covered much of the Carolingian countryside. Against the storm-makers and other folk who offered spells and potions to fend them off, the bishop insisted that only the Father could control the weather. Eighth-century priests at the monastery of Gellone in France, however, adapted to local mores by holding masses for the ripening of new fruits. Generic Latin prayers that were not a part of the church's liturgy also bridged pre-Christian beliefs in the powers of the earth and medieval notions of nature as the Father's miracle. "Now deign with thy benediction," priests prayed, "to sanctify and bless these plants and other fruits."[53]

Nowhere was the confrontation between Christian and earlier beliefs about time, landscape, and place more clear than in the struggles and compromises that surrounded the landscape of the English holy calendar. Husbandmen became not just men who conjured life from Mother Earth but crusaders who transformed wilderness into gardens. When they pulled ploughs around fires on Plough Monday or wassailed apple trees on the Twelfth Day of Christmas to ensure their orchards' and their own fertility and long life, they grafted together two modes of power in an attempt to keep their old world intact while appropriating the powers and promises of the new.[54] Rogations, a procession that occurred in the three days before the Day of the Ascension, revealed a similar blending of older and newer forms of belief and propitiation. Congregants followed their curates in an elaborate procession around the parish boundaries and across the community's fields. Farmers in late tenth-century or early eleventh-century England relied upon the ceremonial march to cleanse their fields, and, in order to secure the Father's blessing, they removed four patches of sod and mixed together oil, honey, yeast, milk from each animal that grazed on the land, a piece of each type of tree that grew on the land with holy water and drizzled the medicine on the roots of the four patches of sod. After an elaborate offer of blessings and prayers, the curate then placed a crucifix in each of the four wounds torn into the earth, replaced the sod, said nine our-fathers, turned to the east, bowed nine times, said a prayer, and then walked clockwise three times around the patches of blessed ground. Then the attention shifted to the plough. Priests reached deeply into Anglo-Saxon notions of land and power and called out in the old tongue "erce, erce, erce" to ask both Mother Earth and the Holy Father for "tall shafts" and "bright crops." After the cutting of the first furrow, the ceremony closed with the declaration, "Whole may you be earth, mother of men."[55]

Within the landscapes and cosmologies of Western Europe that priests and their flocks invoked through both their words and deeds existed a social and economic system that placed the preponderance of power in the hands of landowners and that over time pushed farmers out of freeholder status into that of renters and serfs. By the time of the Norman Conquest, for example, farmers cultivated perhaps only half of present-day England and France. But while only a small portion of England, 15 percent, was woodland, forests covered anywhere from 40 to 80 percent of the French countryside, owing to the weakness of the commons tradition and the strength of manorial power that had grown out of the Merovingian and Carolingian dynasties. In England, however, the Normans transformed the Anglo-Saxon commons and wastes into a landscape more like that of France, or, indeed, like that of al-Andalus, where villages huddled for protection under castle walls. As populations grew, farmers extended their furlongs farther and farther to reclaim land lost to the Black Death so that, by the thirteenth century, the old manorial system began to unravel. In the end the manorial system was ubiquitous throughout Christian Europe as priests and landlords used tribute, custom, and law to tie peasants to their rule in something they believed was a natural order. Medieval Christian fathers also turned to Classical scholars to explain relations between and among people in reference to moral virtue and broader cosmological structures. According to Plato, for example, absolute truth and beauty could only be assayed through an exploration of all things that were partially true or partially good. The gradations of imperfection that supported the ideal and the absolute perfection of truth and beauty, the *scala naturae*, afforded Plato and other Classical philosophers a means by which to fix men relative to one another and to assess the logic of life. "Nature," the philosopher concluded, "does nothing without reason or in vain."[56]

St. Augustine resurrected the lost world of platonic philosophy in the early Middle Ages and fashioned Plato's scale into a Great Chain of Being, ordained by the Father and implicated in man's relationships with men and their world. The Father occupied the highest rank, followed by angels, then men, women, animals, plants and, lastly, the earth.[57] Cosmas Indicopleustès added that men could move up or down within their own ranks owing to their moral character, and later thinkers refined such ideas. The French theologian Pierre Abelard, for example, drew upon Aristotle to tackle the paradox of the Father's immanent sovereignty, the fallibility of man, and the existence of evil in the world that God had created. "All things," Abelard decided, "both good and bad, proceed from a most perfectly ordered plan, that they occur and are filtered to one another in such a way that they could not possibly occur more fittingly." Thomas Aquinas, one of several medieval thinkers to elaborate on the Great Chain, went farther to understand his society in reference to the chain and asserted that agricultural societies like those of Europe occupied the highest ranks of human civilization. In refining his typology, he further declared women to be imperfect men, and he and other Church Fathers undertook to instill among their flock the belief that, just as men ruled animals and men should rule women, their Holy Father ruled them through the divine Crowns of Europe. The ambiguity of all things being linked, of borders being blurred on the edges of categories, however, offset the clear-cut hierarchy that the chain evoked and belied a grander providential design in which evil no longer stood in opposition to the goodness of their god, but rather existed because of him. The Father, St. Augustine and Abelard agreed, had created evil to expose goodness, and the former belonged every bit as much as the latter in the Great Chain that reached from the earth's depths to the king's crown.[58]

Conquests, population movements, disease, and recovery all had a hand in transforming a medieval landscape in which neolithic crops had flourished within a medieval cosmology that looked ever inward. At a time when trade caravans carried news of Cathay and when Christians battled Muslims over the walled cities of the Holy Land, however, the Great Chain of Being provided the means whereby European Christians could recall the ancient antipodes and situate foreign folk in a broader cosmos. Again, Classical authors set the precedent. Pliny the Elder, for example, pieced together the portions of his *Historiae naturalis* on exotic people and monsters from Classical accounts reaching back to the early fifth century B.C. His stories of amazons, man eaters, dog-headed people, and so forth captured the medieval imagination while it pulled the far horizons into sharper focus. Solinus, who had relied heavily on Pliny, reported nations of monstrous people near Ethiopia and Arabia. The Blemmyes of Libya, he wrote, were born headless but could see and speak through the eyes and mouths in their chests. Alphonse de Saint Onge's *Cosmographie* (1544) recapitulated Solinus's recapitulation of Pliny. To the men with eyes and mouths in their chests he added a race of cyclopes on the margins of the known world. Cosmas Indicopleustés reported in the mid-sixth century that in the unknown lands on the other side of the world, the antipodes, the "antichtoniens" lived upside down and Bartholomew Anglicus repeated the story in his encyclopedia six centuries later. Al Hassan bin Muhammad al-Fazi, an Andalusian scribe Christians knew as Leo Africanus, extolled the beauty of cities like Kano and Timbuktu but deplored the libidinous black people who populated them.[59]

The selective copying and editing of Classical sources through the Middle Ages and into the early years of the Renaissance, like medieval uses of Classical cosmology and natural science, replicated forms but altered their meanings in fundamental ways. What Greek travel writers or, centuries later, Pliny took to be monstrous creatures that, while not normal in human terms were nonetheless a regular albeit perilous feature of the landscape, became in the hands of Christian scribes and scholars evidence of the curse of Cain. The monstrous races thus evolved from curiosities to evidence of the Fall. At the same time, the Fall enabled Europeans to conceive of these creatures as flawed if not necessarily evil. The Great Chain of Being lent divine imprimatur to such notions, but the problem of ambiguity that had bedeviled Augustine and Abelard lingered. Clearly Christians held a higher link in the Chain than non-Christians, but where to draw the line between men and monsters and how to connect the lines of men to the patrimony of Adam remained stubborn questions.[60]

Christian scholars used the Great Chain of Being as a spatial as well as a moral map by juxtaposing the Classical division of the world into three continents—Asia, Africa, and Europe—with a biblical genealogy that imputed to the founding inhabitants of each region certain qualities. Even Cosmas Indicopleustés brooked no disagreement with the basic structure of the Classical cosmology that underpinned his and his colleagues' Christian world. Noah's sons Shem, Ham, and Japhet, the argument went, had colonized separate continents. Shem traveled across the Caucasus Mountains where he sired the wild races of Asia while Japhet fathered the temperate people of Europe. Ham, though, who had been cursed for seeing his father naked, took his bane to Africa where he spawned a race of black people. Classical authors had rarely associated dark complexions with monsters, but Church fathers read blackness, darkness, and sinfulness into the skins that, in the words of Bartholomew Anglicus, had been "roasteth and toasteth" by the sun. The antipodal people whom Classical authors believed stood upside down owing to their placement on the opposite side of the globe became, in Christian hands, people whose pigment and morality were also inverted. Classical explanations for dark skin persisted—proximity to the sun ranked high in various explanations for the blue or black skins of Ethiopians—but popular editions of the adventures of Marco Polo and John Mandeville added poor diet, nakedness, and hard toil to the list of the curse's symptoms.[61]

The *mappaemundi* that monks used to illuminate manuscripts and that clerics hung in the apses of cathedrals instructed the faithful in the lessons to be learned from the true faith's history, the centrality of Christendom, and the marginality of exotic lands and their benighted inhabitants. Some illustrators, for example, borrowed directly from Aristotle and Ptolemy and depicted a medieval world divided into frigid, temperate, and torrid bands. Others projected the postdiluvian world in so-called T/O maps on which medieval scholars drew a circle, the "O," a remnant of the Babylonians' and Aristotle's perfect sphere, and placed a tau cross within the circle, the "T," that harkened back to the decorations on the first pots coiled by European potters as well as the puncture wounds Christ suffered when the Romans mounted him on the cross.[62]

The cross of the "T" divided the earth into the three known continents separated by three bodies of water, the Don and Nile Rivers and the Mediterranean Sea, while the ocean surrounded all three and provided the map with its perfect and self-contained circularity. When read through the genealogies of Shem, Japhet, and Ham, however, such maps established the earth as the Father's stage where the world's ultimate salvation would unfold; a world ready to be staked out, carved up, and delivered to the Father. "And the fear of you and the dread of you," the Book of Genesis told the faithful, "shall be upon every beast of the earth, and upon every fowl of the air, upon all that moveth upon the earth, and upon all the fishes of the sea; into your hand are they delivered." What the Church Fathers had done was to replace earlier models in which men and the earth were at the gods' mercy into the chain where men became as gods ruling the land as he ruled them from the heavens. In this way, those who possessed the power to control nature became civilized while those who were a part of nature became savages and barbarians. The promise of such domain, however, came at a steep price. "And surely your blood of your lives will I require," the Father covenanted, "at the hand of every beast will I require it, and at the hand of man; at the hand of every man's brother will I require the life of man."[63]

The Crusades against the Muslim rulers of the Holy Land put such notions of space in motion and sparked important transformations in the medieval view of the world. While abroad the nationalities of western and southern Europe projected a Christian identity, long-distance traveling and diplomacy, military strategy, and lines of supply required a kind of detailed geographical knowledge that the moralizing of the *mappaemundi* and the T/O maps could not provide. While the mapmakers of Christian Europe increasingly crafted exquisite depictions of their place at the navel of Christ's crucified body, sailors and navigators in Italy and

Catalonia crafted an entirely different set of maps born of a faith all their own in currents, winds, and promontories. Their charts afforded detailed topographic knowledge and place names along the Mediterranean coast, measured and scaled distances between waypoints, and charted various features that were necessary to the successful navigation of the Mediterranean, Black, and Red Seas. Portolan maps, after the Italian word *portolano*, "a collection of written sailing directions," improved upon Ptolemy's struggles with proper projection and scale and offered a less theological, more commercial vision of the Mediterranean world. As one sailor from Genoa boasted, portolan charts were "the true description of the world of the cosmographer . . . from which frivolous tales have been removed."[64]

The Italians gained the first foothold in the seaborne trade of the Mediterranean by ferrying Crusaders back and forth between Venice and the Levant and by shipping gold from the shores of north Africa to the Iberian and Italian Peninsulas. The money to be made from the Levantine and gold trades further inspired Italian city-states and principalities along with the kingdom of Portugal to circumvent the Red Sea traders and westering caravans that brought the spices, silks, and other fine goods of the Indies to the bazaars of Constantinople. To outflank the camel trains Muslim merchants ran between the gold and slave markets of Timbuktu and the ports of the Maghreb, Italian merchants began to post themselves along the roads that crossed the Sahara. With increased competition for trade, the portolan charts enabled the first stirrings of Europe's expansion over the waves of the ocean. Even the creators of the *mappaemundi* began to incorporate in their abstract cosmographical works the rhumb lines that tracked the points of the compass rose and that gave the portolan charts their distinctive web of acute and obtuse angles.[65]

The portolan charts that were so useful for navigating the inland seas, however, were useless in opening the uncharted waters of the open Atlantic that lay beyond the Pillars of Heracles. With King Jão I's conquest of the Moroccan fortress Ceuta on the shore of North Africa in 1415, however, the Portuguese Crown began to gaze toward the open seas for a way to circumvent the overland gold trade of the Maghreb that linked West Africa to the Mediterranean. The base at Ceuta emboldened them, for their possession of the town put them in direct contact with Tuareg traders working out of Fez and scattered outposts in the Moroccan interior where slaves from Bilad al-Sudan—"the land of the blacks"—were purchased for service in the homes and courts of Cairo, Baghdad, and Istanbul. In addition to knowledge of the money to be made in trading West African slaves as well as ivory and gold, Tuareg merchants gave the Portuguese a name for the place. Where Greeks and Romans had discussed the sunburned

Ethiops of Africa, the Portuguese set their sights on *Gineus*. Inspired by the Holy Father's promise to repay one converted soul one hundred times over, Jão's son Dom Henrique pushed his sailors past Madeira in 1414 to the Canary and Azores Islands, then to the Cape Verdé Islands in 1444. A little more than a decade after Dom Henrique's death, a Lisbon merchant named Fernão Gomes reached the land called Guinea and landed on a shore he named Costa da Mina where his crew sank a wooden cross into the sand.[66]

Other merchants pushed farther down the continent's coast, where they caught glimpses of the gold trade they so desperately wanted to enter. But while the traders they met were happy to receive cloth, firearms, and other goods, they preferred to take people, so in 1480 a small fleet of caravels sailed up a waterway that the Portuguese named Rio dos Escravos and took on board nearly four hundred captives that they then bartered for gold. The following year King Jão II ordered Diego de Azambuja to build a fort on the Costa da Mina so that his merchants could establish a more permanent foothold in the trade of humans and gold. Azambuja met with Karamansa, a man the Portuguese identified as the King of Guinea, to secure permission for construction to begin, but Karamansa declined the request. Azambuja proceeded anyway and ordered his men to unload the stones, mortar, and tools they had brought with them from Portugal. In clearing a site for the fort, the masons broke a large rock that blocked their way. Their hosts, however, held the rock in great esteem and took the masons' work as an affront to their hospitality. Only by offering gifts was Azambuja able to persuade Karamansa to change his mind and allow the construction of Fort São Jorge da Mina. After the completion of the fort, Jão II took to calling himself "Lord of Guinea" to make permanent in the *mappaemundi* of his mind his own claim to this place. Later commanders set stone rather than wooden crosses into the ground as they worked their way south, and by 1484 Diego Cam had planted three of them along the banks of the Kongo River in a land the people called "Zayre."[67]

The rock that Azambuja's mason shattered had seen it all from the beginning. Indeed, it may have once been a person when long ago another first people began clearing fields, felling trees, cultivating the thorny vines that caused yams to grow in the earth, birthing babies, and founding lineages that allowed them to carve out spheres of sociability amidst the dark and dangerous forests that surrounded them. At the same time, however, neither their gardens nor their homes separated them from the forest they had cleared and, in some sense, had left behind.[68] Some moved farther than others. Bantus, the "people," left the homeland of the yam and the palm, the clearings in the forest, and the civil life of the villages in what is today West Africa for the equatorial rain forests of present-day Cameroon, Gabon, and Congo. The skills to cultivate yams and to manufacture iron followed them to the northern edge of the southern grasslands. Clearing patches for yams made the land they traveled theirs, but it also provided ideal breeding ground for disease-bearing mosquitoes. Perhaps, like other people who also carried horticulture into the rain forests, their blood responded to the mosquito bites by forming sickle cells that inured them to the worst ravages of malaria. Or maybe their ancestral houses, owing to the bountiful crops they raised, bore more children than the forests' diseases could carry off. Their iron tools, weapons, and wealth certainly made them formidable foes for the indigenous people of the forest they met as they pushed their way southward over the course of three millennia. While they continued to clear new fields with each new year, they also set traps, planted beans and gourds alongside yams, and cut down trees to let the sun's light shine on their swidden fields. Other crops grown by the people they met worked their way into their repertoires. Banana trees, for example, offered better yields than yams while requiring less cleared land and providing a less hospitable habitat for mosquitoes. As the banana supplanted the yam in their stewpots, Bantu populations and houses grew and drew the indigenous hunters and collectors of the rain forests into trading relationships that abetted their expansion further south.[69]

Finding the places of this past African landscape is an altogether different endeavor from locating that of either the walking people or the Christians. Documentary sources written by European hands have sustained a long tradition of historical inquiry that has placed the burden of African history on explorers, traders, colonial administrations, and missionaries but left on the margins the people themselves. All of this, in historian Kenneth Onwuka Dike's words, has "tended to submerge the history of the indigenous peoples and to bestow undue prominence on the activities of the invaders."[70] Dike's Africanist critique, however, was as methodological as it was historiographical, for he attacked imperial historians' reliance on written documents and their reluctance to consider indigenous modes of historical thought and memory. In the Africanists' toolkit, oral histories, king lists, proverbs, and artifacts emerged alongside more conventional archival sources to enable the writing of a generation of histories that sought to respect and to speak to an essential African consciousness. Critics, however, have likened oral tradition and history to fetishes, superstitions that diverted the sober gaze of scholarship. But the facts, as some would have it, are hard to come by. Questions of derivation, plagiarism, and reliability plague almost all of the explorer narratives on which the history of Africa between the fifteenth and eighteenth centuries is based. And if the antiquity and veracity of oral tradition are indeed difficult to gauge, it is only so when measured against the imperial assumptions about linear time, verifiability, and objectivity that have informed the invaders' writings about Africa since Azambuja's time.[71]

What is left alongside patchy and, at times, dubious historical documents are the voices that have transmitted the lessons learned by the ancestors and that have distilled the murk of the past into the clarity of a clear-thinking present. Proverbs, for example, afford succinct repositories of community knowledge that are, some Yoruba say, "the horses of speech," for when communication is lost, only they can retrieve it.[72] From the mouths of the well educated, such short and sometimes sharp sayings deployed imagery and allusion to teach lessons learned from generations of past experience. People who used proverbs enjoined one another in artful and witty conversations that bespoke their high status. "To the Benin man," one such proverb related, "you speak in proverbs whereas to the rustic, explanation is made." Given the basic problems inherent in how African history and geography has been and is written, it is reasonable at this point to appeal to the ancestors whose wisdom has informed the present, to doff the rags of the peasant, and to try on for a while the hat of the Benin man.[73]

"It will take a European a long time," some have said, "to understand Benin language." And they were right, for if the complicated story of Portuguese colonization began at a rock, so too did the African experience with Europe begin with the death of a being, that rock, who had withstood wind, rain, and time to bear witness to the dim dawn of the people. So long as Europeans failed to master the language of the land, their comprehension of the places they visited would at best be only partial. In the absence of any knowledge of local names of places and peoples, Azambuja supplied his own. In his mind's map, he knew he could purchase people on the Slave River, he took the title of the leader he met, Karamansa, to be the man's name, and he placed the Karamansa on the throne of a Guinea Kingdom first related by Tuareg traders and later added to the Crown's imperial orbit. Whether or not he intended it, the story of the rock marked a starting point for both immediate Portuguese aspirations and more long-term imperial fantasies of Africa that have endured to the present.[74]

And it was a fantasy. The Guinea Coast was a figment of Tuareg rumors and King Jão's vanity. Calling a body of water the Slave River reduced the commercial and social life of the people who inhabited the series of lagoons and rivers between the present-day Volta and Niger Rivers to an extension of Portuguese needs. Karamansa was not a king's name nor even a man's name but an office related to trade with the powerful Mali empire of the Sahel. Malinke rulers dispatched itinerant traders, known as Wangara—Europeans called them Mandingos—to oversee the gold trade with the villages of West Africa, and men titled *karamansa* managed the exchanges on the coast while at the same time they adjudicated the practice of Islamic law between the People of the Book and the alleged infidels who surrounded them. The karamansa's faith would have entailed a particular view of the world of West Africa quite apart from the locals whose traditions, religions, and politics lay beyond the Law of the Prophet. Azambuja had entered a world of commerce structured by Islam and of daily life predicated upon local customs, identities, and beliefs that defy categorization.[75]

Historians have described men like the karamansa in a variety of ways, most of which have evolved out of Azambuja's search for certainty in a world he did not understand. Early explorers, steeped in the emergent nationalism and state building of late medieval and early modern Europe, mapped Africa in ways that made sense to them but that did not necessarily correlate with life as West Africans lived it. In the nineteenth and twentieth centuries colonial officers, missionaries, and anthropologists perpetuated the problem and have left more recent scholars to grapple with the uncertain colonial foundations of an entire continent's history and historiography.[76] Linguists might group West Africans as Kwa-speakers or Yoruba-speakers while anthropologists might divide cultures into Akan or Mande. Historians instead focus on political identities like Asante or geographical ones such as the Gold Coast. Anthropologist Jan Vansina asserted many years ago, however, that such disparate identities were wholly unsuitable for historical analysis because terms like *Akan*, *Igbo*, or *Mandingo* were too unstable over time to be useful as markers of any kind of contiguous and continuous linguistic, ethnic, political, or historical identity. Take, for example, the term *Yoruba*. While Hausa speakers had long used it to denote their neighbors in the kingdom of Oyo, it was not until the 1840s, when missionary Samuel Crowther published his linguistic work on a language he named Yoruba, that Yoruba gained the legs to walk as a colonial ethnic identity. *Yoruba* was not a neologism, but reading such an identity back into the precolonial past can be anachronistic. "It is quite common in Africa," D. Kiyaga-Mulindwa has warned, "to find presumptive ethnic terms slipping in meaning or reference with time, such that many of the terms now commonly used for population groups in Africa are either older terms of transformed reference or terms of quite recent manufacture."[77]

Problems of terminology become particularly acute when historians of American slavery draw one-to-one correspondences between the putative ethnicity of slaves and their points of origin on the African mainland

and then attempt to extrapolate both peculiarities of ethnicity and generalities of Africanness. It is something of a commonplace in the historiography of American slavery to assert that West Africans shared a basic worldview. Too often, however, such a generalization is posed as an assertion rather than as a question. Rarely is there agreement either on what kinds of cultural features might afford the basis for such generalizations or what constitutes cultural uniformity.[78] In studies of slavery in colonial Virginia, South Carolina, and Georgia, scholars have worked within the ethnic categories that planters used to evaluate the hardiness, docility, or skills of the men and women they purchased. People from the Gambia or the Gold Coast, for example, were sought after as excellent field hands while planters avoided so-called Igbos because of their alleged propensity for suicide. Kongolese people, however, made excellent house servants.[79] But others have begun to question such assumptions and to acknowledge the pitfalls of the language of African ethnography.[80] In many respects then, the problem that faced Azambuja faces scholars today. How do we write about the African past without bending it to the terms of the present or yielding to the temptation to generalize and thereby obscure the historical and spatial layers of identity of early West Africa? "If you eat vegetables for dinner," so the saying goes, "you offend the fish-monger, if you walk on the ground, you offend the horseman."[81]

The people who stayed behind in West Africa after the Bantu had left continued to raise yams, tend palms, forge iron, and carve villages out of the forest. When they looked to the sky and stared down at the earth they understood themselves to be caught between two complementary and, at times, competing forces. To the sun and the sky they attributed manhood, and the fire that was a token of the sun. The earth and the moon brought the unpredictable power of life from underground onto the surface of the earth, and the mingling of the sky's light and rain with the earth's topsoil yielded life. People who inhabited what is today Sierra Leone, Senegambia, and the Ivory Coast, for example, guarded earth's chastity and purity jealously. Menstruating women had to remain in their villages, away from the fields and the forests, lest the blood that made babies spilled onto earth and polluted the blood that made yams. So too could the spilling of semen on the ground interrupt the broader cosmic reproductive cycles upon which men and women depended, for semen ruined what rain was supposed to fertilize. Only special rituals could cleanse earth and render her fit to receive the rain. Any failure to do so might cause a family's or a village's children to be born malformed or with great difficulty. Igbo-speakers of the twentieth century saw in sun and moon a great cosmic marriage between Anyanwu and Onwa that made life on earth possible while their neighbors explained the world in reference to three basic colors—*pupa, funfun,* and *dúdú*—that approximated but were not analogous to red, white, and black. They too linked the redness of the earth's clay to the redness of menstrual blood while the white sky and rain found a counterpart in semen. The black topsoil of the earth kept the rain and the clay separate while also making a place for life to take root just as the skin of a mother's belly interceded between the blood and the semen that men and women mingled in the act of conception. Elsewhere, inhabitants of what is today Ghana as well as the Bantu people of the Congo positioned the worlds they inhabited between a male sun and a female moon, between fire and water, and between red and white. It was up to the people, the ancestors, and the spirits, to make a life between the endpoints of their cosmos.[82]

Clothing mapped these worlds and carried the cosmos into daily life. Yoruba-speaking women wore cloth the color of the soil and of the dark clouds that brought the rains while their counterparts in the kingdom of Kongo agreed that black cloth marked the power to give life. Men across West Africa wore white clothing that evoked, depending on the place, purity, rain, semen, the sea, or death to display their own complementary powers and place in the world. Where black and white came together life emerged. Before burying their ancestors, for example, Kongolese men put on white cloths to mourn the dead while women smeared their faces and chests with black dust to counter the power of death and to reconfirm their own powers of life. Such colors, however, also clothed life. Two sisters, daughters of a Muslim leader known as "the Brak" who governed the shores of the Senegal River, visited a French official's bark in 1715. André, Sieur de la Brüe, had been charged with opening the Senegal River Valley to trade and with obtaining access to the region's gold fields. Brüe invited the sisters and their four attendants onboard his vessel for a lunch of honey-drizzled hard tack and prunes, and, afterwards, an aperitif. In the meantime the two sisters danced to a beat provided by the women who had accompanied them. Fitted out in cloth of white and black stripes, one sister reached out to embrace and kiss the commander, but it was his spine that stiffened. He rebuffed her advance, "her Posture being extremely wanton and indecent," as he put it.[83] And in so doing he also said no to a world where chiefs drew traders into their families by fostering relationships between outsiders and eligible wives and where the meeting of black and white made life possible.

Red was a common color of transition between worlds. Kongolese women, for example, daubed themselves with red pigment during the time they passed from being young girls to wives. Leaders across West

Africa wore red to connote their mediating position between the world of humans and the world of spirits as well as between their people and outsiders in acts of war. The king of Bissaõ welcomed Brüe wearing a cap of red cloth while the king of Benin celebrated his power and dignity by riding through town in an outfit of red cloth on a horse draped in scarlet festooned with bits of red coral. A leader of the Ardra nation tied red feathers into his hair and wore red shoes and cloth while a Jalof prince named Little Brak wore a gown of blue and white-striped cloth and a wide belt of red cloth. His tailor, however, had also sown *gris-gris*, small scraps of paper inscribed with prayers rendered in Arabic script, into the gown and into the belt with red cloth and thread, marking the man as a figure who bore the power of his house, his land, and the book and who was invulnerable to all comers.[84]

Such colors and clothing, however, were but items in a larger legend that enabled people to map the places of West Africa. The power people needed to make their way in the world lodged as well in the shrines that engaged them in conversations with the spirits of groves, crossroads, paths, gardens, fords, houses, and borders. As one visitor to the kingdom of Koto put it in 1727, the land was "crowded with Idols."[85] In the kingdom of Whydah small clay statues inhabited every home, field, and path. Some people placed special shrines at the margins of their villages to mark the boundary between the social and antisocial world, to draw lines between different lineages, or to ward off any evil that might enter the community. Here, on these margins, women could spill blood to give birth. Here too stood special groves of trees that held in their fingers the spirits of the ancestors whose own blood flowed in the palm wine that sustained the lives of lineages and communities. Each family shrine worked as a place of truth and power, a place where an ancestor might have founded a compound, performed a feat of extraordinary bravery, or made an equally extraordinary sacrifice that could be invoked by songs and acts of praise. Once an initiate had caught a spirit's ear, gifts of food—plantains, fish, a goat, a hen, or a bowl of palm wine—convinced the spirit to enter the shrine and make available the power and knowledge that the supplicant needed. With a spirit's backing, people could contest rivals, heal sickness, challenge house histories, influence village affairs, secure a good harvest, or bring misery to an enemy. Some shrines, though, were never permanent, nor were the boundaries they marked, for the forest and its denizens engaged villagers in a constant struggle to maintain their homes and fields against the encroaching bush. If the power of the shrine failed or if the spirit proved too mild, no one would dance for it, no one would feed it. The grass would grow high and cover its face, and the spirit would fade from the memories that had nourished it.[86]

Shrines were discrete points within a broader landscape that was equally alive with power and possibility. People left gifts of wine, oil, bread, chickens, and vegetables at the feet of hills, near rocks, and on the shores of lakes and rivers to honor the resident spirits.[87] One German traveler recorded in the 1640s that people of the area he knew as the Gold Coast poured a portion of the palm wine they drank into a small hole in the ground. The explanation he received, that "the earth gives the wine so one should give the earth some of it back," however, only hinted at the meaning of the earth to these people. In this case the land was the abode of the founding ancestors who had made the trees, the wine, and the people possible. To pour a libation for those who dwelled in the ground was but one way of recognizing the way in which the past, the present, and the future were all folded into the earth.[88]

Lakes and rivers were often beings that had once been human but, owing to various circumstances, had transformed themselves for the benefit of others. The people who inhabited what today is called Sierra Leone never crossed rivers without commending themselves to the water's spirit, and they mumbled words of thanks for the transformation that their ancestor had undergone and for their safe journey as they disembarked their canoes. Near the Danish fort at Akra, a group of people sought to end a drought that had parched their fields by offering a sheep to a lake just beside the fort. After mixing its blood with the water to call forth the spirit, they roasted and ate the sheep and hurled a pot into the lake, at which point they implored the spirit to take the pot to nearby rivers and streams and fill it. Only if the rains came would they know that their offering had been received and their request granted. When the Portuguese occupied the fort some years later, they drained the lake of its water and its power, and killed the ancestor, so the people moved on to find another landscape that had not yet been defeated. The Kongolese too saw bodies of water as sacred places. The rivers that ran through their land foretold the future, and the Mbidizi River was preeminent. All of the other rivers in the region lived as its brothers and children.[89]

Ancestral and yet-to-be-born spirits tied the fields, rivers, forests, dwellings, and villages of the countryside to the lineages, clans, and families that inhabited it and created a continuum of life in and around the house and village. Just as gifts of food fed shrines, hills, and rivers, the spirits associated with families and villages demanded propitiation. Inhabitants of the Senegal River Valley set aside morsels of food to appease a spirit they called *Guné* whom the Europeans identified as the devil. Families always washed before meals and left a small portion of their food for the dead. Such recognition of their power, they believed, ensured that the ancestors would watch over their descendants. Should a person signal that his or her death was near, family members would gather around the bedside and inquire, just as they might have asked of a fetish or a river spirit, whether he needed food, drink, a wife, or a child.[90]

The relationships between lineages and the land made their houses sites where labor, production, land tenure, worship, and kinship found expression across space and through time. Among BaKongo people, for example, the ideology behind the *kanda* social group expressed a number of important domestic conventions as men cleared fields, tended tree crops, and hunted animals while women planted and tended the fields and saw to the upkeep of homes and villages. Children traced their ancestry through both parents, but each *kanda* stood as a collective mother to all of its descendants, and they made both alliances and enmities by selecting particular marriage partners for their members. For all of the social relations that constituted the *kanda*, their relationship to the land grounded them even more fully into the space of the Kongo kingdom. *Kandas* controlled particular fields, and their ancestral genealogies justified the size and scope of their holdings. While the existence of such groups explained the fragmentation of both cropland and kinship, they also traced a fundamental kin and geographical relationship to the king, *mani Kongo*. Before he received the crown he underwent a number of rites that divested him of his former kin relations so that he could become the father to all. As his children, the *kandas* surrendered to him ultimate claim over their land, but, as the head of all *kandas*, the king could belong to none. *Kandas*, however, comprised one part of a much wider social world that is too often rendered as an otherworld somehow beyond the plane of human existence. Indeed, the two worlds swirled together as one in the landscape, so that material and immaterial life were indistinguishable.[91]

Kongolese struck deals with the *bakisi basi* that inhabited the groves that surrounded their homes. Such spirits were keen to acquire goods, so farmers offered food and alcohol in exchange for unmolested use of the land. Goods also appeased the spirits of the dead that inhabited sacred groves. The spirits of title-holders might find bows or arrows on their graves while hunters would find animal skulls, and musicians drums. *Bisimbi* were tutelary spirits that inhabited particular locales—pools, creeks, groves, and rocks. Their white color betrayed their origins in the land of the dead, and they interacted with village inhabitants in the guise of children who allied themselves with particular houses. Other ancestral spirits, *bakulu*, and the ghosts of dead witches, *min'kuyu*, added to the complexity of the non-visible social world of villages and forests. People who had been raised to access the power of the spirits, *ngangas*, made use of the power that inhered in the land, but their efforts on behalf of one person might at the same time harm another.[92]

The spirits and powers that inhered in the land constituted a shadow world, a place where nightfall saw shrubs transformed into men and where the sounds of falling trees troubled the ancestors' repose. Trunks and branches afforded cover for witches or for homes for ancestral spirits, sap flowed as blood in the trees' bodies to provide food for the bodies of others, nuts were eaten as meat, and leaves offered as raiment. According to one traveler the kings who governed the polities of the Gold Coast drew more traders to the roads and villages they controlled by offering food and drink to the trees that stood as their patrons. In Kongo trees marked the boundary between the forest and the village as well as the place where the land of the living and the land of the dead met. French chronicler Jean Barbot noted that palm trees seemed to be the most important, for he claimed to have seen people tear fibers of bark off of trees to twine around their fingers or wrists in order to tap the trees' power. Men across West Africa cleared ground to enable their palms to thrive in exchange for the blood they consumed as wine. Other trees marked places of historical importance or sheltered the fetishes of the ancestors as living beings who inhabited the landscape every bit as fully as did the people. People in present-day northern Ghana still plant groves outside of their family compounds to ward off bad spirits and to provide shade in which people can socialize or welcome visitors to their world.[93]

People in the past did too. The King of Bissão had a reputation for demanding presents from anyone who hoped to stand under his tree and trade with his people. In 1700 he welcomed to his island Sieur de Brüe, who wanted to build a trading post. The king seated Brüe beneath the large tree that stood between a fort the Portuguese had built and the convent of St. Francis that ministered to the community. Much to Brüe's relief, no doubt, no woman came forth to provoke him with her hips, lips, and hands. The king was a powerful man. He wore a red cap of royalty, and around his cap he had wound a double row of hemp cord to denote, Brüe remarked, the "absolute Power which he has of making Slaves." Anxious about what was going on under the big tree's branches, the busy-body Portuguese governor interrupted the proceedings to wag his finger and to crow that the Crown of Portugal would never agree to what Brüe proposed.[94]

The man with the red cap took great offense at the governor's presumptuousness, so he took his visitor by the hand and led him to a different spot under the same tree where small images of various spirits and deities resided in its limbs, a constellation of powers in its leafy embrace and the words and deeds of generations of ancestors in its trunk and roots.

The king's retainers circled him, his guest, and the tree and presented a calabash of palm wine. After his wives and retainers had all touched the bowl, to affirm their place in the circle of their world, the king asked the tree if he should grant Brüe's request to open a trading post. To get, however, one had to give, and the king splashed the palm wine on the tree, poured the rest on its roots, and satisfied its needs in an honorable way. The crowd parted as a holy man led an ox to the circle where he cut its throat and caught the red blood in the same calabash that had held the palm wine, and he sprinkled the trunk and roots with the fresh blood. The tree replied. Dipping his finger into the blood, the king painted Brüe's hand, and told him under the great tree of Bissão, "I take you under my Care and Protection."[95]

Trees marked other important places. The inhabitants of a present-day town called Dwinwinabagi on the Gold Coast trace their origins to a group of hunters who had pursued an elephant through the bush. Taking a break from the pursuit, the party rested in the shade of a large tree they named Dwendwaba. After killing the elephant they decided that the location pleased them, so they called for their families and built a village around the tree.[96] At the mouth of the Gambia River traders noted a large copse on the north shore they called "Pavilion of the King of Barra." The tallest tree was his "Standard." English ships fired their cannons as they passed, signaling their respect and willingness to pay the tribute necessary for trade, usually bars of iron. For the Portuguese, however, while they recognized the power in the tree, they named it "Arvora da Mara"—the landmark tree—and in that way fit it into their own conceptual map of the Gambia.[97] Further up the river the king of a nation called Fereja situated his capital, Paska, around a large tree that locals called the "king's tree." He, however, had to use a force of one hundred musketeers to levy tribute and to cow enemies and traders.[98]

Trees could be contested beings that enabled groups or individuals to challenge either a king's decree, a house's legitimacy, or a faith's efficacy. A tree-like being that lived among the Muslim people of the Senegal River Valley whom explorers called "Mumbo Jumbo" wore a coat made of tree bark with a tuft of yellow straw for a cap. During the day the outfit rested on a pole on the outskirts of the village, but at night it came alive and searched through the village for married couples who were having problems. When he located the right house his mournful cries stopped and he stretched out to his full height of eight or nine feet. Children, however, could sleep easy, for they knew the monster had come for their parents and not them. Into the nearest door or window the beast bellowed a solution to the couple's problems, and villagers expected not only that the creature would offer a reasonable solution to the couples' difficulties but that they would heed his advice.[99] On the Gambia River, in the town of Albreda, a man of little note claimed to be a prophet who could make himself invisible and project his voice wherever he wanted. "God," he claimed, had sent him from heaven to restore order and justice on earth, and, as his message spread, he earned the name "Mamayenbûk," the Great Justice. He welcomed everyone, particularly the well armed, into his camp, and those he called "child" no longer had to tremble before the might of their new father. The new clan that the Great Justice had reconstituted out of the alienated and the aggrieved aimed its strength against leaders who had failed to uphold the normal order of things. The beating of a drum reverberated up and down the paths and over the treetops of the countryside to announce his approach, and curious onlookers flocked to catch a glimpse of his robe, "made," one French trader recorded, "of the Bark of Trees."[100]

The places marked by cloth, shrines, trees, and men and women created connections with space that tied the world of meaning to the landscapes the people inhabited. Some expressed this cosmology in the organization of their villages. Komo people of the equatorial rainforest, for example, set their houses in lines on either side of the road that went from the village clearing into the forests and the villages beyond. They drew clear distinctions between the façade that faced the road and the houses opposite, *ntangá*, with the back of the house that faced the forest, *bá-á-t'éndju*. *Ntangá* was the place where men socialized, wove or repaired baskets, and put together their hunting kits. Between the houses and the forest women and children performed a number of household chores and prepared the family's meals. The people aligned their houses with the east and the west as best they could and associated the small courtyard that linked the two rectangular rooms with the path of the sun.[101]

Others expressed similar relationships through the symbol of the circle and the cross that the Mississippians also knew so well. From the Gold Coast to the Kongo, people mapped the forces that structured their lives as an equilateral cross in line with the sun. Its four arms traced the fundamental relationships of the sun and the moon and the sky and the earth. Each arm of the cross marked one of the four positions of the sun during the day. The upper half of the ideogram expressed masculinity while the lower half invoked femininity, and the horizontal line that bisected the cross, the kalunga line, marked the horizon where the surface of the underwater world that was home to powerful spirits met the sky and framed the world the people inhabited. They would either draw the map on the ground or form a circle around a wooden cross and dance counterclockwise around the figure in imitation of the sun that ordered their world. Women might invoke the moon in such ceremonies by dancing in the opposite direction, and thus express the total system in which the people lived. The dances brought the land alive to send the spirits of the dead onto the next stage of life, to offer aid in some way to the people of this world, or to reproduce the social and spatial order that made their lives meaningful. Others traced the patterns of the dances in their hair, shaving away all but enough to trace crosses or concentric circles on their scalps. Warriors too painted crosses on their bodies before going off either to defend their own sacred circle or to destroy the circle of another.[102]

Inhabitants of the sacred circles of West Africa came together regularly in markets that knitted houses to towns and towns to chiefs, but unlike the close bonds of family and kinship, it was common wisdom that a handshake made in the market did not necessarily follow one home. Bantu speakers derived their word for market from their term for "beach," the place where hunters and farmers met fishermen to trade yams and bush meat for salt and fish while BaKongo people took their verb for selling from their term for setting a trap. Speakers of what is today the Igbo language called their markets after the places, town squares, adjoining fields, or days they met. Each one stood in a calendrical sequence that accounted both for the pride of place of the markets' hosts and for the passage of the moons and of the seasons. Among the inhabitants of the Whydah kingdom, for example, the moon marked market days. Country folk gathered in a field outside of the king's town Sabi under the shade of some great trees. Thousands of merchants came to vend cloth, pottery, and other handicrafts while on the outskirts stood booths where shoppers could buy beef, pork, goat, dog, bread, palm wine, brandy, or whatever else they might need to feed and entertain themselves. Speakers of the forerunner of today's Yoruba language convened their markets on neutral ground, and behind the hustle and bustle, smoking fires, squawking chickens, buzzing flies, and chattering voices lay a deeper order that shaped the spatiality and sociability of the marketplace. While men mingled at a distance, bragged, told tales, drank palm wine, and fought, women from all over the countryside oversaw the buying, selling, and bargaining that put cowries in their purses and food in their pots. Their stalls followed an order determined by the ranks of the lineages that the women represented, and they sat with their backs toward the paths that led to their villages so that in case of trouble they could make a quick escape.[103]

When European traders entered the region's commercial life it was up to the men who wore red, who stood on the margins of the world, to find ways to knit the newcomers into preexisting networks of trade and alliance. Their roles as people in-between the sky and the earth made them the ones to put the cosmologies of West Africa into play in order to accommodate the men who had been coasting the shores of Africa since the middle of the fifteenth century. The contact at first was reasonably balanced. West Africa's well-developed clothing and metal trades cut short Europe's ability to dump cheap metal and cloth goods into local markets. With the exception of a few trading posts and forts, no European power conquered an indigenous polity during the first few centuries of contact, and European diseases also seem not to have decimated regional populations as would happen with the walking people even if, here and there, death and pestilence destroyed whole families and villages. If the economics of contact were more or less equitable, however, the consequences of contact were more far-reaching as each side sought to come to grips with the other. For the people and their leaders, this meant fitting traders, government agents, and missionaries into their own landscapes of spirit, kin, and family.[104]

At the points on the coast and along the river valleys European factors and African kings fabricated new kinds of worlds. Two kings, one of the coastal chiefdom Whydah and the other of an interior kingdom called Dahomé, created such a juncture when the latter attacked the former to tap into the coastal trade. But just as much as the brief war was a struggle over economic opportunities, so too was it a battle between rival cosmologies and landscapes. The king of Dahomé, Agaja, sought direct access to the coast so that he could trade directly with the caravels that bobbed off the shore of Glenhue, Whydah's port. He and his house, however, were not native to Dahomé, so, in order to justify and maintain his hold on power and to muster support for his drive to the ocean, his ruling lineage adroitly adopted the spirits of those they governed. Foremost among Agaja's sacred arsenal was a life spirit called Da who took the form of a python and whose tight coils held the earth together. Agaja's rivals in Whydah also possessed a python of their own named Dangbe who had fled to them from the nearby chiefdom Ardrah, the leaders of which had once earlier captured Dangbe from their rival King Popo of Tado.[105]

With Dangbe, Whydah had grown to be the preeminent power in the region. Between fifteen- and twenty-thousand captives left its shores every year in the early eighteenth century. Agaja, however, found a chiefdom in turmoil for the boy king Huffon was having trouble maintaining the networks of tribute that underwrote his royal seat. Agaja attacked in March 1727, but the advance ground to a halt at a large river that stood between the invaders and the Whydah capital, Sabi, where Dangbe's temple stood. Whydah warriors and priests established their last line of defense at a nearby ford and three times a day called on the river for help. To receive aid, however, they had to give, so the priests threw small pythons into the water in the hopes of persuading the river to crush the invaders when they crossed. But Dangbe meant nothing to the men of Dahomé. They had Da on their side, and they drove across the river, seized Sabi, destroyed Whydah, and shed the blood of four thousand souls to the glory of Da and the shame of Dangbe. Those whose lives they spared they handed over to the traders of Glehue. To commemorate his feat, Agaja took on the surname Hunyita, "taker of ships."[106]

Needless to say, the trade in people altered customary forms of servitude and the cosmologies the people of West Africa used to explain their worlds. The landscape began to reflect the new movements of people as they traveled out of the villages and into the cargo holds of the ships on the coast. Across the region, villages contracted and threw up defensive works in the hopes of either thwarting slave hunters or providing cover for their own raids on the coffles. In 1732 the Englishman Francis Moore visited a town on the Gambia River called Kassam where a log palisade surrounded the town. The inhabitants had chinked the barrier with clay that had hardened to a rock-like consistency while loopholes and towers enabled people to fire guns from behind the wall and perhaps ambush caravans on the way to the coast for captives that they could sell for their own profit. In the Birim Valley of present-day southern Ghana, people huddled behind earthworks for protection while the diseases that the Europeans had brought—measles, smallpox, influenza, and colds—ravaged them. By the early eighteenth century the population had so dwindled that the last holdouts abandoned their towns and fled. None of this stopped a new group of people, the Atweafo, from moving in, appropriating the landscape, and claiming for themselves status as the original inhabitants of the land. The human trade remade the landscape as fortifications spread across the land and villages contracted. Shrines that had formerly brought rain, health, or success now began to protect some people from raids and to facilitate the success of those who hunted them.[107]

People generally assigned the slavers a particular color, white, and a particular place of origin—the world of the dead. In 1506 Portuguese traders were met with fire arrows and shouts of "cannibal" as they worked their way up the Gambia River. In 1603–4, when a German explorer of the Guinea Coast inquired as to why corpses were painted white before burial, he learned that their bodies would travel to a land of "Whites" where elites would continue to enjoy the services of those who accompanied them to the grave.[108] Some years later, at El Mina, a local woman identified a European who was visiting the post as the reincarnation of her husband. "She said it was me," the stunned visitor declared, "and I was her deceased husband, who had become white through death."¹⁰⁹ In 1669 an Ardrah priest informed one French navigator that the small white clay figure that stood by his side had informed him of "the Design you had formed in France to open a Trade here."¹¹⁰ While in the Kongo two small white children from the land of the dead visited a young girl named Dona Beatriz Kimpa Vita. After her encounter with the twins, Beatriz undertook training in the spiritual arts and captured people's attention when the spirit of St. Anthony possessed her in order to redeem the kingdom and to restore the balance of the Kongo world that had been lost to civil strife and slaving. Beatriz framed the world of the slave trade in reference to her land. Whereas her people, she revealed, had come from an ancestral fig tree named *n'sanda*, the Europeans who had beset the kingdom had crawled out of *fuma*, a white clay-like mineral associated with the watery realm of the dead.¹¹¹

Before the slave trade, the spirits of the dead, people believed, descended a mountain and crossed the kalunga line into a body of water. After crossing the water, they reached the foot of another mountain where the soul passed into the afterworld. As slavers worked their way into BaKongo consciousness, they came to inhabit the bottom of the body of water and the lower slopes of the second mountain. By seizing the realm below the kalunga line that was home to the powerful forces of life and death, white spirits could devour African flesh, cut off access to the afterlife, and circumscribe the power and reach of the ancestors. Such spirits broke the circle, set adrift the cross, and ruptured the lines of kinship that had made Kongo society meaningful and whole.¹¹²

Such adaptations to the presence of the slave trade were not, of course, limited to the Kongolese. Captives who passed through Ardrah believed that their captors were fattening them in the pens for sale to cannibals. Growing up in Fante country, Ottobah Cugoano remembered being told as a child that "white people" ate Africans while Olaudah Equiano recalled upon boarding the slave ship that delivered him to the Americas, "I was now persuaded that I had gotten into a world of bad spirits, and that they were going to kill me." After fainting from fright, the young Equiano regained consciousness and asked his fellow captives "if we were not to be eaten by those white men with horrible looks, red faces, and loose hair." Others who feared being caught escaped through the permeable boundary between the village and the bush and, in the process, turned their backs on the humanity they had claimed from the bush millennia before. When prodded by a French trader's curiosity, a Muslim trader explained that the red monkeys that frolicked on the shores of the Senegal River were not actually monkeys but people who had gone wild from refusing to speak. Why had they stopped speaking? the Frenchman asked. Because, the trader replied, speaking would have marked them as human and liable for seizure, sale to the slavers, and transportation to a place that for them was a world worse than death.[113]

The founding peoples' cosmologies—watery worlds of snakes, skies patrolled by birds, circles and spheres and crosses, kalunga lines and cannibals—were each real even if they might not bear today the imprimatur of fact. Without understanding such different cultural constructions of the constituent spaces of the Atlantic world as it informed the creation of the colonial South, however, it is impossible to understand how these cultures operated in space and produced the kinds of societies they did. Moreover, if we discount the meaning of different cultural constructions of space by subscribing to such things as natural facts, we discount as well their depth of meaning. Asserting that the Atlantic Ocean is a natural fact is, then, more than just another instance of that inert horizontality that Natter and Jones identified. It is instead a stark cultural position not unlike that assumed by the Genoese merchant who characterized portolan maps as truths minus frivolities. If we consider the ocean to be a fact, the serpents, the kalunga line, and those enchanting visions of Eden become equally frivolous when they should instead be seen as foundational to the creation of the Atlantic world in general and to the colonial South in particular. The stone Brathwaite imagined skipping across the water's surface left ever-widening circles that, when they reached the limits of their energy, faded and disappeared. If we lose our sense of balance between the past and its places in the asymmetries of knowledge and of power, then we risk allowing the power and the connectedness of the founding peoples that made one modest corner of the colonial Atlantic world possible to recede beyond the horizon of the past, out of sight and out of mind.

Chapter 2

INVASIONS

Christopher Columbus set sail for the land of Shem at an important juncture in the history of Christian Europe. After more than seven centuries of struggle the Crowns of Navarre, Léon, Castile, Aragón, Galicia, and Asturas toppled Grenada, the last Muslim caliphate of al-Andalus. Caught between the foothills of the Pyrenees and the brawling armies of the Ummayad and Almoravid caliphs, the Christians took heart in the castles that studded the valley of the Ebro River and in the faith that their stout walls defended. When Alexander II put the power of the papacy behind their plans to retake lost Christian lands, Castile emerged as the crusading state it remained some four centuries later when the project was completed in 1492. In the end the reconquest transformed the clutch of Visigothic kingdoms that had held out against the initial North African onslaught into the vanguard of western Christianity.[1]

With the patronage of Isabella the Catholic, queen of Castile, and her husband King Fernando of Aragón, Columbus carried Castile's expansionist impulses into the west, an unknown but wholly anticipated region that medieval cosmographers had associated with health, happiness, and paradise. Indeed, as he tracked the expanses of the open Atlantic during the three voyages he made to the Indies, he thought himself closer and closer to a holy paradise that sat atop not the spherical earth of Aristotle and Ptolemy but one that was pear-shaped or, better yet, pendulous like a woman's breast. The cyclopes, cannibals, and other inversions of the natural order that had inhabited the antipodal lands since antiquity, however, were another matter altogether.[2] To his sovereigns, the "lovers and promoters of the Holy Christian Faith, and enemies of the false doctrines of Mahomet and of all idolatries and heresies," Columbus pledged fealty and promised to continue across the seas what the assault on the Alhambra had finished. Whether with a bite of the pear or a grasp at the breast,

Columbus took ownership of a western paradise that medieval clerics had regarded as all but closed to any but the divine.[3]

The great sailor navigated the western seas by dead reckoning, inferring what was not known—his actual position—from what was known—the speed at which he was moving and his ship's relationship to the path the sun traced in the sky. The rhumb lines, compass roses, and meridians of the portolan charts he and others used to ply the Mediterranean and the shores of western Africa were of no use in the open Atlantic, and the farther he sailed, the more his own mind determined the relationships of wind, sun, and water that bore him westward. The same system of navigation showed him his way through the worlds he entered in the west. Only to locate himself on the ground he looked not to the sky but to histories, geographies, medieval compilations, and his own memories to position what he had found in relationship to what he knew. Marco Polo had already named the land, and Columbus sought in vain Cathay, Quinsay, and Chipangu.[4] The dwellings he spied through his eyeglass reminded him of the tents Moorish soldiers pitched on their campaigns. Pliny the Elder explained to him why the trees he saw were so large while Ptolemy and Aristotle enabled him to correlate latitude and skin color. Pierre d'Ailly's 1483 compilation *Imago mundi* provided a T/O map that forced Columbus to reconcile what he saw with what the Bible taught, and a library of other authors prepared him to believe that beyond the island that came to be called Cuba, he would find, he wrote, "one-eyed men, and others, with snouts of dogs, who ate men."[5]

But dead reckoning could only suggest links between fixed objects and fluid positions. The navigator's most primitive craft could not shape new things to suit old referents. Without the aid of a portolan chart to guide him, he simply could not take in the entirety of what he saw. Just a few days after sighting trees unlike anything to be seen in the Mediterranean, he confronted the limits of the world he had known. "But that I do not recognize them," he confided to his diary, "burdens me with the greatest sorrow in the world." Rather than yield to his own crisis of confidence, however, he made his own fate and his own world all the while believing that his god had handed him both. Wherever his crews made landfall, ringing axes felled trees, cross-cut saws hewed timbers, and carpenters assembled crosses to sink into the beaches to cow the forests, to bring order to the bays, rivers, and plains that opened before them, and to remake their desires into an actual world.[6]

The wooden crosses, Latin prayers, and linen flags that accompanied each ceremony of possession situated such places on a mental map of dominion that Columbus revised every time he rounded a point or sounded a shoal. And the knowledge he sustained through the names he bestowed on the land bent the unfathomable origins of the place he had entered to the known genealogy of the creation and the Crowns that he served. As the days passed into weeks, though, the world he crafted moved farther and farther from what he might have read in Pliny or Aristotle, seen in the *mappaemundi* that graced the walls of churches of Genoa, Lisbon, or Seville, or measured in the portolan charts that stopped short on the far shores of the Canaries.[7]

The people posed a particular challenge. He called them "Indios," a term that reflected his own erroneous assumption about where he was and whom he saw. But the meanings he attached to the term as he navigated the island seas came to denote so much more than a people who inhabited the Indies. The edenic qualities the navigator attributed to the islands he surveyed suggested that Columbus wondered whether or not the Fall or the Flood had ever happened there. If they had not indeed occurred then the "Indians" were a people who had lived outside of time as he understood it. And if they were innocent, their poverty, simplicity, and, ultimately, degradation made them ideal candidates for redemption before the One True Faith in vassalage to the Crowns of Castile and Aragon.[8] As he reported to his sovereigns, the "Indians" were "fit to be ordered about and made to work, plant, and do everything else that may be needed, and build towns and be taught our customs," and, lastly, "to go about clothed."[9]

The place that Columbus brought into being, however, was neither blank nor empty, nor particularly new, for where he saw Muslim tents, cycloptic monsters, and unknown Edens, the people who lived there held altogether different conceptions of the land and what it and they meant. To limit the story of colonization to the narrative of conquest that so often follows from Columbus's voyages predetermines the outcome of the story and leaves unchallenged Christian notions of what the land and its possession meant. While explorers charted spiritual, political, and commercial cartographies, their encounters with other people and places challenged the stability and veracity of the maps that guided them. Columbus, for one, saw a people who lacked all of the accoutrements of civilization as he knew it—towns, customs, clothing, and a work ethic. We do not know what deficiencies his hosts saw in him. Probably a lack of generosity, a suite of bad manners, too much hair, and an unwillingness to become a part of their world that galled them every bit as much as their alleged indolence appalled him. But in order to contest the land the invaders imagined and the very real processes that transformed it into colonies, we need to know, in a fundamental way, how all of the parties to the encounters understood the places they inhabited, shared, and contested.[10]

As each side sought to place the other in their own particular understandings of place and of peoplehood, the accommodations, disruptions, and oppressions that comprised the formation of what Europeans called "the New World" exposed the frailty of the *mappaemundi*, the limitations of the circle and the cross, and the need for new ways of thinking about place and self. To make sense of the peoples and places that came together in the Columbian encounter requires the ability to imagine points of contact as whole places with their own particular meanings and practices.[11]

The men who followed Columbus into the Indies shared his late medieval gaze. Hernán Cortés saw Tascalteca as a larger, more populous, and more powerful version of Granada. Lucas Vásquez de Ayllón drew upon Ptolemy and the reports of slavers to depict the shores of present-day South Carolina as a new Andalusia while the hamlets and maize fields of La Florida reminded Alvar Núñez Cabeza de Vaca of the Andalusian countryside. For Cortés, the parallel was apt, for he and his men sliced and shot their way through the countryside to wage war against the enemies of his faith and his lord, Emperor Charles V. As he smashed the temples and icons of those he vanquished he explained that they would have to adore and worship the Christian god. While such worship would save their souls, it would also bind them to two chains, one in vassalage to the Crown and the other in service to the divine order of creation. Cabeza de Vaca and his party, however, experienced none of the triumph of Cortés as they bumbled through the sawgrass of the present-day Florida panhandle. Instead, they imagined themselves beset on all sides by "giants" who could fire arrows through oaks, never mind the cuirasses the men wore for protection. With diminishing hope, supplies, and health they named a river they found "Magdalena" in the hopes she might deliver to them the succor they so badly needed.[12]

In 1514 Hernando de Soto set out to find his fortune in the "Indies of Castile." He went on to win fame as a conqueror in Panama, Nicaragua, and Peru, and Charles knighted him in the order of Santiago, a confraternity whose oaths of poverty, chastity, and obedience had bound knights and foot-soldiers in service to the Crown against Muslims since 1170. After a few short-lived attempts by others to carry the conquest to La Florida, the Crown granted him permission to take up the cross and the sword. As part of his mission, the Crown required him to read the *requerimiento* of 1514 that stipulated, in Castilian, that the "Indians" to whom it was read had a choice—to surrender their souls to God and their sovereignty to the Crown or to be put to the sword and sold into slavery. Whether or not he stuck to the script is difficult to say, for he improvised from time to time. He might plant a wooden cross in a town square to exorcise the devils he had encountered or declare to anyone in hearing distance that Christ had suffered on the cross, that he was a god and a man, and that he had fashioned the heavens and the earth and all things in-between. The fantasy of conquest, domination, and conversion, however, was too unstable when stretched over the months and then years that the expedition wound on. When food ran short, when freshwater pearls failed to satisfy his greed, or when the expedition's burdens proved too great, the knight of Santiago depended on whatever he could extort from the devils he met: maize and beans here, young women there, and any able body who could carry a pack, in chains if need be.[13]

The people Soto and his men fought and the hardships they encountered forced them to adopt some of the practices of the people they sought to conquer, both to survive and to be successful. At the town of Cale, where the men found a field of maize budding with dry ears, they praised their god and, as the women of Cale would have done had they not fled, they shucked the ears and pounded the kernels in the mortars fashioned from hollow stumps that sat about the abandoned town. But they were so clumsy with the heavy log pestles that they had to sift the crushed kernels through their chain mail to get any meal for their efforts. Several of the men simply refused to pound their own and parched or boiled the kernels they had harvested.[14]

While others pounded maize for him, Soto began talking like a priest beholden to two congregations. In order to remake La Florida as a new Andalusia, he invoked the power of Christ against the idolaters he faced down at every ford, town, and crossroads. But, in order to accomplish the conversion of the people and the land, he had to engage their world in ways that went beyond a lance's tip or a mastiff's jaws. At a town called Achese the people fled his approach, but a captive found the town's leader on the other side of a nearby river and, after some discussion, he agreed to meet Soto. The knight wasted no time to declare that "he was a son of the sun and came from where it dwelt and that he was going through that land and seeking the greatest lord and the richest province in it." The leader acknowledged Soto's proclamation and passed him on to an even greater town called Ocute. Before he left, however, Soto had his men erected a cross in Achese's public plaza and commanded the people to honor the suffering it commemorated. "They signified," one chronicler wrote, "that they would do so."[15]

The people of Ocute welcomed rather than fled Soto's army. Their gifts of rabbit, wildfowl, and bread were a sight for sore starving eyes. But the soldiers appreciated most the dogs they received, and they devoured them like "fat sheep."[16] What might their hosts have thought as they watched the newcomers, the self-proclaimed sons of the sun, butcher and barbecue animals associated with household offal and town garbage? Had the hairy Christians passed or failed a test? Without a doubt the people felt ambivalent about these raiders who emptied their granaries, seized their young folk, and held their leaders hostage, but, at the same time, by managing the newcomers in this way they acted as real and true people who had always been there living in-between.

The chief of Tascaluza was a giant of a man. His headdress reminded the Castilians of an *almaizar*, a turban, that, one of the invaders wrote, he wore "like a Moor, which gave him an appearance of authority."[17] His voice carried from the top of the mounds that loomed over the town and across the public plaza to his anxious audience. He spoke about his world as he stood beneath a circular piece of black fabric marked by a white cross and held aloft by his aides. No doubt he had heard of how the Christians had sunk their shafts into the young women of nearby towns; how their Toledo blades had opened the bodies of boys and men; and how their frightened kin had had no choice but to leave the dead in the field to be gnawed by rats, dogs, and opossums. When Soto demanded porters for his baggage train, the leader, according to one chronicler, replied, "that he was not accustomed to serving anyone, rather that all served him before." Perhaps confronting for the first time the limits of his own power, the chief of Tascaluza urged Soto and his army to move on, to take the cross of the Son, and to leave the circle over which his sun presided. Soto and his men did leave but not before devouring most of the town's stores of food and seizing the chief to guide them to a nearby town, Mauvila. Here the chief promised to deliver what Soto wanted.[18]

The leader of Tascaluza, however, had dispatched runners to alert the inhabitants of Mauvila that a red path of war was opening and that their circle was about to be breached. Mauvila's leaders lured Soto's army through a gateway in the palisade that surrounded their town. Soto's men, however, spotted the warriors hiding in the houses, retreated, rallied in a nearby clearing, and returned to set fire to the place and kill everyone they could. Scores of bodies reduced to charred bone and crisp crackling littered the smoldering town, and while the invaders tended to their wounds, the townsfolk fled into the countryside to spread the alarm. The battle removed any doubts the people might have had about the invaders' sanity and propriety. Clearly they were not going away and, if they were to be stopped, the leaders and warriors of the real and true people would have to find other means, either diplomatic or military, to thwart their invasion.[19]

In the end, though, it was malnutrition and disease that felled Soto and undid his expedition. Starving and without a friend in the country, the survivors built a flotilla of rickety boats and made a miserable escape down the Mississippi River into the Gulf of Mexico. Knowledge of the alleged wealth of La Florida, however, circulated widely in Europe in spite of their failure to find gold just as news of the hungry yet insatiable knights circulated throughout the region. Both rounds of gossip came face to face on the Atlantic coast of La Florida where two rival leaders, Saturiwa and Outina, men who were every bit the equal of the chief of Tascaluza, sought to absorb into their nations the Huguenots who had invaded their land. French explorers and writers shared Castilian opinions that the first people were little removed from beasts, but they did not imagine them as "Indians," denizens of a particular place. Instead, they used a term, *savage*, derived from the Latin term for forest, *sylvaticus*, to mark the people's ostensible lack of civilization and their intermediate position on the Great Chain between Christians and animals. A people the explorer Giovanni da Verrazzano had described as "rough and ignorant" became in the hands of cosmographer André Thevet "a remarkably strange and savage people without faith, without law, without religion, without any civility whatever."[20]

Such preconceptions informed Jean Ribault's uneasy relationship with the first people he met in La Florida in 1562 when he led a group of Huguenots to found an outpost from which privateers could interdict the Spanish treasure fleets. To signal his arrival he planted a stone column on which the arms of France had been carved overlooking a river that he named May after the month in which his group had found it, the present-day St. Johns River. There Ribault praised God for leading him to the strange place before turning northward with the current where his crew found a large sound they named Port Royal. Here they founded Charlesfort. One of Saturiwa's allies, a leader named Audusta, provided the newcomers with food in order to oblige them to defend him against his enemies, but the colony was beset with problems and succeeded more in depleting the countryside of food than in either abetting the expansion of Saturiwa's chiefdom or preying upon Spain's lumbering galleons. After Ribault returned to France to procure more supplies and people, the men he left behind abandoned Charlesfort and fled to Audusta, who promised them food in exchange for help in his wars. Another regional leader, Stalame, however, offered a bow and arrow to draw the Huguenots into another alliance that to this point could only be communicated in signs and gestures. In the end, however, the garrison decided to try to sail back to France rather than remain at the mercy of their sylvan hosts.[21]

René de la Laudonnière, one of Ribault's captains, returned to La Florida in 1564 with around three hundred colonists. Rather than settle at Port Royal, however, the party decided to stay on the May River and to establish themselves near the pillar Ribault had left behind. Laudonnière's men were surprised to find it encircled by baskets of maize for the comfort of the French when they returned to hold up their end of the bargain originally struck between Ribault and Saturiwa. Four hundred people welcomed him ashore and Saturiwa greeted Laudonnière as "the brother of the sun . . . [who] would go to make war with them against their enemies." Not surprisingly, Saturiwa granted the party permission to start construction on a fort, the walls of which traced a distinctly European pattern with three bastions keeping watch over a perimeter the men had cleared of trees and brush. Within the wooden walls, however, Saturiwa's people topped the invaders' timber frame buildings with thatched roofs, giving the place a look that was not altogether out of place. But Laudonnière could not bring himself to accept the mixing of worlds that was occurring all around him. To him the locals were no more than "thieves," and the invaders held to their leader's vision of creating a Mediterranean paradise. After all, he reported, the abundance of grapevines with fruit so thick was such that one could hardly avoid stepping on grapes. Saturiwa, however, accepted the newcomers not as savages or infidels but as a people who could be real and true and where Laudonnière could stand next to him as a brother of the sun.[22]

Saturiwa wasted no time ordering the sun's brother to join him in a war against his rival Outina, who governed a powerful chiefdom further inland that sat astride an important trading path. Laudonnière, however, refused to walk the red path by telling the chief that he did not want to make enemies. In the meantime, however, he had dispatched scouts to locate other chiefs who might help him escape his new family. Word of mouth led his men to Outina, but Saturiwa, who, of course, knew of such back trail murmurings, forced Laudonnière's hand by telling him again to fight Outina. When the brother of the sun refused his host's final call to go to war, Saturiwa cut him loose. Without the supplies of maize and other foodstuffs on which they had come to depend, mutinies tore the Huguenots apart. Locals were willing to trade wild food, fish, or acorns for bits of cloth and metal, but, without a relationship to the sun, no one would give them civilized food like maize or beans. Even the people of Outina's land came to hold in contempt these people who could not feed themselves, people who, by the end, came to be seen as less than people. "They burst out laughing," Laudonnière despaired, "and made fun of us."[23]

In August 1565, while preparing to abandon the village they called Fort Caroline, lookouts spotted a relief fleet under Ribault's command bellying on the horizon. Ribault found, however, that the settlement had not quite worked out the way he had planned. Instead of claiming a piece of the "New World" for France, he and the people who had followed him had entered into the complicated world of Saturiwa's circle. But even Saturiwa's grip on the region was loosening. On Saint Augustine's Day in September 1565, Pedro Menéndez de Avilés chose the site for Spain's first permanent settlement in La Florida, adjacent to a town called Seloy. He took possession of the land in the name of his king, Felipe II, and had his men parade along the beach with banners unfurled and trumpets blaring. Gunshots echoed as he knelt and kissed the cross, pledging to clear the land of Huguenot blasphemy and "Indian" deviltry. Not a Protestant was left after he had completed his bloody work.[24]

The feudal relationships that Castillians knew were not so far from the ways that Mississippian chiefs had ordered their own societies, and the two styles meshed in La Florida to remake a landscape that had been devastated by diseases deposited by Soto and other adventurers. Starting from St. Augustine, Menéndez de Avilés coasted the peninsula offering gifts and favors to local leaders, all the while taking pains to recognize their hereditary statuses and ranks. Among the Calusas of present-day southwestern Florida, for example, the governor went so far as to abet his incorporation into the ruling lineage by accepting as his bride the sister of a leader whom the Spanish called Carlos. To the dependents of Outina he presented gifts of beads, cloth, and metal tools, and to still yet others he and his adjutants stood as baptismal sponsors lending their names to the leaders who had decided to borrow their faith. Not all leaders, however, accepted the newcomers, and when the scattered Jesuit outposts and garrisons that Menéndez de Avilés planted along the coast began to succumb to mutinies and raids, the governor went on the offensive. Mixing wars of conquest with presents of peace, the Spanish extended the One True Faith and extracted from the walking people tribute in the form of labor and maize. Indeed, the men of the presidio of St. Augustine set themselves up as something of a chiefdom that was not necessarily out of place in post-contact Florida.[25]

The Spanish went where there was maize because without it they could not sustain their imperial efforts. For this reason missions did not appear among the non-horticultural Tequestas, Hobes, Calusas, Ais, and other nations of the South. Instead, the Franciscans, who had replaced the Jesuits as the bearers of the One True Faith, settled themselves among the Apalachees, Guales, and Timucuas. Prior to contact, their towns and villages devoted the produce of specific fields to their leaders, priests, and other notables while large communal fields yielded the harvest that would serve as the peoples' reserve against hard times or drought. Missionaries and officials simply inserted themselves into this indigenous order, what they called the *sabana* system, to provide the tribute they used to knit disparate peoples into a provincial order under the rule of the presidio at St. Augustine.[26]

The collapse of the *encomienda* system by which Castilians had parceled out Mexican land and labor to colonials led the men behind La Florida to invest their hopes for food and power in the missions that radiated out from St. Augustine across the region. One of the earliest outposts, Santa Elena, built in 1566, extended the Crown's authority to where Charlesfort had once stood and guarded La Florida's northern flank. The mission's founders followed a blueprint mandated by the 1573 Laws of the Indies. A church and the *cabildo* framed a central public plaza that held the center of a rigid grid of streets that would guide the future growth of the town. Beyond the order of the town, the surrounding fields and forests loomed as a powerful threat, what Spaniards called *la confusión*. But they could not repudiate completely local customs and imperatives. As was happening in Saint Augustine to the south, a shortage of Spanish women led the men to seek relations with local Guale women, who brought into the households of Santa Elena pots made of local clay for preparing local dishes. People also paid their tribute to the friars in pots full of maize, squashes, and beans, but the blood and body of Christ they received in return were poor recompense for their hard labor. Requirements that the missions had to remit twenty-five pounds of maize for every male, an annual levy of between twelve and thirteen thousand pounds of maize, as tribute to the granaries of St. Augustine tipped the balance, and in 1597 the walking people rebelled. They put Santa Elena to the torch and strewed about the plaza the bells that the priests had named and blessed, and in unmaking the mission they hoped to make whole their sacred circle.[27]

The Guale rebellion worked. Governor Gonzalo Méndez de Canço ended the payment of direct tribute in maize and replaced it with a scheme whereby the inhabitants of the missions had to pay tribute to the presidio with their labor instead of with their produce. Toiling away in the invaders' fields, they raised most of the maize on which the colony subsisted, and colonial officials exchanged coins, metal tools, or cloth for additional stores of maize, beans, and other foods to see the colony through each year. While wheat was grown at the mission of Santa Catalina and in the Apalachee and Timucuan mission provinces, it was too scarce to depend upon. What little quantities were to be had were probably used to prepare the host for communion rather than their daily bread. The dependence on maize was thus progressive, for in spite of imports of wheat flour, royal stores of maize increased from around three thousand pounds per month in the early seventeenth century to nearly twenty-five-thousand pounds per month in the 1690s. Sixty percent of the maize in the latter period had to be imported from New Spain and Cuba, but the remainder came from either the tribute or the trade that bound the walking people and the invaders in an extensive regional network.[28]

Changes in the tribute system presaged others as well. Such was the shattering impact of the Guale revolt that afterwards governors were reluctant to enter into marriages with prominent women to gain entry into their lineages. As well, the custom of having governors and other high-ranking officials stand as baptismal sponsors or as godfathers for local leaders and their kin declined as invaders and first people settled into two distinct political and social orders, or republics, that afforded a way for the Spanish to govern and to extract tribute from their indigenous vassals and for the first peoples' leaders to secure their own positions of power and authority against further Spanish encroachment. While Guale leaders returned slowly to the fold to renew their vassal status, others, particularly in the interior of Florida, repudiated the new order. Ocales and Potanos of Utina province stripped their landscape of alien trees and plants, cattle and hogs, one priest wrote, "wishing to leave no trace or smell of us."[29]

In his effort to expand the Crown's influence, Menéndez de Avilés had dispatched Jesuits to probe a bay he had visited in 1561 and named Bahía de Madre de Dios. They erected a mission in 1570 only to retreat in the face of a prolonged drought that led them to conclude that the Lord had chosen to chastise the country. English navigators had identified the bay the Jesuits had abandoned as the most likely spot for finding a passage to the east, so Elizabeth I asked her courtier Sir Walter Raleigh to locate a fort capable of supporting the search for the passage and for raids on the Spanish galleons that followed the currents up the coast. Such a site, Raleigh boasted, would make the English "lords of navigation."[30]

In the summer of 1584, a man named Granganimeo welcomed the group of English explorers dispatched by Raleigh to a land governed by his brother Wingina. Just off shore, two barks bobbed in the pass that opened into the gray-green waters of the sound between the island and the mainland. The weary crews probably packed the gunwales to watch Granganimeo and his party roll out a mat on the sandy beach. While the headman sat at one end, four beloved men took their places at the other, maybe even at the four corners. The other forty men stood at some distance, and all watched the captains of the two barks, Masters Arthur Barlowe and Philip Amadas, and a group of sailors clambering through the surf while hauling their ships' boats above the thin line of waterlogged wood, seaweed, and jellyfish that the high tide had left behind. The harquebuses they had brought made the task doubly difficult. Matches and powder had to stay dry in case there was trouble.[31]

Despite the aspiring lords of navigation having come armed to the teeth, Granganimeo stayed sitting and motioned for the company to join him on the mat. Barlowe and Amadas probably would have preferred to stand or at the least to sit in chairs, but they dutifully took their places on the mat. Only then did Granganimeo acknowledge their presence and allow their entrance into his world. Professing his love for the newcomers, the leader welcomed them to his land at its margins, for the beach was some days' walk from Dasemunkepeuc, where Wingina was convalescing from wounds sustained in a recent battle. People made their way in such places by giving particular things to particular people and expecting something equally valuable in return. Granganimeo claimed pride of place among the delegation seated at the beach, so Barlowe handed him a tin plate, a copper kettle, some beads, and other items that he had drawn from his pack. The plate caught the leader's attention, but he did not eat from it. Rather, he clapped it to his chest and, after the meeting, he or someone else made a hole in the outer rim so that he could wear it as a gorget and stand out from the other beloved men who sported similar tokens of shell or polished copper. Granganimeo then returned to Barlowe a bundle of skins and furs that clinched the deal and created, for a moment in time, an English place in Wingina's land. The four beloved men who had remained seating throughout the encounter murmured among themselves.[32]

But would there be a place for the hosts in the New England that Barlowe had imagined and was in the process of making? After being released from the ceremony on the beach, he breathlessly reported, "Wee found the people most gentle, loving, and faithfull, void of all guile, and treason, and such as lived after the manner of the golden age." Just as Adam and Eve found their every want satisfied in the original Garden, so too did the first people, Barlowe concluded as he added but the latest chapter in the book began by Columbus so many years before. "The earth bringeth foorth all things in abundance," Barlowe remarked, "as in the first creation, without toile or labour."[33] His inability to recognize the work that went into the dishes of maize, beans, and venison that the women fed him and his men after the initial welcome was neither idle nor innocent. For in the old medieval formulation of land tenure and use, only those who put labor into the land could rightfully claim it as their own. Moreover, the Father gave land only to men who could exercise dominion. After one of the founders of the Roanoke colony discovered a plot Wingina had hatched against the invaders, he beheaded the man to the cry "Christ our Victory!"[34]

Beyond Wingina's land lay Tsenacommacah, the "densely inhabited land," home of people who also greeted outsiders by spreading mats and offering their affection and food in welcome. The people of Tsenacommacah preferred to locate their homes on ridges or hills between the hardwood forests of the uplands, where they hunted deer and collected acorns and hickory nuts, and the marshlands that opened below into the rivers where they found mussels and fish. In a society where canoes afforded easy travel over water between towns, such places garnered names like Namassingakent, "plenty of fish;" Assaomeck, "middle fishing place;" and Namoraughquend, "fishing place," that inscribed in the land the longstanding importance of underwater resources to the region's people. But the arrival of maize had enabled these people to build upon the world of their forebears. They situated oval long houses made of bowed saplings roofed with either bark or woven mats among the fields of maize, beans, and squash that provided the bulk of their sustenance. Families tended crops of gourds, sunflowers, and tobacco in small gardens. Smoke trailed from open holes in the houses' roofs, where the families slept on platforms along the walls. Sweat lodges and menstrual lodges enabled men and women to socialize apart from one another and to isolate the imbalance that followed whenever men shed blood in war or when women bled with the moon. This was not, however, a society of equals. The new forms of class and status that accompanied the cultivation of maize further to the south appeared in Tsenacommacah as well. Elites set themselves apart by wearing shiny copper bands on their arms or the wings of birds in their hair to denote their ties to the sun. On their bodies, etched in their skin, ran the blue-black outlines of serpents that carried the power of fertility and a capacity for disorder of the world below. They also inhabited larger homes and supervised warehouses where they stored the skins, furs, and crops they received as tribute. And they enjoyed exclusive access to the bones of deceased leaders and priests who resided in other structures made of bowed saplings, giving the appearance of arbors planted specifically for the purpose. The eastern end of the houses of the dead was open to allow the full morning sun to shine in. At the opposite enclosed end sat the bundles of bones along with gifts of maize, skins, copper, and pearls, tribute paid by leaders to leaders to ensure that in death as in life the basic order of the world remained.[35]

The people of Tsenacommacah projected their sense of the material, social, and political landscape in a view of the world that encompassed a communal sense of history, place, and power. *Pawcorances* dotted the countryside to mark important events, places, and people. Parents taught children to honor these piles of stones that could be found on paths or in woods and to leave gifts of tobacco or blood to acknowledge what their ancestors had done before them to warrant such commemoration—feats of war, a successful hunt, or the making of powerful medicine. Gifts also calmed troubled waters. When storms whipped whitecaps on the rivers and bays, a token of the sky, a shiny piece of copper, or some tobacco whose smoke the sun favored, could restore the world's balance and becalm the roiling waves. The forests that ran between and around towns, paths, and bodies of water, however, lay beyond the kinds of power and control that ordered life in Tsenacommacah. Here, in their own version of *la confusión*, elders sent boys on the cusp of manhood through a gantlet, and while the older men beat their shoulders, backs, and arms with reeds, women mourned the impending loss of their children. Those who endured the gantlet entered the forest to gestate for nine months. Upon their return elders cleansed them of the disordered state that had caused their transformation from genderless and purposeless children to men who hunted and warred and whose newfound status was marked by the honorific title they each bore, "he has a new body."[36]

Into Tsenacommacah came a group of adventurers from England who had sworn to their god to overturn the papal donation that had granted the land to Spain and to extend their majesty King Charles's dominion. Empowered by biblical injunctions to subdue the land and to plant the garden, the shareholders of the Virginia Company of London, according to prevailing Aristotelian and Ptolemaic notions of latitude and temperature, expected to find on the Chesapeake a climate conducive to growing grapes and incubating silkworm eggs. The first landfall brought the small party of adventurers to the shores of Kecoughtan where they feasted and were introduced to the *werowance* of Paspihe who invited them to settle in his domain. At first glance, the site he offered seemed well suited for the purpose. It was low and level, and the bottom of the river dropped so precipitously that ships could moor close to shore. To John Smith the place was "a verie fit place for the erecting of a great cittie." George Percy turned to his bible for inspiration and declared his new home a "Paradise," a "Garden." But what they celebrated as utopia was, in fact, a place where no sensible inhabitant of Paspihe would live. And the location of Jamestown was not an accident but rather a point of strategy, for the site all but ensured that the newcomers would be dependent on their hosts for food and would have to walk far to find clean fresh water. While the first people might camp seasonally on the shore to harvest fish and shellfish, they preferred to build their permanent habitations on bluffs near the marshes, forests, and prairies upon which they depended for much of the food they hunted, collected, and cultivated, and far from the salty waters of the coastal estuaries.[37]

Trouble came to the garden when a fight over a hatchet broke out between one of the *werowance*'s warriors and one of the Englishmen. After an exchange of arrows and musket fire, the guests marked themselves as foes in the country by raising a palisade mounted with a number of small cannon around their camp. In the meantime a small party set out to find the man who claimed the allegiance of the people of Kecoughtan and Paspihe. As they sailed their way to Powhatan's town, they hailed those they met with the land's word of welcome, *wingapoh*, and people offered them strawberries, bread, and fish. In return, Captain Christopher Newport held forth bells, pins, needles, and beads. At last they arrived and saw the town perched—where else?—high on a hill overlooking the river. Between their boat and the palisade and homes that sat atop the ridge stretched a broad plain filled with growing maize, beans, pumpkins, gourds, and tobacco. Harvest time was approaching, and this was good fortune, for Powhatan sent out word to welcome the strangers, and at a feast he invited them to join his confederacy. Newport had other ideas. He was exploring, and he insisted that his party continue just up the river where the people showed him a falls that blocked further travel by boat. To mark this discrete limit of both his knowledge and grasp, Newport had a cross driven into the ground and inscribed upon it the name of his king and the year of his dominion. When Newport explained the monument's significance to the people who had gathered to watch, however, he returned to Powhatan's invitation and likened the cross's timbers to the arms of Powhatan and himself bound in league to one another. Upon their return to Jamestown the men found the siege lifted and their stores replenished. "It pleased God," George Percy reasoned," after a while to send those people which were our mortall enemies to releev us with victuals, as Bread, Corne, Fish, and Flesh." But it was Powhatan who had given the command, for he now had a new town, and a vulnerable one at that, to add to his growing confederacy.[38]

At the point between Eden and God's helping hand, the men of Jamestown sought to fashion a world they could master. Its potential, however, remained untapped for it had not been inhabited by, John Smith wrote, "industrious people" who could draw from the land both pleasure and profit. To begin to wrest the land from those Smith argued who "make so smal a benefit of their land," the invaders initiated a number of claims. The cross the party had erected on the river shore above Powhatan's town was but one of several they planted at various falls where their explorations of the region's rivers terminated. If no cross was to be had, they improvised and carved them into tree trunks or secreted in hollow limbs and trunks notes or small brass crosses to demonstrate to all who followed that "Englishmen had beene there." The crosses, however, failed. As Jamestown's leaders continued to bicker over the organization of the company's labor, the dispensation of food, and so forth, sickness ravaged them. From the foul and brackish water that surrounded the town and strained their kidneys to the ravages a novel diet of maize wreaked on their bellies to the intermittent delivery of supplies by Powhatan's allies, Englishmen began to die and to wonder why their god was so angry with them.[39]

Eventually the behavior of the invaders, more so than the actual location of their town, determined their place within the large space of Tsenacommacah. Rappahanocks called them "strangers," people who had "come from under the world, to take their world from them."[40] Powhatan's cosmographers shared similar conceptions of the strangers' disruptive and dangerous powers. After Smith's capture during a foray into the forest a party of warriors brought him back to Pamunkey, a town governed by Powhatan's brother Opechancanough, where the warriors set him in a house. The next morning seven men entered the dwelling painted in the colors of their world, red for war, black for death, and white for life and peace. Around the fire that blazed in the center, its smoke trailing out of a hole in the ceiling up to the sun in the sky, they danced, rattled, and sang, and at the end of the song one of them sifted between his fingers a line of ground maize with which he traced a circle around the fire. The meal produced by the women of the town in large mortars fashioned out of hollowed stumps bespoke the transformation of a plant that thrived at the meeting point of the earth and the sun. The people, as well as the hungry men of the Virginia Company, depended on the women's work and power to subsist, so perhaps the dancers explained this to Smith as they marked the map's first and closest boundary. Beyond the circle of cultivation represented by the pale grains of meal, the dancers laid concentric circles of whole kernels of maize, perhaps to stand for the fields that surrounded their towns or the towns that comprised their confederacy of maize. The farther the mapmakers got from the fire, however, the less domesticated their world became, and they scattered small sticks amongst the kernels to connote the forests that bounded their world and that had also been the first thing the Virginia Company had felled in the construction of their fort.[41]

"They imagined the world to be flat and round," Smith concluded from the ceremony, " . . . and they in the middest." But his own conception of his own people's place was not so different. When Opecanchanough inquired after Smith about his ivory compass, Smith obliged by drawing on an intellectual tradition that reached back to Bartholomew Anglicus, Isidore of Seville, Pliny the Elder, Aristotle, and even old Thales of Miletus. The sun, Smith explained, ordered the universe and marked the predictable rhythms of time. It chased the moon in an endless cycle of days. If he understood Smith, Opechancanough probably nodded in agreement. Against the immutability of the sun's celestial order, Smith went on, planets embodied change, mortality, and imperfection because of the erratic movements they followed through the sky. To emphasize the point, Smith traced their imperfect orbits across the sky with his finger, and Opechancanough followed. Each planet in Smith's universe brought a unique mixture of heat, cold, dryness, and moisture to bear on the earth, which when combined with air, fire, soil, and water produced the variability of human life, and he related how the globe was covered with a variety of nations and people of different colors.[42]

The places enacted by the dancers who visited Smith that morning in Pamunkey or demonstrated by Smith in the conversation around his compass each made room for other kinds of people, albeit in different ways and for different reasons. To the dancers, Smith had a place in their world sitting on the edge of their map while, for Smith, the Pamunkeys and the English were bound to one another as antipodeans, forever locked in cosmological opposition. The invaders' basic need for food, however, eroded Classical and Christian boundaries and drew Tsenacommacah and Jamestown together into a common space defined by maize. Jamestown's first hard years coincided with some of the worst drought of the past millennia. Seeing his town short of food and long on dissension and disease, Smith dispatched small groups to live in the towns that held the ridges and bluffs and that had better access to fresh water and fertile fields. His strategy, however, did more than see the invaders through a difficult time; it taught them the value of adaptation and, on a basic level, of the blending of worlds. "Many were billetted amongst the Salvages," Smith reported, "whereby we knew all their passages, fields, and habitations, how to gather and use their fruits as well as themselves."[43]

Historian James Horn has written of Jamestown's early years that the company exerted little effort to create a world where the English and the "Indians" could live together. "Such a vision," he concluded, "was beyond the grasp of a nation intent on colonial expansion and assured of its own superiority." Such things may have been true of the English nation, but more can be said on this point. Under the tutelage of Smith the invaders attempted to build a confederacy around Jamestown that was organized along the same lines as the one that Powhatan governed and that the invaders hoped to supplant. Indeed, pre-existing political boundaries, trade routes, and alliances bounded the horizons of the English imagination in Virginia and forced them to reckon with what they found on the ground. The process began early. The chief of Kecoughtan had feasted the Virginia Company after their first landfall, and when Smith returned to trade for maize he received fish, oysters, bread, and venison in exchange for his sheets of copper, hatchets, and glass beads. The people of Paspihe and

Chickahominy likewise engaged Smith in reciprocal relationships that involved kinship and alliance as well as trade. Even when Opechancanough's warriors had seized Smith and brought him to Pamunkey, where he had first watched the map dance, the town's women fed him bread and venison, civilized food, as a way of showing that he belonged. The *werowances* who hosted Smith treated him as any other rival or potential partner and mediated his relationship with their people and other towns in order to obtain the exotic prestige goods like copper or glass beads that he possessed and to yoke his power to their own interests. Building ties with the strangers enhanced their leadership and added to their renown. Indeed, when Powhatan dispatched Smith to subjugate two enemy towns, he named Smith a *werowance* and proclaimed publicly that Smith was as entitled as any other leader to the maize and loyalty of Tsenacommacah.[44]

Smith understood full well the position in which Powhatan and Opechancanough had put him, but the captain was adept at the game as well. Armed with a passel of presents from King Charles, Smith invited Powhatan to receive them at Jamestown. The old leader knew he would be asked to place his authority under that of the king, so he replied, "Your father is to come to me." Having lost his gambit, Smith opposed taking up Powhatan on the invitation. Smith's superior, Christopher Newport, however, forwarded the gifts by boat—a bed, furniture, scarlet cloak, and other goods—to Powhatan's residence at Werawocomocco and promised to follow soon to make the man a subject of Charles. The ceremony that followed was as awkward an event as can be found in the annals of invasion. "But a foule trouble there was to make him kneele to receive his Crowne," Smith regretted. "At last by leaning hard on his shoulder," Smith continued, "he a little stooped, and three having the crowne in their hands put it on his head." Things came undone after the affair of the Crown. Powhatan had grown disappointed in Smith's constant scheming and his refusal to accept his position as *werowance*. "I never use any Werowance so kindely as your selfe," Smith recalled Powhatan saying to him, "yet from you I receive the least kindnesse of any."[45]

Whatever suspicions Powhatan had of Smith were well founded, for the captain traveled the countryside looking for towns he could pry from Powhatan's league and attach to his own. In reply Powhatan withheld the maize on which the company depended, so Smith went on the attack, and Nansemonds, Chickahominies, and others saw their dwellings fired, their fields destroyed, and their granaries emptied. Smith, however, by chance suffered terrible burns when a store of gunpowder accidentally ignited. While the first people may have told tales about the avenging fire of the sun, he departed for England, never to return. The colony's fortunes plummeted without his astute exploitation of his position as *werowance* and his understanding of the politics of tribute, trade, and hierarchy. His adaptation of the walking people's ways was neither an affectation nor an empty convention of rhetoric because the colony starved when Powhatan shut off all trade. What had been a reasonably healthy outpost of five-hundred people dwindled to sixty or so ragged survivors during the starving time that followed Smith's exit.[46] Subsequent governors like Thomas Gates and Thomas Dale lacked the rapport with Powhatan that Smith had enjoyed, and they too learned over time the advantages of structuring Jamestown's external relations along lines similar to Powhatan's confederacy and of belonging to rather than standing apart from the world into which they had stepped.

At first Governor Gates sought to undo the close ties that had formed between the two people when Smith first sent settlers to live with their hosts. He instructed the invaders to evict first people who might be living in their homes, to post sentinels to keep first people away from their fields and herds, and to undertake whenever possible the conversion of "these murtherers of Soules" to the Christian faith.[47] But the degree to which Gates had to concede to the rules of the land offset the invaders' separation, suspicion, and missionary efforts. The Board of Governors in London ordered him to ensure that invaders built their plantations on dry land close to clean freshwater, and officials undertook walks similar to rogations to mark the boundaries of their fields, only now the ceremonies had been stripped of their religious content as settlers asserted not so much a sacred relationship with the earth and with the Father but their ownership of private property in the face of their hosts' occupation of the land. Virginia had supplanted Eden just as surely as maize had supplanted wheat. Plantations came to look like indigenous towns where palisades defended their homes. Besides their own fields, families worked common fields as well for the maintenance of the public. Each able-bodied man deposited a portion of the maize he raised in the surrounding fields to a common granary overseen by the town's highest official. The governor too oversaw a common store of maize at Jamestown that he used to reward friends and to punish enemies by either forwarding or withholding scarce supplies. Nearby nations also paid tribute to the governor in the form of maize. The Chickahominies went so far as to accept subjugation to King James and to adopt the name "Tassantessus," or "strangers" as they called the English. The English accepted the bargain and paid out hatchets for every two bushels of maize they received. Gates had to be active as well, however, to assert his own paramountcy, and Powhatan was his target. "You must make him yor tributary," the Virginia Company's directors ordered the governor, "and all other his weroances about him first to acknowledge no other Lord but King James." The key was to use trade goods to direct tribute away from Werocomocco and toward the Virginia Company warehouses and granaries at Jamestown.[48]

Similar imperatives of trade, alliance, tribute, and reciprocity that had characterized the invasions of La Florida and Tsenacommacah drove the history of South Carolina and Georgia years later as early pronouncements of yet another Eden offered by God to his chosen people yielded to the actual demands of living on the land.[49] Taking a page from lessons learned elsewhere, the Lords Proprietors and a number of local officials in the Carolina colony identified trade with the first people as the best means to purchase peace and power. Indeed, when William Hilton first scouted the coast for a suitable location for the envisioned colony, he met a Spanish captain, Antonio de Argüelles, who was purchasing maize from some Guales in Santa Elena. After having a drink the two men parted ways and Hilton recommended that the Lords Proprietors found their colony a few miles north of Santa Elena at a place the Spanish called San Jorge. Walking people ravaged by disease or alienated by the Spanish mission system, or both, began moving into the land surrounding Charles Town to take advantage of the trade possibilities the newcomers offered. The Westos were one of the earliest and most important groups, and they found their place in the new order by training English guns on Spanish friars and their *congredados*, whom they traded back to the Carolinians for sale into slavery. The Yamassees were another such group who found their national identity in the collapse of the Santa Elena mission province. A man named Altamaha led them to settle at the mouth of the Savannah River. By 1720 colonial officials reckoned they had bound twenty-eight thousand walking people to their interests at the cost of ten thousand pounds of trade. But their projection of power had its limits, for the network of trade and tribute that knitted together Carolina's defensive perimeter was, from the other end of the trading paths, a perfectly normal way of building alliances and interpersonal relationships that ensured due regard for the autonomy and power of its constituent nations.[50] When, for example, in 1693 a party of Savannahs killed an invader to square away the murder of one of their own, the proprietors counseled Governor Thomas Smith to ask the Savannahs to punish the guilty men. The Savannahs would have none of this. "Wee are informed," the governor regretted, "that Indians are apt to revenge the death of their Relations upon that Nation that put him to death."[51] For the Westos, Yamassees, Creeks, and others, the trade and tribute network that Carolina built with its allies made the colony a nation beholden to the customs of the country.

And such customs changed the way that the invaders had expected to live. In a pamphlet aimed at prospective immigrants to Carolina, the author created a stock settler named James Freeman to explain to interested readers that, while in England one sowed seed in rows, in Carolina one planted maize, or "Virginia wheat" as it was popularly known, in small hills and intercropped them with peas that, like beans, would climb the stalks. Ploughs were of no use in the colonies because of the deeply entangled system of tree roots that in Europe had been cleared out of the fields millennia before. Like the first people, settlers felled trees by girdling them, which, by Freeman's calculations, left the roots intact for twelve to fifteen years after. Hoes were all that aspiring farmers needed or could really use to draw life from the rich soil, and when the colonizers adopted the locals' practice of burning the land every fall they were able to replenish their fields with ashes instead of muck and manure. No longer would the Europeans need to live alongside their cattle and hogs, for the beasts could range freely in the forests where they competed with deer for forage and trespassed on first peoples' fields. Hedgerows were, likewise, also absent from the colonial landscape because the invaders, like the first people, preferred to move to new land when they had exhausted their gardens' soils. The technology and knowledge that had evolved in a cloistered and cluttered European landscape that required fertilizing and fallowing to remain productive simply had no place in the region. Indeed, according to naturalist Mark Catesby, maize was superior to its Old World analogues. "Oats thrive well in *Carolina*, though they are very rarely propagated," he remarked, "*Indian Corn* supplying its Use to better Purpose."[52]

As elsewhere, maize was the staple in Carolina. Dr. Francis Le Jau, a missionary for the Society for the Propagation of the Gospel in Charles Town, set up house for himself and subsisted on "Indian cornbread" and water with the occasional morsel of meat to round out his diet.[53] During his visits to towns and farms Reverend Charles Woodmason encountered people who ate the same food as the Catawba and Cherokee warriors who raided them from time to time. As much as he despised the people to whom he ministered, he loathed their diet even more. At Cane Creek in the winter of 1767 he survived for a week on nothing but "Indian corn meal" and milk. And after a particularly hard journey through foul weather he happened upon a small cabin where the "poor woman" who lived there welcomed him by her fire, but she had nothing more to offer him than "Indian Corn Bread and Water." The diet of the people who had settled at the Cheraws was just as sparse. "No Eggs, Butter, Flour, Milk, nor anything," he regretted as he pined for the fare of his home country, "but fat rusty Bacon, and fair Water, with Indian Corn Bread."[54] And those invaders who subsisted on maize also learned to make their homes in places that had drawn human inhabitants for millennia. In 1731 the colony's government created nine townships to settle the drainages of five major rivers, the Savannah, the Wateree, the Edisto, the Congaree, and the Peedee. Fredericksburg Township on the Wateree, for example, lay astride the Catawba path that tied the colony to one of its closest allies. The Quakers who had turned the square plots into homes in the 1740s positioned their meeting house on high ground overlooking Pine Tree Creek and engaged in a ceramics trade with other nearby settlements over the paths that had bound people together in the region for so many years.[55]

The invaders, of course, had their own myths to explain the land they claimed. Expanding upon General James Oglethorpe's intent to dedicate the colony of Georgia to "a Christian, moral and industrious way of life," Sir Robert Montgomery, an early booster of Georgia, described the colony as "*Paradise* with all her virgin beauties." But the womanly garden did not belong to the first people who had made her. Georgia was nothing less, Montgomery declared, than "our *future Eden*." To erase any doubts in the minds of his readers, he calculated that the new settlements occupied the same latitude as the Promised Land.[56] Oglethorpe remarked that the land Creek women farmed would "produce almost everything in wonderful Quantities with very little Culture."[57] Another visitor to Georgia went so far as to applaud the "spontaneous" wealth that sprung from the soil.[58] Abundant oak trees pointed colonizers toward champion land where they could produce raw silk, potash, flax, hemp, cattle, and fowl with little or no effort.[59]

The leaders of yet another real and true people who met Oglethorpe in 1735 gave the lie to the myth of Eden, however, and dramatized their own conception of how their people had come to be and how they saw the English fitting into their land. The Kasihtas informed him that they had crawled out of a hole in the ground, a mother cave, and had fought their way across many red rivers to arrive at their present home. While offering the Englishman a white token of peace to mark the opening of a clear bright path between the two peoples, they, at the same time, drew Oglethorpe and his followers into the landscape so that they could share the same world. In pointing out to the Georgians how best to conduct themselves in this new relationship, the man reminded Oglethorpe that in the past his people had never shirked from setting aside their white feathers when outsiders violated the balance of their relationship. At such times, the real and true people had, the group informed Oglethorpe, painted their hatchets red and marched to war down crooked paths against former friends who, through their ungrateful behavior, had shown they did not belong.[60]

Such lessons had not been lost on the invaders who founded La Louisiane. While scholars tend to recognize the colony as French, the men who undertook its founding were Canadians who had gained invaluable experience working with first people in the St. Lawrence Valley and, for this reason, shared none of the utopian fantasies that inspired their imperial rivals. Talk of Christ, Eden, and trees as tall as the sky did not figure into their imagined sense of place when they coasted the shoals of present-day Alabama, Mississippi, and Louisiana. When, for example, a party visited the abandoned remnants of the town of Mavila in 1700, the men found a large cross erected by the Spanish. But the impact of the diseases impressed them most. Pierre Le Moyne d'Iberville's experience told him epidemics must have torn through the countryside. This was not a landscape of grapes and gardens. "I have found almost everywhere," he noted, "abandoned Indian settlements," and the people he met were the survivors of the ravages that Soto and others had loosed upon the land.[61]

When Ribault's party had coasted La Florida, they had chosen names like Seine, Loire, and Jordan for the rivers they sighted, but Iberville, whose father had labored for four hard years at a Jesuit outpost on Lake Huron, who had mastered a number of native languages, and who made his name in Montréal as a translator, had grown up in a different kind of landscape from Ribault's Huguenots. He sought not to recreate the old world of France but to register by names the people and resources that would be important to his endeavor and, not to be forgotten, his claim of ownership in the name of his king. The "Baye des Pascagoulas," for example, marked the way to visit one of his important allies while the "Rivière aux Poissons" or the "Pointe aux Coquilles" reflected where fish could be caught or shellfish collected. The Canadians Iberville stationed at Fort Biloxi were as experienced as he was, and they spoke to the Pascagoulas, Bayagoulas, Biloxis, and Mobiliens in Iroquoian tongues to little effect, much to their own chagrin. Owing to their experiences in Canada, Iberville's party had no illusions about invoking royal dominion. Instead, he sought to strike up partnerships with the local nations more in line with their own sense of the world. At Fort Biloxi, for example, it was Iberville who rolled out the welcome mat and called several leaders together to smoke a calumet he had had made for the occasion, for he knew the importance of protocol, tobacco, and smoke. Artisans had crafted his pipe in the shape of a ship and decorated it with a white flag bearing fleur-de-lis and glass beads. He gave as well blankets, shirts, axes, and knives, and received furs and pledges of food and military support in return. He knew what he was doing, and, more importantly, he made at the outset a place for the Canadians in the lower Mississippi Valley.[62]

Owing to the relationship between place and space, Iberville was able to translate the good relations he enjoyed with the first people he met into the support necessary for the colony's survival. Unable to scratch a living from the sandy soils that surrounded Biloxi, starvation forced the Canadians to depend on their neighbors for their sustenance. In 1700 the commander of the garrison of Fort Maurepas at Biloxi dispersed his soldiers among the Mobilien people, where they could find adequate sources of food, as John Smith had done nearly a century before. The Mobiliens' maize, what the French called "Indian wheat," beans, squashes, watermelons, and peaches, as well as the pots in which to cook the food saw the struggling colony through its first year. Five years later Canadian farmers attempted to grow wheat along Bayou St. John between Lake Pontchartrain and the Mississippi River to nourish the slowly growing colony. Seed damaged by the voyage across the ocean, high humidity, and scorching summer temperatures, however, conspired against their efforts to plant a little bit of Europe in the old fields of America. Only maize flourished in the invaders' gardens, and, just as the walking people had been doing for perhaps five centuries, the settlers hilled their maize but did so in straight rows to facilitate weeding and, no doubt, to act out their own linear compulsions. Accommodating themselves to the taste and texture of maize was difficult, however, and only in 1706 could the colony's governor write that "the men who are in Louisiana are accustoming themselves to eat it, but the women who are for the most part from Paris eat it reluctantly."[63]

Obtaining supplies of maize, beans, and venison required ongoing efforts at cultivating and maintaining relationships. Gift giving, smoking of the calumet, and pledging friendship enabled Iberville both to integrate La Louisiane into broader regional networks of power and to situate first Biloxi and then New Orleans as important nodes in those networks. But it took practice and effort to make it happen. Under the deer moon, for example, the first moon of their calendar, a real and true people whom the Canadians called the Natchez welcomed him to their country in much the same way as Tascaluza had greeted Soto a century and a half before. The body of their leader, the Great Sun, mapped his people's world in the blue tattoos of the sun and serpents that covered his arms, legs, and chest. As a group of men bore the sun to meet Iberville, the Canadian understood the degree to which land and power fused in the body and the lineage of the man before him. The living map welcomed Iberville to his world with gifts, a white cross to evoke the sun's power and the sanctity of the man's authority, and a pearl, an object from the watery world of the earth, that situated the explorers in the same in-between place that the real and true people called home.[64]

A sacred fire burned in the temple that sat atop a mound adjacent to the Great Sun's home. Inside sat the cane boxes that held the bones of the deceased suns that had preceded him, tying his family's line to the original mother, the earth. Wooden eagles perched on the roof, watching the world on behalf of the sky. Outside of the temple, the chief performed his own sense of place and space. The architecture of his home and the mound, his body's markings, and the cross and the pearl came to life as he shouted to the west, lit his pipe, and blew smoke to the four points of the cross. His visitors shared in the pipe ceremony, letting their clear voices fly into the air to take wing toward the west, signaling their own concurrence, if for only a moment, in the poetics of his place and space, his in-between. When the Great Sun instructed his guests to blow smoke to the sky, the earth, and, lastly, the horizon that separated the two and that marked the in-between world where he and his guests lived, he held out the promise that they too could become real and true.[65]

The Great Sun, and leaders like him, were as good as their word. The settlers who followed Iberville up the waterways of La Louisiane found first people whose knowledge of portages, passes, and waterways made settlement possible. Shell middens, deposited by shellfish collectors over thousands of years, marked the spots where first people built their camps. And, as the middens trapped wind-blown soil and acorns, they sprouted to life, sustaining the large oak trees that caught the invaders' eyes. Old town sites yielded new homes and fields such as at Bayou St. John, Bayagoulas, Tchoupitoulas, and New Orleans where the scarce high and dry ground had been home to a Quinipissas town and a major portage between the river and Lake Pontchartrain. Once they realized that wheat would never grow, they planted maize, beans, and squash on levees and burned the land in the fall to prepare it for spring planting, gaining for themselves a foothold as a people by adopting the practices and places of those they had pushed out and replaced.[66]

The replacement of people in the landscape, however, involved more than the invaders, for they brought with them people whom they had enslaved and whom they had enlisted to remake the land in their own image. Enslaved people troubled the real and true people, who first encountered colonial slavery in 1521 when, on the day of the feast of Saint John the Baptist, two caravels commanded by Pedro de Quejo and Francisco Gordillo eased into what today is called the South Santee River and made contact with a group on a nearby beach to whom they offered linen shirts, kerchiefs, and red caps. The landing party received in return a meal of venison, maize, and other local food. They named the river Jordan and rowed their ships' boats up and down the shore, in and out of the inlets and mouths of creeks looking for people to grab. After trading and exploring for ten days or so, the two captains invited a number of locals on board and set sail. In the end, they had captured perhaps sixty walking people whom they carried to their employers for sale in the markets of Santo Domingo.[67]

Another kind of enslaved people came from afar, and it was they who emerged as the third of the region's founding peoples. The first few contacts between first people and enslaved people from either Africa or the Indies are inscrutable. In 1526 a revolt in Lucas Vázquez Ayllòn's short-lived colony on the coast of present-day South Carolina let loose a few enslaved people into the countryside, but no one knows what happened to them. Soto's *entrada* and Juan Pardo's search into the interior for a trail to the silver mines of New Spain also put enslaved people of African ancestry and real and true people in contact with one another, but again the substance of such contact has been lost. Far more certain are the experiences of enslaved people who arrived in the South through the middle passage that opened between the Americas and Africa in the wake of Columbus's voyages. But where he found a world of wonder and possibility, the captives who were crammed between decks on slave ships and suffocated in the reek of vomit, feces, urine, and blood had, one ship slaver wrote, "a more dreadful apprehension of Barbados than we have of hell."[68] In addition to the horrible living conditions, inhumane treatment, poor food, and bad water; the passage severed their connections to the ancestors, to the spirits, to the trees, and to the worlds they had made together. Captives on the slave ships looked on in horror as the slavers, wise to local notions that only intact bodies could make the journey below the water to the afterlife, knowingly mutilated some captives to cow the others into submission. Captives watched with horror as one ship's captain beheaded a man accused of killing a crewman and threw the body across the kalunga line into the ocean. Without his head the man had no chance of finding the afterworld where his ancestors awaited his arrival, and with his death an entire family tree fell into the sea and sank to the bottom.[69]

But out of these early fragments comes a story that, while taking different turns depending on where the enslaved people were placed, followed a fairly common plot. Enslaved people did not arrive in the Americas as members of intact communities. They stumbled out of the holds at the end of social life and on the edge of death. Relationships that reached back to their homelands or that had been forged in the holds could come undone in the sales. The effort to reconstitute the places of their former homes or the homes of their forebears and to adapt old practices to a new environment took place almost immediately, however, and was an important part of their broader struggle to make new families and new communities under the worst of circumstances. The cycles of the moon had to be recalibrated for both planting and birthing, the sun crossed the sky in a wholly new direction, new seasons had to be overlaid atop old calendars, new medicines had to be fashioned from unfamiliar plants, and the screeches of owls and the colors and patterns of new snakes' skins had to be added to extant lists of omens. In Carolina and Georgia, woodcarvers found supplies of cedar and cypress at hand to fashion into boats, mortars, boards, and drums, and basketmakers located banks of rushes which could be bundled with grasses and made into baskets, containers, and rice fanners while, on the farms of Louisiana, enslaved people often used baskets and containers fashioned by enslaved first people. African crops, those plants that had first distinguished the world of people from the world of animals, held important places in the enslaved people's gardens. Yams first sprouted in Barbados in 1627 and spread across the Caribbean. At the same time indigenous plants known as sweet potatoes, batatas, or Virginia potatoes played important roles in sustaining invaders, first people, and the enslaved. Okra and "Guinea corn," as sorghum was known, also enabled families to recreate in partial form the gardens and dishes of their ancestral places and to provide poultry for stewpots from Charles Town to New Orleans.[70]

Their homes likewise signaled their ability to rebuild the past out of the materials of the present. Across South Carolina rammed-earth dwellings typical of the West African countryside transformed what plantation owners called slave quarters into human settlements. The thick earth walls dried to a rock-hard finish and provided cool shelter in long summers and retained warmth for short winters. A variety of African roofing technologies were used, from palmetto thatch to split planks with gabled ends, and, as in African dwellings, the people designed their settlements, when they could, to allow for a wide range of communal outdoor activities. Hard-packed floors flowed out of the homes and into the courtyards where women transformed maize, okra, sorghum, and other foodstuffs into the stews and sauces characteristic of African cooking and worked local sands, clays, and shells into the pots they used to cook and serve their food. Regular sweeping held at bay the constant invasion of the forest and kept the children busy in the routine of place-making.[71]

The domestic landscape of their villages belonged to a series of larger relationships between place and power and that rooted the people in more than just their homes, gardens, and courtyards. As in Africa the enslaved people measured time by the cycles of the moon and by the seasonal rhythms of their lives. In Carolina and La Louisiane, maize planting time was followed by rice planting time while harvest time heralded cooler weather and sorer backs. They could look to the time and space they inhabited for guidance, and they enjoined their surroundings in conversations. Perhaps people sought out prominent trees in nearby groves to strike up conversations as one enslaved man in New York did, or, to find the comfort of kin, as one enslaved boy in Alabama found under the shade of a big oak tree that he called his nurse. The Cooper River became home to a water spirit whose ability to read the future, alter the weather, and protect the people merited a number of gifts. On the bottoms of the pottery pieces that people threw into the river, people traced the circle and cross maps that both first people and enslaved people shared as a basic cosmological referent and that brought the kalunga line across the sea to the plantations of Carolina. People left similar pots filled with food in the graveyards that were adjacent to their villages. The spirits that relied upon such gifts to sustain them were thereby able to remain in the land and to intervene in the lives of the living.[72]

As with the river and its gifts, so too did the herds of cattle they managed bespeak the promises of the ancestors to their descendants. Though the cattle were owned by invaders, the enslaved men who tended them in Carolina, La Florida, and La Louisiane employed techniques and technologies born in the highlands of the Senegambia and Niger River Valleys. Turning cattle loose in the salt marshes of the coastal plain echoed prior practices in Africa and in Jamaica, while the nightly herding and penning of the animals called for the construction of cowpens and wattle fencing that anchored small African settlements beyond the towns and plantation districts closer to Charles Town and New Orleans. In Carolina, over time, as the herds multiplied, nightly penning became impractical and British practices such as using salt blocks to tie herds to particular locales merged with African antecedents to yield new forms of animal husbandry while in La Louisiane, first people and enslaved people continued the early methods well into the nineteenth century.[73]

In the Senegambia Valley, whence many of the cowboys came, women's cultivation of rice played a complementary part of the regional economy. Wetland rice cultivation, which relied on flooding and rain for water, was the earliest rice-growing complex to appear in South Carolina. In West Africa men and women rotated field use, allowing cattle to browse the stalks of harvested rice while enriching the fields with their manure. Such practices may have occurred in the Carolina low country before the cowboys moved the herds farther away from the coast. The cultivation of rice, the timing of planting with the full moon, hoeing the rows side by side while singing worksongs, and fanning the grain after the fashion of their forebears drew women together in ways similar to those enjoyed by the men who herded cattle. Rice, like cattle, too tied women to the land

and, even though the grains their efforts yielded were owned by the very men who owned them, rice cultivation provided crucial links to the sacred potential of the land. Over time, African workers augmented the floodwater rice complex by building holding pools and irrigation ditches much like those built for rice farming in the mangrove areas of West Africa, but it was the floodwater complex, most likely established by the women, that gave them a first purchase on the land.[74]

The gardens that fed them, the homes that housed them, the graveyards that held their ancestors, and the rivers that contained powerful spirits enlivened a landscape that brought the meanings of the particular places of western Africa to the fields, forests, paths, and towns of slavery. Such places created the kind of depth they needed to build a sense of time and place attuned to their own needs. The landscape the enslaved people made reached further, however, and began to knit together far-flung communities in local and then regional networks of contact and exchange. Enslaved people marked Sunday as the one day a week when they gathered in cities and towns for market. Upon his arrival in Charles Town, Francis Le Jau remarked that "I[t] has been Customary among [slaves] to have their feasts, dances, and merry Meetings upon the Lord's day."[75] Le Jau hoped he had found not just a ready pool of converts to his ministry but a respect for Sundays on the part of owners and the enslaved people that would facilitate his mission. Practice did not square with theory, however, as Le Jau complained to his superiors that many enslaved people refused to attend his Anglican services on Sundays, preferring instead to clear ground and to plant crops for their own use.[76] In spite of invaders' complaints that the Sunday tradition had filled the streets of Charles Town with dissolute "negroes" and portended doom for the colony, the practice found legal sanction in the proceedings of the colonial government of Georgia and in the customs of the country.[77]

People packed their produce and traveled to towns to vend and trade what they had raised, grown, made, or taken. In Mobile, New Orleans, and Natchez, enslaved people vended their owners' produce as well as the products of their own labors, and it was the women who held the positions of greatest prominence as they barked from their stalls, bartered for goods, and perhaps skimmed a bit of cash whenever they could. In New Orleans a stretch of land between the levee that held the river at bay and the first row of town houses hosted the main market. In Charles Town it was the green. On one Sunday in the fall of 1732, for example, two hundred people that the editors of the *South Carolina Gazette* identified as "negroes" took over the green, the town's principal civic place, to drink, to talk, and to fight.[78] The markets that sprouted on Sundays, what a grand jury in Charles Town declared in 1734 to be a "great Grievance," afforded important places for enslaved people to interact, to acquire, and to dispose of their own property, and to constitute regional and rural geographies in condensed urban settings.[79] The markets of the South where enslaved people vended their produce undoubtedly bore certain similarities to African ones, but, as historian Gerald Mullin has indicated, signs of African holdovers in the colonial South are extraordinarily difficult to find. The markets provided places for exchange and spaces for social interaction above and beyond marketing. Both men and women hawked their wares. Bacchus and Quaco, for example, were well known in the Charles Town market where they vended greens, fruits, and veal that Quaco had raised.[80] Apparently men like Bacchus and Quaco could be formidable salesmen, for settlers complained that the markets in maize, peas, and poultry on which they depended for their household subsistence charged "exhorbitant prices."[81] But the vendors drove more than hard bargains, for the men and women who set their calendars by the seasons, the moons, and the marts persisted to create places and time for themselves within the wider coercive space of slavery.[82]

Markets provided places for broad social interaction between scattered communities of enslaved people and laid the foundation for networks of kinship that transformed economic relationships into familial ones that were deeply implicated in their constructions of the landscape of the enslaved. The bonds of family that reached beyond the here and now of blood relations to the past and future lives of their kin emboldened many enslaved folk to flee and reconnect with lost loved ones, drawing the South together in a network of ancestral energy that crackled from Charles Town to Chota. A number of explanations have been offered for the motivations of runaways as well as for the predominance of male runaways, all of which hinge on protesting the conditions of enslavement. Neither flying to freedom nor escaping terrible living conditions, however, reflect anything that might be called a particularly African motivation for flight. But it is possible that certain general African imperatives may have also been at work that while connected to slavery also predated it, and, if so, they can probably be seen in the most common explanation owners offered for the flight of the people they enslaved: their desire to reconnect with family members and restore their fragile lineages.[83]

In a world where the living inhabited the same places as the spirits of both the dead and the yet-to-be-born, young adults, who were the majority of runaways in colonial South Carolina, were the least grounded members of society. They were caught between the stages of life that distinguished mature mothers and fathers from genderless children and, in the same way, between the interstices of the kin hierarchies that tied mothers, fathers, aunts, and uncles to the communities they inhabited. Among African societies family provided essential support and resources for young people to become adults through marriage exchanges and circumcision and scarification ceremonies. One could not become an adult without a family, and the frequency with which people fled to reunite with distant parents and children reflects their struggles to retain the communal bonds and lines of lineage that had structured life in Africa, as truncated as they might have been in the colonies. Hector, for example, fled to a plantation in Christ Church, South Carolina, to be with his mother and father while a slave named Dick rejoined his father in Wando Neck, and July reconnected with his father on William Gibbons's plantation in Georgia. Hagar, who had given birth to a "mustee" daughter named Fanny likewise sought support on Mr. Barksdale's place at Wando Neck where her brother and other family members lived. In 1749 Cuffie fled presumably to locate his wife and child whom his owner Catherine Cattell had sold.[84] None of these people left journals, and none had their travels and deeds recorded for posterity. Instead, their owners placed advertisements to find them, and in the owner's search we can see another search—for family, kin, and friends—that wove the places of slavery into the space of the South and put a third founding cosmology into play.

In some respects, slavery was a by-product of the biblical imperatives that impelled the invaders to create their own places. Over time neither Eden nor the cyclopes were serviceable as reference points for the exercise in dead reckoning that Columbus had begun. While the fantasy of dominion and conquest remained an unshakeable component of the invaders' gaze, they confronted people whose own values, practices, and desires made the creation of a "New World" impossible. Instead, the invaders had to adapt to survive and yet in so doing failed to see that the new monsters that inhabited their horizons—"negroes" and "Indians"—in fact shared the center with them. The integrity of the enslaved people to the region's places came from their labor; from the first people it came from their power and their knowledge. Whether in the maize that fed the invaders or in the honored titles that made them brothers to the sun, the rules and practices that were already in place drew the trajectory of colonization away from the linear patterns of progress and onto the intersecting and elliptical paths that had grown from millennia of human occupation and sociability. The founding peoples were making neither a New World, a white world, a red world, nor a black world, but something else, something in-between, a creole world.

Chapter 3

PATHS

In 1732 James Oglethorpe and twenty other trustees for the colony of Georgia received a royal charter to settle land west of Carolina and south of the Savannah River for the purposes of building a place that would know neither slavery nor poverty. The contours of the land to which they laid claim were quite clear in their minds. It was, Oglethorpe wrote, one of several "vast Tracts of waste Lands subject to the Crown of *Great Britain* in *America*," a "Receptacle of wild Beasts." Hoping to attract the "the better Sort of the Indigent" from the overcrowded streets of London, the trustees expected that removing such folk from the idleness, vice, and misfortune that came with city life would provide the makings of a new world of prosperous and pious smallholders in Georgia.[1] Aristotle and Plato, as repackaged by the compilers and editors of late medieval Europe, had told the trustees that the land they had received from the Crown would yield silk, wine, and olive oil owing to its location along the same latitude as China, Persia, and the Madeiras Islands. The capital city Savannah too would be a model of order with its latticework of streets embracing modest town homes and gracious public gardens. As anthropologist Ann Laura Stoler has suggested, however, it is too tempting to read such idealistic designs as plans of conquest. On the contrary, such fantasies of order are, as she put it, "blueprints of distress." The plan that must have seemed so plausible when put to paper in a London parlor fell apart as soon as the first shipment of 114 men and women arrived in November 1732 at a place whose names challenged the plausibility of the trustees' design.[2]

Some people called the place Yamacraw Bluff after the walking people who had only recently moved into the area after the first people who had lived there before them disappeared into the slipstream of the Carolina slave trade. Other people had given the spot another name from another place. When the Castilians cut their way across the islands they called the

Indies they borrowed a word, *sabana,* from the Arawaks who lived there to signify the marshy treeless floodplains that were so different from the more arid rangelands of home where they pastured their cattle. As time passed, enslaved Africans from either Senegambia or the highlands of Foula Djalon, *sabaneros* the Castillians called them, ranged cattle for their Iberian owners in the Indies and had spread the word as well as an entire way of raising cattle from Hispaniola and Cuba to English plantations in Barbados and Jamaica. By way of cowboys who had either ranged north from Spanish haciendas near St. Augustine or had been brought to Carolina by the founders, the name *Savannah* fell into place where the men turned the invaders' cattle loose to forage in the forests—"receptacle of wild beasts" indeed. It was enslaved people and first people who had made the tract of "waste" into a place, and the trustees ignored the lay of this land at their peril.³

No matter the trustees' vision of a place isolated from both the evils of Carolina's slavery and the dangers of the savage forest, the town was but one place in a much larger space, and the land Oglethorpe claimed was not a disembodied thing. It was neither a champion field for "Indians" to lose and for invaders to win nor a frontier that separated civilization from savagery. Whether the invaders had no doubt about the existence of a frontier between them and the "Indians" or that the boundaries created by European conquest should stand as the unyielding center of any history of the Americas is beside the point. The concept of frontier relegates such points of contact to that inert horizontality that Natter and Jones warned us about. Nor is it enough to switch our gaze and face east rather than west if we persist in calling them "Indians," for there is no more westward facing word than that one.⁴

Other portals offer other entries into this world and can take us beyond the limitations of the concept of "Indian" or of frontier. A trail that started at Savannah's waterfront, for example, ran through the grid of streets and parks into the nations beyond and worked as an axis around which the next several decades of life in the town revolved. It was more than a path in the sense of a cleared trail cutting through an otherwise difficult landscape. It was a conduit for relationships, a bearer of obligations born of the world of the sun and goods shipped from the land of clouds eastward across the open sea. Let us follow the walking people for a while and see the colonial South from such paths.

It is easy to take the talk of paths that was so common around council fires as just talk, but in the real and true peoples' concept of the world, paths expressed the poetical quality of relations between neighbors. In theory, places tend to break down the opposite forces that come together within them and to hold the people who share them together in new kinds of relationships. In the colonies and in the nations, as the paths became blocked or cleared, crooked or straight, or bloodied or cleansed, the people who traveled them meandered from being strangers to friends to family to being enemies and back again. Being a so-called "Indian," "white," or "black" was important to be sure but did not necessarily determine either the nature and quality of the paths or the relationships that linked the founding peoples together. What the paths did was make possible the creation of the colonial South out of the moments of invasion and first contact.

The red and white paths that crossed in and around Savannah were neither simple nor linear. They had been long in the making, and, as such, they were complicated, overlapping, elliptical, and, at times, contrary. Remember, when the invaders came they stepped into a landscape that had been in the making for millennia, and no matter the powerful effects of their guns, their germs, and their steel, they were in no position to impose their own kind of order. Looking back today we can see that centuries of conscious effort to wipe the old paths from the region's face have mostly succeeded even though today they linger still if one looks hard enough. But in the process of colonization as it unfolded on the ground, notions of Eden, of temperate zones, and of antipodal beasts gave way to hard-nosed preoccupations with the landscape at hand and the people who inhabited it. Enslaved people of course had to make their way as well, and while their servitude left them with little force they did have the power to create, to attribute meaning, and to make their own places that at once echoed life in Africa and laid bare the powerful disruptions and discontinuities of life in America. From the invaders' perspective at least, a landscape populated by savages and negroes, whose existence at once threatened and was integral to the reproduction of invader society, needs instead to be seen as one that the founding peoples created together.[5]

One white path opened between the first people and the Jamestowners when Powhatan recognized John Smith as a *werowance*. After Smith's departure for England to recover from the powder burns he had sustained, however, the Virginians starved, sickened, and began to die. Lord de la Ware sought to help out by building two forts, Henry and Charles, but in so doing he forsook the white path for one that was red. Taking a page from the walking peoples' handbook on where to settle to survive, he positioned the forts as if they were indigenous villages—on ridges near springs at the intersection of woods, marshes, and fields. Both happened as well to be near the town of Kecoughtan that had first welcomed the Virginia Company's men before they moved on to the unhealthy spot where they founded Jamestown. Behind the wattle and daub walls of the invaders' homes and the log palisades that protected their towns, the invaders set about to create their own rival confederacy premised on the collection of maize as tribute. Officials mandated that each eligible man must clear, sow, tend, and harvest three acres of maize annually, and, in 1611, Governor Sir Thomas Dale ordered settlers to pool their own maize harvests for collective use while plantation commanders supervised the redistribution of the surpluses. Allied nations also surrendered baskets of maize for the support of the invaders so that by 1619 the English system of maize tribute yielded the colony twelve hundred bushels of maize and put the place back on a reasonably sound footing.[6]

But the policy of remaking the colony of Virginia as a confederacy predicated on the politics of maize put Jamestown in open competition with Powhatan for land, labor, and authority. New pales sprouted to defend Jamestown, and new fortified settlements like Bermudas, where the pale stretched for two miles from one riverbank to another, crawled across the land.[7] The ability of the invaders to project their power on the land signaled to their neighbors their hostile intentions, and Governor Gates cultivated a distance between the invaders and their neighbors as well. "Make little estimaçon of trade with them," the Virginia Company directors ordered their new governor. Pretend to be self-sufficient, the company urged, and show the first people "that you neede care for nothinge of theires." The process of disengagement that such rudeness fostered blocked the white path Smith had blazed and took Virginia farther down a red one that they were not quite prepared to walk.[8]

Self-conscious incivility antagonized the colony's neighbors and resulted in the disappearance of any number of tools, firearms, and swords as first people reasserted their humanity and ownership of the land by denying the invaders theirs. To bring Powhatan to terms, Captain Samuel Argall, with the help of some first people who saw Jamestown as a more likely seat for the confederacy than Powhatan's town, lured the leader's kinswoman Pocahontas on board a ship in Jamestown harbor where Argall held her in ransom for the missing items. Powhatan offered instead five hundred bushels of maize, but it was not enough. Governor Dale led a column of 150 men to press Powhatan's brother Opechancanough to come to terms, but, in the moment of crisis, they as well as Opechancanough's warriors had to relent. Harvest time was approaching, and each side needed its maize if it was to live to fight another day.[9] A more formal peace and the restoration of the clear bright path came with the subsequent marriage of Pocahontas to John Rolfe. The marriage of Powhatan's confederacy and of the Virginia Company restored the imbalance that had come with the forts, the incivility, and the resentment. The walking people used the new path to make up their losses while other nations who had sided with the

English plotted to redden it anew. A party of Chickahominy warriors, for example, brought the governor two fat bucks and received in exchange copper gorgets emblazoned with King James's face. They took up one end of a shiny copper chain as the English took the other and pledged to protect one another while they connived to supplant Powhatan.[10]

What the Virginians did was not unique. Just as the Jamestowners adopted indigenous practices and politics in ways that imprinted their production of a colonial landscape, so too did the invaders who followed in later times and in other places. Several hundred miles south and nearly seventy years later, for example, shell middens marked the spot where a group of Barbadian adventurers decided to settle and search out the passage to India. They originally named the spot Oyster Point for obvious reasons, but the Lords Proprietors hoped to use the ancient gathering place as a base for the construction of a kind of feudal new world. Oyster Point became Ashley Point, after one of the lords, and then Charles Town while the founders named a river that probably had as many names as nations that traveled it Ashley.[11]

But as in Virginia, aspirations counted for little in the early going. Indeed, the Lords Proprietors who sponsored Carolina's founding instructed their men in the colony that "it is absolutely necessary that the trade be carried on with those nations so that they may be supply'd with commodities . . . by which rewards a firm and lasting peace shall be continued." The advice was sound, for subsequent generations of invaders found that gifts and goods enabled them to transform themselves from outsiders beholden to either force of arms or grace as guests into social beings who could influence outcomes within the confines of preexisting codes of conduct and belief. Just a decade after the founding of Charles Town, for example, Kasihtas, Savannahs, Yamassees, and Westos who had benefited from the proprietors' willingness to trade in guns and captives impelled hundreds of other walking people to flee to the border country of La Florida. At the same time the clatter of metal pots that heralded the arrival of pony caravans from Carolina drew people to the towns of Creek country where English traders handed out muskets and hatchets to those they hoped to enlist in furthering their slaving efforts. To leaders who before had received small gifts of exotic Spanish clothing that they displayed much as their predecessors would have made a show of exotic feather or shell adornments, the abundance and quality of English goods was attractive.[12]

Trade and gifts, in the world of paths, made possible deeper human relationships. Brims, the leader of the Creek town Coweta, earned his influence through control of trade goods and used his power to tie the newcomers to his people as kin. Coosaponakeesa, his niece, completed the opening of a white path when, in 1716, she married the son of a trader named John Musgrove to conclude a treaty that allied Carolina and Coweta. A number of Coosaponakeesa's relations decamped on Musgrove's land at Yamacraw Bluff, and their leader Tomochichi welcomed the invaders with a buffalo robe on which had been painted an eagle's head and feathers, tokens of the sky and of the sun. The gift embroiled Oglethorpe in a wider social world. Tomochichi explained that Brims and the leaders of Coweta, a town that had been born of Kasihta sometime in the late seventeenth century, had pushed him and his people to the coast. In the genealogy of towns that confronted the invaders in Savannah, Yamacraw Town was the youngest and, therefore, the one most in need of protection, and when Oglethorpe accepted the skin he accepted in his embrace a small group of people who shared their leader's preference for trade ties to the English. In this way, Tomochichi was able to more firmly establish his leadership of Yamacraw Town, Coosaponakeesa and her husband won the privilege of opening a trading house on the bluff, and Oglethorpe was able to secure a revision to an earlier peace made with Coweta in 1716 and send his pious poor south of the Savannah River.[13]

The invaders caused problems, however, for just as soon as permission had been granted a party of Yuchis complained to Oglethorpe that some Carolinians had "swam a great herd of cattle over Savannah river, sent up Negroes and began a plantation." The cattle, Tomochichi explained to Oglethorpe a year later, were destroying the Yuchis' fields. But rather than follow the Kasihtas' example and chide the Georgians to stay on the white path and off of the red one, Tomochichi's wife Senauky, like Coosaponakeesa before her, used the occasion to bring people together as she would have greeted visitors to her home. She fed them and remade Oglethorpe and his adjutants as her kin. They were lucky, for within the language Senauky spoke lived grammatical structures and conventions of thought that, in words at least, would have constructed Oglethorpe and his men as women whose menstrual blood flowed uncontrollably. They were the height of pollution and all things dangerous, so perhaps she threw a portion of the venison she served them into the fire over which she had cooked the meat to ensure her success and safety. By accepting the food and the relationship to the land it expressed, the leaders of Georgia signaled to their hosts their acceptance of the place they had entered, its order, and its obligations, first and foremost of which was that they now had to offer something in return to complete the opening of the clear white path.[14]

What could the colonists give back in exchange for the food, nourishment, and kinship that Senauky had given them? Senauky knew. She was a mother, and mothers owed their children their upbringing. She handed to the missionaries who had accompanied Oglethorpe two bottles, one containing milk and the other containing honey, to constitute her place as a promised land and to enjoin them in the education of her family's and perhaps her people's children. Reading and writing would thus enable the next generation to be conversant in the invaders' way of life and close even further the gaps that separated those who gave food from those who ate it.[15]

The officers of La Louisiane too used gifts to open white paths and accomplish what they could never by force. Mingo Chito, a prominent leader of the people the French called Choctaws, sought to tread a white and clear path in spite of the disorder that had come with contact with the invaders. In 1729 he had tried to expand his power by enlisting war chiefs who could bolster his own authority and perhaps cultivate some trade ties with the packhorsemen operating out of Charles Town up among the Chickasaws. When colonial officers refused to allow one of his subordinates, a war leader named Red Shoe, to visit Mobile and collect the presents the colony gave to reward its supporters, Mingo Chito was outraged. Not only had Red Shoe been embarrassed but Mingo Chito's standing as a "Great Leader" hung in the balance. To express his contempt for the invaders' bad manners, capriciousness, and arrogance, he tore from his neck the shiny medal his partners in Mobile had given him and threw it into a nearby stream, where it sank into to the watery and womanly source of chaos that always threatened to upset life in-between.[16]

The governor, however, needed Mingo Chito and was not about to allow the king's medal to languish at the bottom of a muddy creek. He dispatched an officer named Régis du Roullet to repair the friendship and restore the balance. As he approached Mingo Chito's town, Roullet entered a cross marked at each of the four points by an oak tree. A group of honored men presented him a calumet, and for a while they shared tobacco and smoked. After enough blue smoke had risen to the sky, the men led Roullet to the town plaza, where all manner of public business was transacted. Roullet, however, did not belong to this public, so one of the men beckoned him to climb onto his back. While the beloved man scurried across the ground, the others shielded the conspicuous officer with a blanket from the peering gaze of the sun. Once they were cleanly at the plaza's center, the men deposited Roullet at Mingo Chito's feet, the talks began, soothing words were said, and the breach between the chief and the French was repaired with promises of goods and good faith. Mingo Chito had his medal retrieved from the stream, and the sun once again shone on La Louisiane and its path to the Choctaws.[17]

The values that had led Senauky to serve strangers or a beloved man to bear a French officer on his back, all for the sake of keeping white paths open, were, of course, not just limited to one place or one time. They sat deep in an age-old repository of manners and morals that outlived first contact and continued to inform social relationships. An inhabitant of the Creek town Okfuskee, for example, greeted an English agent by invoking the reciprocity that was integral to any healthy relationship. "[We] must all provide for him," he told the townsfolk, "that he may not want anything that your town can supply him with."[18] Stung Serpent, one of the men who led the real and true people that the invaders in La Louisiane called the Natchez, informed his colonial counterparts that "the same sun should enlighten us both, and that we should walk as friends, in the same path."[19] The Raven of Hiawassee extended the same sentiments to South Carolina Governor James Glen when he named Glen "my Father" and promised that "the Chain of Peace of which the Great King George holds one End, and we the other, never will be spoiled, nor broken." Hagler of the Catawbas also called Glen "Father," but while Glen retreated into his own visions of treating his red children with paternal love and protection, he knew enough to reach into his "own pocket" to provide his hosts with presents of powder, bullets, and guns, which was what real fathers did on the white path.[20] Superintendent John Stuart drew upon similar ideas when he met Chickasaw leaders at Mobile in 1765 and used gifts of cloth, metal, and firearms to cast the English as real and true people. Only he supplanted Chickasaw notions of matrilineal descent with English preoccupations with the father's line. "The King looks upon your Nation as a Son," he informed the gathered leaders, "brought up in the House of his Father." And this novel kinship entailed responsibilities that Stuart expressed in the Chickasaw vernacular. The King would, he pledged, make safe and clear "the Paths from your Towns to every Country Round."[21]

White paths augmented each side's power, influence, and respectability, but their maintenance was a tricky business that required negotiation and mutual respect. Without respect they collapsed and left gaps in the land that could only be filled by red ones. But it took conscious effort to block in any permanent way the white paths that made friendship possible, and it is important to remember that violence on the paths turned them red and marked the failure of the white ones. In Virginia, for example, Governor Argall contrived executive orders to ensure that invaders and walking people remained separate. He mandated "no trade with ye perfidious Savages nor familiarity lest they discover our weakness" while his successor George Yeardley approved bans on the sale and trade of English dogs, firearms, and munitions to first people. Anyone caught engaging in contraband trade, the Virginia Assembly decreed, would be hanged as "a Traytor to the Colony."[22] Settlers who had moved beyond the pales to plant tobacco had to return "in one seat and territory that so also they may be incorporated by Equal and like Law and orders with the rest of the colony."[23]

But closing the white paths and retreating from civil life with the first people ensured neither the creation of the Garden nor of the king's dominion. The land had to be remade at the same time it, or one particular interpretation of it, was remaking the invaders. Just as sassafras, tobacco, sarsaparilla, sumac, walnut oil, and honey had replaced silk, wine, and olive oil as the produce of the American Eden, names like Elizabeth City covered "savage" names like Kecoughtan to abet the construction of a different kind of world. Still, what to do with the walking people? The directors of the Virginia Company sought to make them disappear just as Kecoughtan had vanished from the colony's map, only God would erase the problematic existence of the people who most seriously challenged the Virginians' vision. To do so involved relaxing social boundaries and allowing social contact once again but under the rubric of conversion, not confederacy. Opechancanough agreed in fact to disperse his families, as Smith had done a decade before, among the Virginians' plantations to plant maize, work in households, and observe the invaders' way of life. By bringing the two societies together on the path of peace, Governor Yeardley believed, English dominion could be achieved. The plan fell apart, however, because the Virginians were unable to accept fully the conditions for maintaining white paths. The respect and good intentions that went with such relationships were impossible to sustain in an imagined geography of the civilized against the savage. Rather than work toward the assimilation of the men, women, and children Opechancanough had dispatched to the settlements, farmers put them to work hunting deer, pounding maize, and fishing.[24]

Over the first fifteen years of the colony's existence, the invaders had gradually pushed beyond the pales of places like Bermudas, Henrico, Charles City, and Jamestown, but they continued to live like the walking people did, in small groups scattered about on the ridges that ran between creeks and rivers and swamps which they found useful for hunting and collecting food to supplement their stocks of maize and beans. Even their homes looked more indigenous than English. Officials scorned the typical invader home made of logs set vertically in the ground and covered with boards, and they lamented the scarcity of framed houses. Making a place in the land, however, involved more than mimicry; it involved recognition of the moral landscape that gave meaning to the physical topography, and the colony's antisocial behavior demanded from its partners the kind of lesson that elders had for so long taught the boys with the coups they landed on their backs when they beat them before sending them into the wilderness to find themselves as men.[25]

On 22 March 1622 the pales around Henrico and Charles City burned as did farmsteads across the land. The invaders' food stores would have been at their lowest in spite of a winter's worth of parsimony. The moon in the sky was at quarter phase, a period of incompleteness and transition, and the holidays associated with the crucifixion and resurrection of the Father's Son stood as a tempting target for the men who fought on behalf of the sun. The coup that followed left more than three hundred lifeless settlers, many of whose bodies were dismembered, scattered across the countryside. Cattle, horses, and pigs lay dead in the fields while the bloodied feathers of chickens blew about the yards of smoldering homesteads. Those who lived stopped planting maize and retreated behind their pales for fear of the warriors who held the countryside. What little they managed to plant was quickly put to fire, and anyone who ventured into the fields did so under armed guard.[26]

The invaders, it must be said, did not sit still and take their lesson as the ill-mannered children they had showed themselves to be. In their own way they found themselves as men. Just as white paths turned on exchanges of beads, bells, maize, and beans, they opened their end of a red path with blades, balls, and mastiffs. Militiamen burned towns, dismantled fishing weirs, looted stores of maize, and set fire to fields. Roving parties ambushed groups of first people along paths that the Virginians had come to share and along the rivers they paddled to interdict any possibility of trade, for trade, Smith had taught, was how one made friends and enemies in Tsenacommacah. At the same time, the governor drew upon the other members of the league who had reached for and grasped the copper chain that had bound the Chickahominies to the invaders to trade for the maize he needed so badly. In exchange, his militia provided important protection for his new allies and their fields. Turning the principles of the original league to the invaders' own use, John Martin recommended that if his people could acquire more land they would be able to force Opechancanough's people to be dependent upon them for maize. And what land they had taken was now theirs for the price of blood, shed first by maize farmers caught unawares and then by first people who were to be pursued until they vanished from the face of the earth.[27]

By April 1623 both sides had exhausted themselves and needed to plant maize for the coming season. While Opechancanough asked for peace, settlers surmised that the coming harvest might afford an ideal chance to strike a decisive blow and, Governor Francis Wyatt believed, "Ruinate them." Opechancanough had similar ideas, but he promised to call off his warriors so that the invaders could plant their own fields, and he pledged to return the men, women, and children whom his warriors had seized.

In return, his foes dispatched a cargo of beads to redeem the captives. A fragile peace settled on the land, and the General Assembly ordered that 22 March be made a holy day to commemorate the colony's greatest test. The same orders included a requirement that every invader's home be surrounded by a pale.[28]

While the first people would again strike at the colony some years later, Tsenacommacah had indeed waned and the new confederacy of Virginia supplanted it. The first people's presence in Virginia diminished, the original paths closed, and by the 1660s the few enslaved people who had entered the colony were joined by hundreds of others from Africa and the Caribbean to expand the invaders' tobacco operations and transform the landscape yet again. Historians have debated for a long time the significance of the "20. And odd Negroes" who arrived in Virginia from the West Indies in August 1619 and whether this cargo marked the colony's first step toward slavery. Opechancanough, however, knew what the shipment meant and recognized the dilemma that bondage posed for his people. While he believed that for the sake of peace first people had to live together with the invaders, he resented their custom of treating his people's children like "black boyes."[29] The word *black* is tough, for one wonders whether Opechancanough meant "negro" in the language of the day, whether a translator added the word on his own, or whether Opechancanough used the color to denote not so much dark skin as death. Whichever may be the case, Opecanchanough's observation is instructive and points to broader opinions about the meaning of servitude, for the blackening of boys was but one factor that led him to wonder whether or not "the time of peace and League" that he and his counterparts in Virginia had enjoyed had come to an end and whether the new governor coming in 1622 "woulde contynue the League or nott."[30] Slavery had settled on the land and created its own sets of red and white paths.

One hundred years after Opechancanough's observation about the relationship between color, status, and servitude in Virginia, similar claims were made elsewhere. The Natchez used the idea of slavery as a gauge whereby they measured their own colonial standing. "In a former time our nation was very numerous and very powerful," the Great Sun recalled. "Why did the French come to our land?" he wondered. "Did we not live better before?" his counterpart Tattooed Serpent asked, "Was it all for their white, blue, and red blankets?" The ultimate impact of contact and trade, to Tattooed Serpent's mind, had been to reduce him and his people to "slavery." The Great Sun agreed and admitted that "the sacred fire has been rekindled with a profane one that has brought disease and death to the family of the Great Suns." The deaths of the Great Sun and of Tattooed Serpent in the 1720s opened a broader debate over whether or not the poetics of place and space in the colonial South had enslaved or empowered the Natchez. While warriors traveled the countryside to threaten the colonists who encroached on their land, female chiefs, the most powerful mothers and cooks, counseled the people to remain fast friends of the French. "When you are hungry," Serpent Woman said, "the French will give you food, they will give you tobacco, they will give you alcohol because they were friends with your father the Great Sun." "Do nothing to spoil your friendship with the French," she commanded, "They will give you the things you need."[31]

Slavery also blazed red paths between Chickasaws, who tended to trade with the English, and Choctaws, who found their own supplies of guns and powder in French storehouses in Mobile and New Orleans. Fed up with the grasping nature of English power, however, a Chickasaw war leader named Terrapin Chief denounced the Carolinians who came to the towns offering rum, horses, cloth, and guns for captives as "impure and covetous . . . peoples." He tried to open a white path to the Choctaws in order to persuade some of their warriors to join him on a red one to extirpate the outsiders and their slave trade.[32] Many Choctaws shared Terrapin Chief's concerns. English trader James Adair, for example, reported that they refused to allow "the English the name of human creatures—for the general name they give us in their most favorable *war-speeches,* resembles that of a contemptible heterogeneous animal."[33] Historian Alan Gallay has calculated that between 24,000 and 51,000 walking people were seized into slavery in the colonial South between 1670 and 1715, but, as he points out, such numbers cannot do justice to the horrors of it all.[34] While disease had ravaged La Florida for nearly two centuries, English-sponsored slave raids obliterated the colony. Colonel James Moore of South Carolina delivered the death blow when in January 1704 he led a party of fifty Carolinians and one thousand Creek warriors against the Apalachee mission province. Hundreds perished in the raid while another thousand faced a solemn march back to the Charles Town where they were sold into slavery. Subsequent raids wrecked the last vestiges of La Florida's mission system and drove the last of the region's first people to seek refuge in Havana.[35] The story, however, was replayed over and over in other places in later times. On 11 February 1756, for example, Choctaw warriors took two Chickasaw men, one woman, and two children, probably in retaliation for losses sustained in an earlier slave raid. The next day a party of Chickasaws set out to track the Choctaws to, as one trader put it, "redeem the beforesaid slaves."[36] But the trader saw the captives as commodities to be traded, sold, or, in this case, redeemed. He did not see the men as hunters, warriors, and husbands, the women as carriers of the clan, and the children as the future of the clan and of the nation. Looking beyond just one incident to decades of raids, counter-raids, and the placing of real and true people under the control of the monstrous strangers, Chickasaw warriors like Tuska Mobby and Piamallaha pledged "to defense our Lands & prevent our women & children from becoming slaves to the French" and to guard their world against the invaders.[37]

The lessons Cherokees, Creeks, and Catawbas learned were no different. In 1759, when Cherokees were embroiled in a war against the invaders, they too likened their situation to slavery. A debate in the townhouse of Keowee resulted in an agreement that the middle towns were enslaved by Carolina, and that, the leaders concurred, "they could not move without being watch'd by the white People." No one doubted the conclusion that they reached. Governor Lyttelton's intention, the Cherokees reasoned, "was to destroy all their Towns and make Captives of their Women & Children."[38] Oakfuskees worried that English forts in Cherokee country would engross their land while enslaving them. They dreaded this moreover because to be a slave was to be naked, bereft of the kin and company one needed to obtain food, clothing, and shelter. Meanwhile an officer in the South Carolina militia warned a party of Catawba leaders that a group of North Carolinians who wanted to erect a fort on their land planned to seize their land and, in a short time, the people for the purposes of enslaving them all.[39]

Enslaved people, however, were not just an idea that informed the making of a coercive and closed landscape or served as a metaphor for weakness. Rather, they were the creators of places and paths of their own. Indeed, of the many forms of resistance to slavery, one of the most important was place-making. The missionary Francis Le Jau worried as early as 1709 that the enslaved people who lived in and around Charles Town devoted so much time to the cultivation of their gardens on Sundays and to visiting spouses and kinfolk on various plantations that it was impossible for him to collect enough souls to subject to his Sabbath ministrations. What he noted, however, was more than meets the eye. Planting gardens and meeting people are two of the basic preconditions for place-making because they create the necessary spatial and social connections for the formation of a community. The paths that emerged between plantations led to certain common points, like the shores of the Cooper River just outside of Charles Town where Governor Glen saw what he described as a "floating market." In spite of prohibitions on enslaved people owning boats and a 1686 act that prohibited trading with enslaved people, brightly colored pettiaugers that enslaved boatbuilders had hewn from cypress logs plied the river, bringing produce down from the country and returning clothing, shoes, manufactured items, and news in return. The relative isolation of low country plantations further facilitated the growth of trading paths that made possible in turn the development of independent social and economic networks in the country around Charles Town. In the city's marketplaces enslaved people defied municipal and colonial codes to peddle their wares, purchase contraband, and hire out their own labor. The power of these places and paths drew people and goods from all around. Friends met, rivals fought, and the news of the land was swapped along with vegetables, fruits, chickens, cakes, and cloth. The women who dominated the proceedings in Charles Town, just as they did in Savannah when its public market opened in 1755, sported "gay" clothing that set them apart from the common folk and perhaps indicated social divisions or status like the clan and village ties that had underscored the organization of the markets of West Africa that their parents and grandparents had known.[40]

What kinds of links tied the white paths of the enslaved people to the walking people are difficult to discern, but it is reasonable to conclude that each people's shared history of servitude played a part. As well, enslaved walking people were part of the normal order in the early colonial South. In 1708 for example, census takers in Carolina counted 2,900 enslaved "Negro" men and women and 1,400 "Indian" men, women, and children. Relations between the few thousand first people who endured life as slaves in Carolina and Louisiana and their counterparts whose ancestors may have hailed from either Africa, the West Indies, or even Carolina and Georgia produced lineages with far-flung roots. One such woman named Sarah kept Stephen Ford's house. In the summer of 1732 the twenty-five-year-old woman fled, Ford surmised, to either the Creeks or the Cherokees, where her kinfolk lived. A pair of so-called "mustees," Peter, who liked to be called "PP," and Abraham, used horses to escape to freedom either in Saint Augustine or among their relations in the nations while "Indian Jack" simply lived out in the open with a group of Creeks at Smith's Ferry and dared the Pon Pon planter who claimed title to him to come and get him. Who knows what connections Sambo might have made during his work as an oarsman on one of the colorful boats that plied the waters of the Ashley and how they might have influenced his desire to flee to the nations. Primus, a Pon Pon slave, probably absconded to the Creek nation while Sampson, Molly, and their two-year-old child were caught by patrollers twenty miles from Augusta on the Creek path. One young man owned by the publishers of the *South Carolina Gazette* fled his job delivering papers in Charles Town up the "Path" to the Cherokee nation. His facility in English, French, and Dutch may have helped him along the way, but so too might connections he made while walking the town's streets handing out the news. When Cudju and his wife, who spoke English and Chickasaw as well as a smattering of French, fled a Savannah river plantation for points unknown they carried with them the possibility of the invaders' worst fears that followed all of these flights—the union of the people the invaders called "negroes" and "Indians" in an alliance against them.⁴¹

For those who escaped the patrollers and arrived in the nations, a whole new world of social possibilities opened up. Outsiders to the sacred circles of the South could always acquire the status of insiders through adoption, and those who found a new home in the nations typically had something special to offer their hosts. One man named Abraham made a name for himself as a dependable letter carrier on the path that connected Charles Town to Fort Loudon, Carolina's outpost among the Cherokees. His success may have related to his possession of news, for while the post commanded only a patch of cleared ground, the Cherokees still held the forests through which the fort road passed. Catawbas adopted a man who was also adept at mediating news. While he stood out to the invaders because of his skin color, in the absence of an official interpreter, South Carolina Governor James Glen tapped the "free Negro that lives among the Catawbas and is received by them as a Catawba," to translate on his behalf. A man named London acquired such a good reputation for mediating relations with the Chickasaws who lived on the south bank of the Savannah River across from the town and for being "acquainted with the Path & been used to the Nation" that his owner, John Pettigrew Jr., hired him out to guide a delegation of Carolinians to the Creeks and to translate all that was said. Neither London nor the Catawba fellow could have accomplished what they had without some sort of kinship standing in the nations they served, for to speak before a council fire required the offering of a woman's food or a lineage's lodging before entry into the social world that the fire anchored.⁴²

The invaders did not sit idly while such white paths were being made. Across the region, colonial officials offered blankets, guns, beads, and other goods to walking people who would retrieve enslaved people who had fled. Such payments may have brought an end to a man named Michael's experiment in freedom. He had lived for two years in the Creek nation before a group of young warriors returned him to a Georgia workhouse. To have remained for so long suggests he too had made the necessary family connections to obtain food, land, and belonging, much like one man captured by Creek warriors who had been setting up a town on the fringes of Cherokee country that would have given refuge to people the invaders identified as criminals, debtors, and runaway slaves. And the same was probably true of three other men who had lived among the Creeks for seven years before being captured and returned. The young men who returned Harry, Bear, and Sampson to an Augusta workhouse where their former owners could claim them undoubtedly upset the social relations that had knitted the three into Creek society, but that is what warriors had to do to gain the goods and the prestige they needed to underwrite their own rise to prominence and power in the colonial South.[43]

Colonial officials counted on the imperatives that drove slave catchers to perform their dangerous work to inform more broadly the white paths they sought to open with the nations and to suppress any sympathies that might form between real and true hunters and their enslaved prey. A treaty signed by Cherokee leaders in London in September 1730, for example, declared that warriors would seize enslaved people who fled toward their nation in exchange for a musket and a matchcoat. Indeed, in negotiations with the Choctaws and Chickasaws at Mobile in 1765, the governor of West Florida, George Johnstone, insisted that Choctaw warriors "agree to bring in any Negroes who may desert their Masters Service." For Johnstone the brightness of the path was at stake. "These are the Principles," he admitted in council, "on which we wish to Establish a Lasting Peace, between the White & Red Children of the King."[44] His counterpart in South Carolina shared similar concerns, worried that men like Harry, Bear, or Sampson might transform Creek and Cherokee country into "a plentiful refuge to the runaway Negroes from this province who might be more troublesome and more difficult to reduce than the Negroes in the mountains of Jamaica."[45] As the English superintendent of Southern Indian affairs wrote, such policies could not "fail of having a very good Effect, by breaking the Intercourse between the Negroes & Savages which might have been attended with troublesome Consequences had it continued."[46]

Think back to the fears that men like Opechancanough, the Great Sun, Tuska Mobby, and Piamallaha, among others, had voiced. They were as deep and pervasive, as fundamental to their view of the world, as anything that made Governors Johnstone, Bull, or Lyttelton shiver behind closed doors. For every white path a man like London could open, the red ones that slavery could open were many more fold. In the early 1700s warnings to stop the trade in slaves began to drift back to Charles Town, and the Yamassees, who anchored Carolina's network of trade and tribute after the Westos and the Savannahs had had to run for their lives, stood out as the nearest threat to the colony's safety and good fortune. Officials in St. Augustine took great pains to explain to walking people the future that English colonials had in mind for them and took note of worries that English control of trade might eventually enslave them. Indeed, in the years before the Yamassee War first people who had been enslaved in Carolina started spreading the word amongst the people who had crowded up against the border with La Florida that English traders would soon ensnare them and package them off for sale. One such group, the Apalachees, in fact found themselves face to face with Carolina traders who promised to enslave them if they failed to pay off their debts.[47]

Governor Charles Craven dispatched a team of negotiators to plead the colony's case before the Yamassee leaders. After a day's discussion his delegates turned in for the night, confident the crisis had been averted. While they slept the leaders who had listened to them continued to hold council around the fire, and the next day, 15 April, Good Friday, dawned to two parties of warriors painted red and black moving through the countryside to lay waste to Port Royal and nearby plantations. Most of the members of the delegation, like the traders who resided among the walking people, fell dead that day. Thomas Nairne, who in his capacity as agent had attempted to defend Yamassee interests before the government in Charles Town, stood at the center of the ritual of mourning and retribution that opened the attack. Knives opened slits in his skin for the insertion of lights and splinters of kindling. Whether he screamed or remained impassive as the flames crept into his flesh is not known, but the fact that he endured the ordeal for several days before the death blow stilled his heart and closed his mind suggests he had won the Yamassees' respect in his death as he had in his life. That they would kill such a man showed the townspeople of Pocataligo and their brethren in Carolina the gravity of the situation. One delegate who had managed to escape death, for one man always seems to escape these terrible encounters, fled to the Port Royal settlements, so that as the war parties arrived the people huddled for safety in boats and canoes just off shore. Rural folk, however, received no such warning. It was Virginia all over again—a coup delivered to instruct the newcomers in the ways of being real and true people. More than one hundred invaders and enslaved people fell to balls, knives, and hatchets before the warriors returned to Pocataligo with the captives and the plunder that would make a start toward redressing the balance in the relationship that had been lost because of the threat of slavery.[48]

The same path confronted the Natchez. How to strike a balance between demand for useful trade goods and maintain a relationship with an imperial partner? The conciliatory words of Serpent Woman had patched over tensions for the first few years after the Great Sun's and Tattooed Serpent's deaths, but the continued growth of La Louisiane made it increasingly difficult for the Natchez to juggle a place that was in-between within a space of expanding settlements, tobacco fields, and slavery. In 1729 the commander of Fort Rosalie decided to build a large house for himself, and he selected the site of White Apple, a Natchez town, for the new dwelling. White Apple Sun asked the officer to delay construction of the home until the maize crop had ripened. He knew how to take by giving, and in exchange for an offer of maize and poultry to the commander, he received some time.[49]

The leaders of White Apple immediately debated their next course of action. At council one man remarked that it was time the Natchez realized that contact with the invaders had caused more harm than good. "We walk as slaves," he declared. The council at White Apple agreed that the world had changed and that they could no longer posit themselves as insiders against colonial outsiders. They had begun to conceive of themselves as inhabitants of a different world, and they began to put together a new poetics of place and space that might fit better the new colonial context. What position they occupied in the new scheme of things, they decided, depended on their next course of action. One leader, who sensed the Natchez's loss of control over their place in the world, despaired that sooner or later the invaders would begin to whip them just as they whipped their "Black Slaves," so he advocated war.[50]

Enslaved people were not innocents in such dangerous talk. John Brown, for one, attracted a lot of unwanted attention when a leader named Mankiller, who favored maintaining the white path with Carolina, reported to the colony's officials that Brown was out opening a white path between Chota, the mother town of the Overhill Cherokees, and the French garrison of Fort Toulouse. The fort was about seven days' travel from Chota, twenty-one from Charles Town, and it sat astride the trail that Carolina packhorsemen followed into Chickasaw and Choctaw country. Besides checking English influence, the post offered Cherokees another source of trade goods and power. But it sat on the land in other ways that may have been equally significant. In 1717, just after the Yamassee War had smashed Carolina's commerce, the Alabamas invited the leaders of La Louisiane to build the fort on a level fertile plain that sat atop a high bluff overlooking the junction of the present-day Coosa and Tallapoosa Rivers. Old mounds already succumbing to erosion marked the site as one of ancient significance, and perhaps the Alabamas had this in mind when they looked on the new post's palisade in anticipation of the exotic goods that might restore earlier networks of trade, friendship, and power. Uncovered and wanted by the Carolina government, Brown fled to Chota where he hoped to secure the protection of Old Hop, the man behind the overture to La Louisiane. Old Hop held a white wing over Brown, and neither the garrison commander at Fort Loudon nor Mankiller dared risk the old chief's retribution by killing Brown. As Captain Raymond Demeré admitted to Governor Lyttelton, "I am at a Loss to know what steps I must take to French John." In the end, Brown absconded to New Orleans, but not before Old Hop admitted to the governor that he had indeed used the formerly enslaved man to open a path to the old mound site to counterbalance the power of the men who lodged by the old mounds of shell.[51]

The intrigues set in motion by John Brown and Old Hop were but one step along a broadening network of relationships that knitted the places of Carolina, La Louisiane, and the nations into a colonial space. Carolinians had worried for a while that the Canadians who carried the French trade had positioned themselves so securely in the landscape that they would begin to foment slave rebellions "by Artfully Giving them an Expectation of Freedom."[52] Governor Glen himself admitted that people also feared such efforts would spark an "Indian War." [53] Efforts to use trade to control the Overhill Cherokees, "a Bridle in the Mouths of our Indians" as Glen put it, led to talks concerning the construction of a fort among the Overhill towns that would make the towns "Tributaries" who would be liable, Glen planned, "to pay an annual acknowledgement of a few skins for their Protection."[54] In the summer of 1753 Richard Coytmore accordingly drew a strand of white beads from his pack to confirm the peaceful relations between his home of Carolina and the Cherokees he visited. But at the same time, he hoped to instigate a war and handed over a strand of black beads and a hatchet which he requested his hosts use to bring death to the garrison by the mounds on the Tallapoosa. When middle town Cherokees fretted about the degree to which Carolinians had bent them to their purpose, they dispatched their own strands of black beads to their kinfolk in the Lower and Overhill towns to express their own fears about this looming red time.[55]

Being Cherokee, of course, did not mean being of the same mind when entangled imperial alliances came to issue, and even Old Hop changed his mind when his supply of English goods was put at risk. Instead, he drew his Catawba allies onto the same path by placing strings of white beads around the necks of three of their warriors who had come to hear him take up the hatchet against the French.[56] South Carolina Governor James Glen appreciated the support and reciprocated by explaining the red path in terms Cherokees would readily understand. He told Old Hop that the French "lay upon the Banks of your Rivers like Great Snakes ready to devour you," at once casting the French into an alliance with the murky, dangerous, and feminine underworld while claiming the light of the sun for him and his Cherokee brethren.[57] Two other leaders, Tistoe and the Wolf of Keowee, dispatched strings of beads to Governor Lyttelton on the understanding, and it was a reasonable one, that the English had bought into their world and understood it on its terms. "This black wampum is the path where the French go and come," they explained, "to kill our Brothers, the English, and we went [on] this path, and took revenge for our Brothers loss."[58]

Such kinship alliances, however, shifted with time and tendency, for invaders who were brothers one day could find themselves on the outs the next. Catawbas and Cherokees regularly chastised Carolinians to try to keep them on the white path even if it meant opening red ones from time to time. The party of Catawbas who surprised Widow Pickens in the Waxhaws in the early days of spring, 1757, for example, had probably chosen her for death because, to their minds, old women embodied the life blood of the clans and of the communities they led, and so they bashed in her head with a wooden shovel. Other nearby families saw their horses and cattle disappear and their fences and fields burn as Catawbas struck to drive them back.[59] Invaders on the Saluda River who lived midway between Charles Town and the Cherokees were more sanguine, pledging to "Defend Our properties from the Heathen Enemy."[60] Just before Christmas, Cherokee warriors rode up to Thomas Williams's small trading house on the Broad River about seventy miles north of Augusta. Even though his brother John had fled at the first word of imminent hostilities, Thomas remained put. The leader of the war party dismounted, approached Williams, stomped on the ground, and announced that this was his earth, this was his war, and that he would kill Williams. Whether Williams ran or stood his place is not known but he nonetheless tumbled to the ground when the warrior's tomahawk cleaved his skull. Other parties fanned out and brought back to their towns the scalps of the men, women, and children from their homes in the Yadkin, Saluda, and Broad River Valleys. Across the region, invaders retreated back into Carolina and Georgia while those who remained huddled together behind hastily erected pales waiting for higher powers to bring peace back to the land.[61]

But what to the people who fell along the banks of the Saluda or the Yadkin was undoubtedly a red path, to the architect of much of their misfortune, the Catawba leader Hagler, was an ongoing effort to blaze a white one, for he was positioning his nation to hold the center of a confederacy that would entangle Cherokees and Carolinians in a web of his own making. He already received shipments of maize, tribute, from Carolina to reward him for the ongoing raids he organized against La Louisiane, and the deaths of people like Widow Pickens pushed Governor Lyttelton to hand over another 450 pounds of maize "on condition that they leave off plundering the White People."[62] Cherokees marveled with open mouths at the willingness of the Carolinians to forgive Catawba violence. "The white people were afraid of them and made too much of them," one Cherokee official surmised of the white path between Carolina and the Catawbas, else the Catawbas would not have dared "to behave so, to those from whom they get both their food and Rayment."[63]

The Cherokees who wondered why the Carolinians did not understand their relationship to the Catawbas and the Carolinians who clearly understood the power of trade and tribute were each walking the same networks of paths, looping in and out of one another's lives while building a space larger than the places they called their own, even if they were at times at cross-purposes. This is what had happened in and around Savannah and, in its day, was cause for celebration. In the fall of 1757, just over two decades after its founding, the maize was in, the deer were dropping their antlers, and the hogs were fattening on acorns no one bothered to gather any longer. More than one hundred riders from across Creek country assembled to travel three hundred miles and pay their respects to the people of Savannah. A party of rangers rode out to meet the Creeks, as did the gentlemen of the town. When the group arrived at a patch of open ground someone, enslaved people no doubt, had erected a large tent where they talked for a while. The party then proceeded toward town along the path to the waterfront that had been worn over the years by the *sabaneros* who herded cattle, by the walking people who visited the coast, and by the traders who plied the country with rum, cloth, and guns. A battery of cannons boomed a salute as they passed the town's gate, and reports from shore batteries, vessels moored offshore, and the muskets of a company of Virginia Blues who happened to be in town signaled the Creeks' entry into the colony's council house. The men and women from Creek country were resplendent in buckskin leggings, scarlet trade shirts, calico blouses, layers of petticoats, and silver armbands, gorgets, and earrings. And the scent of smoke and bear grease trailed behind them as they filed between two lines of militiamen before meeting with and receiving the hand of Governor Henry Ellis.[64]

If Ellis's wife presented his guests with gifts of maize or venison, no one recorded it, and it probably did not happen, but in spite of all the burned powder, blue smoke, and gaudy militiamen, the people of Savannah had to admit the Creeks to the center of their place. The first people had, after all, been there all along making the paths that drew together the region's hamlets, towns, and countryside into a space in which everyone had their place. And no matter the trustees' original utopian intentions, they could only do so much to make the town in their own image. Space encompasses the places people inhabit, and no amount of denying the personhood of either the first people or the enslaved could offset the truth of the place that Savannah occupied. The meeting between the Creeks and Ellis enjoined them in the self-conscious making of both a landscape and a cosmology that tied them together as one people.[65] The path that linked Savannah to Creek country was, as Tomochichi and Senauky had shown Oglethorpe not so many years before, not just a road but a relationship that required respect and good faith to keep it white. All across the region, people had used paths to work their way from a time of contact to one of cohabitation, and in the process they created not so much a New World in contrast to an Old one but something altogether different, a world that was old and new where time and space blended in novel ways. Together the founding peoples had laid the foundation for the creation of the colonial South, an Atlantic world where the paths that had guided the walking people for so long took in the invaders and the enslaved people, encompassed them all, and made them belong for better or worse.

Chapter 4

CREOLES

The man the Capuchin missionary identified as the Taensa chief had come of age in a world of gifts and greetings, sun and water, and order and chaos, a landscape framed by eagles and snakes, the endpoints of his particular compass. Between the sun and the earth stretched a filigree of white and red paths that sustained a moral world inhabited by walking people, standing people, and the three sisters—squash, beans, and maize. It was a world where men used white wings and women plates of food to domesticate colonial officials and missionaries who had come from beyond, and hatchets and guns to make bloody their enemies' bodies. Where armed invaders sought to tame the earth and civilize the savages who crawled upon the land. Where hunters who had formerly pursued the hides of deer now trained their sights on the scarred backs of the enslaved. And where the enslaved in turn looked to the rivers, to the trees, to the sky, and to one another for deliverance from the cannibals who threatened to devour them all.

The Taensa chief knew as much, and, in so many words, this was what he told Father Raphael about the world as he understood it. The knowledge of what had happened, how things had come to be, and how they ought to unfold held the man's mind as he searched his memory back to the beginning. Long ago, he explained, seating himself in the unbroken circle of creation that had put him where he was, there had been a cave, a cave that was more than an opening in the earth. It was the opening through which the first mother had birthed the real and true people. Out of the deep wet dark a white man, a red man, and a black man had emerged to dry themselves in the light of the sun. The white man left his mother first and found a good hunting ground. The red man left next, strayed off of the "good road" that the white man had followed, and claimed a less abundant territory for his own while the black man "got entirely lost in a very bad country."¹ What the man explained to Father Raphael was that he and his people recognized that they were no longer the only real and true ones. They were now one constituent population of a broader society that included different kinds of people who could be identified by their different colors, their competing claims to the land, and their respective fates. But no matter natal differences of color and character, each man traced his roots to a common place of origin—one cave, one mother, one earth. They were one people.

Seeing colonial societies, as we so often do, as a world of "red Indians," "white settlers," and "black slaves" makes some sense, for such categories have enormous implications in terms of power, agency, and history. They also have drawbacks. Historian Joyce E. Chaplin has argued that the basic racial categories that underpin racism today are specific products of the history of the Atlantic world. When those same categories work as scholarly building blocks, it is worthwhile to consider the degree to which our modern historiography rests on racial terms whose origins lie in the colonial period we are studying and to what degree our work is therefore implicated in the reproduction of colonial categories of thought, knowledge, and power. After all, language, as critic Walter Mignolo found, is "an instrumental tool for constructing history and inventing realities." What is at stake in thinking about the close relationship between the history of the colonial South and the Atlantic world is the degree to which our most basic social categories might obscure other possible ways of imagining that same past while they ensure instead the perpetuation of certain others.²

What we can take from the so-called Taensa chief's story, then, is that while the founding peoples were different they were nonetheless also one and it is the oneness that gets lost in the language of race. It is hard to find a language to express this oneness, which is what literary critic George Handley meant when he argued that we cannot see other possible pasts and the people who inhabited them if we do not know how to name them. *Métis* has a certain currency in Canada while *mestizo* has spread from the specific literature on Latin America to afford opportunities in other fields to code cultural hybridities. Interpretive models like the "New World" or the "middle ground" likewise favor the notion of hybridity at points where the "Indian" and the "European" met. But too often those points stand as peripheries on the margins of distinct imperial worlds. Points of contact can be centers too. It all depends on one's point of orientation in the landscape of the past and the expansiveness of that view.³

One of the most promising approaches to rethinking the history of the South's founding peoples is to be found in the historiography and literature of the francophone and anglophone Caribbean whose practitioners see the inhabitants of the Americas as creoles more than as "blacks," "whites," or "Indians." The concept of the creole has had a wide and varied history in North American historiography. For students of United States history creole signifies either a particular group of people in Louisiana or, more simply, descendants of the original invaders whose attempts to mimic their home societies only amplified their creoleness. Latin Americanists have tended to see creoles as a particular class of patriotic nationalists whose writings were instrumental in creating political, historical, and social arguments for the distinctiveness of their societies. Creole ideologies, patriotisms, and epistemologies challenged the peninsulares' grip on power, office, and prestige, and attracted figures as disparate as the Inca rebel Tupac Amaru and the Mexican intellectual Carlos de Sigüenza y Góngora. By the time of the revolutions of the late eighteenth and early nineteenth centuries, however, the corporatist and racial underpinnings of creolism foundered against newer ideas of liberalism and republicanism. Proponents of subaltern studies of Latin America consequently have cast the *criollo* project as racist and oppressive. As such, the creolism of Latin America constituted not so much a broad post-contact process of social formation but a political and intellectual movement specific to a particular time and place.[4]

Creoles in Caribbean historiography, however, are entirely different from their United States and Latin American counterparts. Both the Spanish and the Portuguese used the term to denote the animals, plants, and people that had been born in the Americas out of contact between Europe, Africa, and the Americas, and enslaved people used the term to distinguish between those born in Africa and those born in the Americas. Following from historic uses of the world *creole*, Raymond Relouzat recently defined creoles as people who adapted their beliefs and practices to the physical and social environments of the Americas. The creole persuasion neither denies nor overturns the materiality of power as practiced in colonial contexts. Rather, it stands alongside, at once questioning and undermining the racial verities of colonialism and historiography while pushing us to recognize the composite nature of life in the Americas, the oneness, at the expense of such atavistic hybridities as European American, African American, and Native American.[5]

E. K. Brathwaite authored the definitive statement on creolization as a form of American social formation. Writing in a present, the early 1970s, marked by racial division and political unrest in Jamaica, Brathwaite sought to locate in his island's plantation past an elusive unity that could offset the prevailing polarities of blackness and whiteness. While giving due attention to the importance of the metropole and the Crown's other colonies in the Atlantic world, Brathwaite saw the generative power of Jamaican society in the sugar fields, the slave cabins, the planter's dining rooms, and the overseers' beds where, he wrote, "a cultural action—material, psychological and spiritual—based upon the stimulus/response of individuals within the society to their environment and—as white/black, culturally discrete groups—to each other [occurred]." The contact could be cruel, but in this cruelty Brathwaite found another possibility. The failure of Jamaican society was not so much its reliance on the horrors of slavery to compel economic production but its inability to "recognize . . . its own creativity."[6]

The society failed to understand its own creativity as creolization because of the mystifying powers of past and present racial thinking. By defining the basic structures of society in reference to race, colonizers and plantation owners had crafted a political, economic, and social system that was unable to accommodate the colonial situation on the ground. Bonds that formed in the towns and plantations of the Jamaican countryside cut across lines of race and class, and the more time passed, the more the racial underpinnings of the society crumbled and threatened to give way in the face of creolization. But, so long as the scholars who studied them drew upon the same racial categories as the invaders had, they perpetuated the power structures that the colonizers had created to achieve mastery in the first place. Brathwaite adopted creolization as an interpretive approach to revise the black/white model of the history of Jamaica. "The process of creolization," he proposed, " . . . is a way of seeing the society, not in terms of white and black, master and slave, in separate nuclear units, but as contributory parts of a whole." As one critic put it, Braithwaite's advocacy of *créolité* was "less a discourse of resistance than a discourse claiming centrality."[7]

The creole persuasion that Caribbean writers and scholars have articulated focuses on broad processes of social formation in the post-contact Americas. In particular they are interested in how first people, invaders, and enslaved people built together new kinds of societies that, while divided by ideologies of race, were nonetheless bound together by trading, praying, warring, and coupling. The conditions under which such contacts and exchanges occurred varied from place to place and from time to time, as did the degree to which the founding peoples resisted one another, borrowed from one another, or simply found common ground between one another. But the creole people who emerged from such contact did so not necessarily as in-between characters. They were not half this and half that—bicultural or biracial, mestizo or mulatto—but rather whole people who carried within themselves the diverse set of practices and beliefs that made them citizens of the places they made.[8]

What is a creole landscape? What does it look like? No matter the confluence of thoughts, beliefs, and social categories that enjoined first people, invading people, and enslaved people in a common belief in red, white, and black people, they shared connections that transcended race. The colonial period, the time from first contact to the Seven Years' War, was very much a time of becoming for the founding peoples. When the man Father Raphael identified as the chief of the Taensas was a young boy, he would have learned how his people set themselves off against the others who inhabited their world. He would have seen men planting tree trunks into the ground to form the palisades that protected the town's temple and the sun's house just as the Mississippians had done for centuries before. As well, much of the architectural grammar of the previous time would have informed the landscape of his present, but not everything had survived first contact. His people, for example, no longer built mounds. Why this was so is difficult to say. Maybe they lacked the will, or the desire, or perhaps even the numbers to build mounds. Or, given that we know most mounds were the result of incremental additions of soil deposited over decades if not centuries to cover the ashes left behind by sacred fires, perhaps his people simply had not been in their place long enough for their ceremonies to have yielded a mother they could climb to reach to the sun. The skulls that the men impaled on the tree trunks marked the palisade as a boundary that made a work of defense into an aggressive assertion of place and peoplehood. Just as fields of maize, squashes, and beans surrounded the town, marked limits, and supported life, so too did these rows of sharpened trees—standing people turned to the needs of walking people—delimit an interior place of life from an outside space of strangers and, in time, colonies.[9]

Within the protective embrace of the palisade, the town's leaders clutched together several objects to bolster the protection afforded by the pales and by the warriors. Sheets of polished copper, probably taken from Spanish kettles, surrounded the chief's house and glinted in the sun. Inside his home visitors saw a Spanish sword and the rotting remnants of three old matchlock guns that substantiated his lineage's claims to powers that reached beyond the palisade and into the broader space that the real and true people inhabited, a space, however, that was now also home to men like Hernando de Soto and Father Raphael. If the assemblage of Castilian objects expressed the rulers' worldly reach, the heads and skulls arrayed along the top of the town's palisade proclaimed the consequences of their power and the lines they were willing to draw between people.[10]

When outsiders entered this world, they understood neither the rules nor the consequences of their behavior and, therefore, posed an even greater danger to the ties that bound the real and true people to the earth and to each other. The chief himself had probably heard about or perhaps even witnessed one of his people's earliest encounters with a party of Canadians from New France who had come to his home to look for the mouth of a very large river. When the *voyageurs* entered the temple to gawk at its sacred objects, a steward followed them through the building and wiped with his hand each spot where their feet touched the floor, such was his concern with their filth. The steward's painstaking efforts, however, came to naught. Only a few years later another party returned, and one of the officers put a stop to the execution of several men and women who were supposed to accompany a deceased leader into death. After black clouds rolled in, a bolt of lightening razed the temple and the real and true people were aghast and sought to halt the sky's terror by smearing their bodies with the earth's mud. The priest attributed the calamity to the officer's intervention and, while fat raindrops sizzled on the temple's blazing ruins, he called for several young children to be hurled into the flames. In a Taensa world where parents took their children to water, perhaps it was appropriate that a priest would, from time to time, take them to fire. One of the Canadians managed to cut short the remedy only after seventeen young ones had perished in the name of covering the newcomers' ignorance and impropriety.[11]

The series of disasters that occurred inside and outside of the temple were but one small part of the ongoing processes of world destruction and creation that had followed on the heels of contact between various groups of real and true people and the Christians, Crown subjects, and enslaved people who had invaded their places and their space. In addition to their bad manners and their own sense of self-importance and divine mission, adventurers from Europe, Canada, New Spain, and the Indies brought to the prairies, fields, and rivers that the real and true people called home various lethal pathogens. Lacking resistance to such maladies as influenza, smallpox, and measles, the real and true people as well as scores of other nations that considered themselves equally, if not more, real and true, witnessed the loss of balance in-between and the destruction of the world as they had known it. Everything was turned upside down and inside out. Weeds choked gardens, brambles closed paths, young healthy folk lost either their bodies or their lives to wet coughs, oozing pustules, and dimpled scars, and the elders whose minds and hearts held the knowledge that had held life together in-between passed away, unable to use what they knew to halt the advance of something they did not.[12]

Diseases and the famines that too followed on the heels of Soto wrecked the first peoples. The nations that are familiar today—Choctaw,

Creek, and Catawba, to name a few—were born of the dislocations and disasters that had followed first contact. Tascaluza's people vanished, as did other polities visited by the Spaniards. Here and there survivors banded together in new places to form new peoples and to graft new ways onto older forms that had survived and that could afford the survivors some way to account for the losses of the dead, the prospects for the future, and the beginnings of the slave trade, colonial warfare, and commercial hunting—the beginnings of what historian James Merrell called the "Indians' New World."[13]

The invaders engaged the land as a "New World" in order to make it comport with the body of classical and medieval knowledge that had structured their cosmological gaze and, Edmundo O'Gorman argued many years ago, to see it "as capable of becoming another Europe." Indeed, the invaders' efforts to construct a "New World" implied the creation of a physical space, but it referred instead to the wholesale creation of the moral and spiritual places that underpinned their colonial efforts. At the same time, however, the men enjoined in the project admitted that they were intellectually ill-prepared for the task at hand.[14] On one side of the Atlantic, cosmographer André Thevet cracked, "Ptolomeus, and others knew not the halfe," while, when confronted with the terrain of Carolina, naturalist Mark Catesby marveled at how his assumptions about man's descent from Adam now made no sense. Indeed, the power of the medieval mind faded in the face of not so much an imagined "New World" but the actual people and places that made it a space beyond the guiding hand of Providence. The creation and reproduction of slavery, the acquisition of land that pitted the invaders against the first people and the enslaved people, and the resulting struggles over landscapes and places forced the invaders to shift their frames of reference.[15]

As red and white paths and red and black people supplanted the wind, the sun, and the one true faith as the referents for the invaders' art of dead reckoning, new notions of space, place, and sociability emerged to situate them firmly within this Atlantic world while at the same time encoding differences in ways that could only be sustained by violence. In his struggle to put into words all of the things he saw in Carolina that astounded him, Francis Le Jau lengthened the shadow Columbus had cast over the Americas. "Many Masters," Le Jau wrote in 1706, "can't be persuaded that Negroes and Indians are otherwise than Beasts, and use them as such."[16] Invaders in the hamlets of the low country were so afraid of the enslaved people, those beasts, that one Georgian revealed "that upon all the Festivals, such as Easter, Whitsuntide, & Christmas . . . Patroles of Horse are always travelling to and fro,' to prevent [enslaved peoples'] Assembly in numbers." "At Charles Town itself," he further confided, "'tis so dangerous to walk the Streets late at Night."[17] Even the towns were forests.

But such prejudice was not unique to the invaders, for they too appeared from time to time to be dirty and dangerous beasts. After what had been an isolated fight between men over horses in Virginia became a full blown war between Cherokees and Virginians, it gave occasion for the walking people to degrade their enemies. "They say Publickly that it is now War with the white People who they can kill like Fowls," one South Carolina agent reported, "that the white People are as it were drunk or asleep."[18] The Carolinians' transformation from brothers to poultry was startling. White and red paths were never solid states but expressions of contingent and evolving relationships. Just as one would never kill a brother, a chicken was just about the most contemptible animal on the face of the earth as far as Cherokees were concerned. The insult had a long pedigree. In 1526, for example, a party of Guale warriors yelled at a passing boatload of Spaniards that they "were hens and worth nothing." Choctaws, meanwhile, had explained to early French visitors, chickens "eat filth," and Creeks too at times likened settlers to "dunghill fowl" and made no distinction between knocking the head off one or the other.[19] People who had imbibed too much rum, moreover, were likewise contemptible for they were incapable of thinking the clear thoughts and speaking the clear words that white paths demanded. Accordingly, the real and true people made allowances in their mental maps of the region for the disruptive presence of the invaders. In 1760, for example, a man whom the invaders had named Aleck and described as a Kasihta, referred to the town of New Orleans as "Balbanja," the town of strangers.[20] Likewise, a Chickasaw leader informed a British delegation that met his nation in Mobile in 1765 that "I was told by the Creeks & Cherokees, wherever the English went they caused disturbances for they lived under no Government and paid no respect either to Wisdom or Station."[21]

One party of Hiawassee warriors believed as much when they converged on John Kelley's house by the Notley River in the Carolina Piedmont and informed him that they had come to kill him. Kelley protested that he had done them no harm and in fact had lived as their friend, but at once Kelley's individuality fell away. "They answered," one officer wrote, "that he was a White Man." To prepare Kelley for death they blackened his face to mark him with the color of the cold and barren north. Down by the riverside the warriors knocked in his skull, dismembered his body, and scattered his flesh and joints in the bushes nearby to emphasize their refusal to grant the invaders any humanity.[22] Another party of ten Creek warriors painted themselves black for their killing task, perhaps to loose the scourge of the north wind on the cowboys who were infiltrating their place. Christian Lirre and John Ulrick Giger met the party on the Congarees River and were told to go home or else be scalped. The herdsmen ignored the warning but after a second encounter packed up camp, fled the area, and returned it to the Creeks.[23]

It is easy to read of John Kelley's death or that of the Widow Pickens, who fell to a party of Catawbas in the previous chapter, and assume that the violence of the colonial South made sense, that of course "whites" and "Indians" would kill one another. Indeed, categories like "white" and "Indian" construct violence as a natural and normal by-product of contact and leave processes of creolization as incidental and, by comparison, less important to the real work at hand. As Chaplin put it recently, "Indians and English may have allowed their cultures selectively to bleed into each other so that they could get on with the task of shedding each other's blood." The way scholars have represented such violence has made it easy to dismiss the early colonial years as a kind of violent prehistory beyond all reason—to detach the acts from their larger cosmological context, and consign them instead to the world of savagery.[24]

Take for example when, in 1757, Hagler, the leader of the Catawbas who was trying to enlist Carolina in his confederacy, asked the Cherokee leader Little Carpenter to provide warriors to assist South Carolina and the Catawbas to fight "the French and their Indians." "The Path," Hagler promised, "is plain between us to pass and repass from one to another to See one another we are all Brothers, all one Body that came from one Women."[25] In spite of Hagler's best attempts to draw the Cherokees onto the same path as the Catawbas, so that they could walk the same ground as brothers, relations between the two nations fell apart. In the spring of 1759 Cherokees complained that Catawba warriors had killed a Cherokee woman on the path that led between the Cherokee towns and Virginia. In retaliation, and to put an end to any pretensions that the two nations were brothers who shared the same mother as well as to protect their own budding relationship with the French, Cherokees seized a Catawba woman, bludgeoned her to death with tomahawks, and divided her scalp into five pieces, presumably to share as the signs of the killing. But they were not finished. As if to drive home the point that these warriors were neither the Catawbas' brothers nor kinsmen, and, perhaps, not even inhabitants of the same world, they threw the woman's corpse into a river where any number of terrible things could have happened to it. Whether her spirit was devoured by the great water snakes that might also have feasted on John Kelly's remains or was entrapped forever in the world of stones and whirlpools, the Cherokee warriors sought to finish their grim business two days later by retrieving the corpse, tying a rope around the neck and dragging it behind a horse. To finally obliterate every last mortal and immortal trace of this woman and the Catawbas' pretensions, the men then fed her remains to their hunting dogs.[26]

The violence that Kelley suffered was more akin to what the Catawba woman suffered than not, so thinking of one as a white and of the other as an Indian can be misleading. They both paid a price for their behavior, or, rather, for the behavior of their broader families, that marked them for death to Cherokee eyes. But when two different parties of Cherokee warriors scattered these two bodies to the four directions they enacted a poetics of space and place to which both victims and killers belonged. They may have identified Kelley as a white, but the treatment of his body was of a kind reserved for insiders, albeit for contemptible ones. In such deaths the places of the colonial South came together in space, and if invaders were not the primary movers in this collision and creation of worlds, that should not distract us from the fact that the violence so often attributed to the great clash of cultures may have in fact been a product of the painful merging of worlds.

Indeed, bonds forged through violence were everywhere, engaging the founding peoples in a collaborative process of place-making that involved them all. The invaders' constructions of walking people and enslaved people as beasts that inhabited their own landscape had another side, for if the two groups were united in their degradation, they too possessed the ability to join arms in revolt. The walking people and the enslaved people who had linked up over the paths from the colonies to the nations understood this, as did the invaders who nervously fretted about such possibilities. The Natchez, who had regretted the loss of their land and resented their slide toward slavery, struck hard against La Louisiane in November 1729. At a prearranged signal, a gunshot, warriors across the area struck the invaders. Of the original population of 200 men, 82 women, and 150 children, some 145 men, 36 women, and 56 children lay dead. Warriors rounded up the rest along with 300 or so enslaved people and holed up in two forts they had constructed in anticipation of war. In light of the Natchez's fears of slavery, they welcomed the assistance of several of the captured enslaved people in their war against the invaders.[27]

French revenge was neither swift nor all that effective. With their reluctant Choctaw allies, the invaders retaliated in January 1730, but the Choctaws beat Governor Perier's force of free and enslaved militiamen to the punch. A Choctaw leader named Alibamon Mingo negotiated the release of many of the Natchez before the French arrived in exchange for the captured women and enslaved folk. After torturing and burning the leaders of the enslaved people who had fought with the Natchez, Alibamon Mingo traded some back to the colony. Many of the others, however, appear to have either fled or been traded to the Chickasaws, who then bartered them to English traders. If the war had decimated the French outpost among the Natchez and scattered that nation among its neighbors, it also served as a warning. "The greatest misfortune which could befall the colony . . . would be a union between the Indian nations and the black slaves," the governor of La Louisiane reflected, "but happily," he told himself, "there has always been a great aversion between them which has been much increased by the war, and we take great care to maintain it."[28]

Carolinians sought too to divide the people they regarded as little more than beasts, but, at the same time, their precarious position forced them to acknowledge the degree to which they needed the other two founding peoples. During the Yamassee War, Governor Charles Craven opened the militia to 400 enslaved men and 170 first people who joined ranks with 900 Carolinians and Virginians. Putting the force on a professional footing, Craven mandated that each colonial would receive eleven pounds per month while owners of enslaved soldiers received two pounds monthly. The first people who served received no regular pay but were allowed a cloth allowance plus a bounty for each scalp they took. Each segment of the colony's militia suited a particular purpose. The colonials enabled their officers to deploy European-style formations of closed ranks that were formidable in the open field while the warriors knew the lay of the land and the art of the ambush. Early experience, however, showed that massed formations of gunmen simply did not work, for the Yamassees and their allies refused to stand and be shot. Instead, the colonials learned and mastered the same ambush tactics practiced by the real and true people. The enslaved men added their own expertise to the force born of their experiences as *sabaneros* and as traders. They too knew the paths and the waterways, so their scouting capabilities were crucial, as was their knowledge of the walking people's languages. Indeed, one Cherokee leader who opposed the Yamassee's war asked the governor for the service of thirty enslaved troops who, the Cherokee foresaw, would be "very serviceable to them in running after the enemy."[29]

The alliance of enslaved people and first people on the side of Carolina was met by an equally balanced alliance on the side of the Yamassees, for the same connections that made the *sabaneros* and traders such good fighters also enabled them to make common cause with people in the nations. In particular, enslaved men sought to extricate the Cherokees from their friendship with Carolina by exacerbating tensions between the two fires, as John Brown had tried with Old Hop. What one agent of Carolina dismissed as "a parcell of Lies" was probably a serious effort to coordinate an assault on the colony that would undo it from within and from without. "2 Rogues of negroes," the Carolinian reported, had set back the colony's efforts to secure the Cherokees neutrality in the war by spreading tales of colonial perfidy.[30] In the end, the Cherokees did not take up the red path with the Yamassees, but the plot fanned colonial fears about potential communities of interest between one set of beasts and another.

The world the invaders wanted to make came to reflect the threatening power of the other people who lived with, among, and around them on the paths. As they made their own way in this world, they deployed their faith and their power to confine first people and enslaved people to their proper places almost as if insisting on difference could obliterate creeping similarities and propinquities and humanities.[31] Such efforts, however, could neither defuse nor deny the incredible tension and fear that coursed through and constituted the landscape that the invaders surveyed. Well aware of the need to offer gifts to keep paths bright, Governor James Glen understood that the first people, from his perspective at least, afforded a "natural Fortification" for Carolina's defense as well as a constant source of political might and economic wealth.[32] Georgians relied upon a group of Chickasaws who had received a land grant on the Broad River opposite Augusta in 1748 for their protection. Under the leadership of a man known as "The Doctor" their young men gave the people of Augusta invaluable service, for the invaders lacked scouts who could distinguish between their Cherokee enemies and Creek friends, and they fretted that the accidental shooting of a Creek might exacerbate an already precarious situation.[33]

What the governors of South Carolina and Georgia appreciated as a strategic benefit, however, alarmed others. Indeed, after touring Carolina, the Reverend Charles Woodmason bemoaned what he took to be the invaders' perilous situation. "There is an External Enemy near at hand," he warned, "These are our Indian Neighbours." "Common Prudence, and our Common Security," he counseled his congregants, "requires that We should live like Brethren in Unity, be it only to guard against any Dangers to our Lives and Properties as may arise from that Quarter." But that was only one side of the story. "We have an Internal Enemy, Not less than [100,000] Africans below us." "Over these," the reverend urged, "We ought to keep a very watchful Eye."[34] Even the invaders who relied upon enslavement to reproduce their colonies were afraid of slavery and were apprehensive about where the institution fit in a world of white and red paths.

Saint Augustine loomed particularly large on the landscape because of the overt challenge it posed to slavery. In 1738, by the beat of a drum, the governor of Saint Augustine promulgated a royal decree that offered freedom to enslaved people who fled either Carolina or Georgia and who agreed to bear arms against their former owners. One colonial official predicted that the order might "entirely ruin" South Carolina while another saw in the enslaved people who comprised the majority of the colony's population enemies who were prepared "to revolt on the first Opportunity and are Eight Times as many in Number as there are white Men able to bear Arms."[35] They were right. The regular flight of enslaved people down the cow paths of Carolina and Georgia to freedom at the presidio of Saint Augustine or behind the walls of Gracia Real de Santa Teresa de Mose added to the invaders' anxieties, and the colonial assemblies set to work on legislation to prevent insurrections and runaways. Shortly after the drumbeat announced the proclamation, words flew to the frontiers where a group of enslaved *sabaneros* who worked for a Captain Macpherson put to use their knowledge of the cattle trails that led south to La Florida to send out the call for others to fly to freedom. They made their own escape after wounding the captain's son and killing another man, and news of their escape from the rangers that pursued them doubtless traveled the paths that led up the Pon Pon Road back to Charles Town.[36]

Those who fled to La Florida, however, had come from a particular place born of the interconnections between the invaders and the enslaved. As historian Philip D. Morgan has noted, the vast majority of eighteenth-century enslaved people lived and died outside of the family of the Father, but those few who gained entry assumed important positions of power.[37] The small brick churches with their cedar shingle roofs that dotted the country of Carolina served the invaders but also afforded alternate nodes of power to the markets that drew enslaved people into the towns from the countryside. As congregations were able, they often enlarged their rectangular churches by adding wings to transform the buildings into crosses that sat as charters to the land, and the knowledge they contained was fundamental to its control. Enslaved people flocked to these edifices too, crowding around the windows, as Father Le Jau noted in the summer of 1710, craning their ears toward the pulpit as he preached to the congregation of Goose Creek parish, to listen and learn about the cannibals who had barred the door to them. The congregation squirmed, and the priest learned to fear the eavesdroppers, particularly those who were able to translate what they had heard into competing visions of divine cosmology. Such "scholars" Le Jau wrote, were "generally very bad men."[38]

The same year that Le Jau preached the Word to the free and enslaved inhabitants of Goose Creek parish, an enslaved man began to cite holy revelations he had read in his Bible. His eyes had seen sin where before they had seen only slavery, and he foretold a day of judgment. To the man who owned him he prophesied that "a dismal time" was coming and that "the Moon would be turned into Blood, and there would be death and darkness." The owner called in Le Jau, who arrived to give counsel while fleet feet and colorful pettiaugers carried up the paths and waterways of the countryside word that an angel had come and spoken to a man, to one of them, and that the angel had revealed to him a book and would raise fires to signal the approach of the end. In this doom, however, lay the creation of something new, a world reserved for the righteous. In some respects, the man's creed fit within the millennial traditions of Christianity, but the new place he envisioned also reached back to the towns and homes of both Africa and the first nations where people associated the moon with blood, women, and the creation of new life.[39]

Far from simply representing discontent with slavery, conspiracies and revolts actually represented the culmination of the enslaved people' abilities to reconstruct out of their received African practices and the exigencies of the Atlantic world a place that had meaning and purpose for them. And that world was not the land of Shem, nor was it a plane that held the middle ground between the sun and the earth. It was a hell that the enslaved people made humane, to the best of their ability, by creating places for themselves in the quarters and in the markets, and on the paths that connected them within a space of coercion, servitude, and inhumanity. Clearly the revelation of the blood moon that the Goose Creek man had had was widespread and a regular feature of the enslaved people's cosmology that parents and preachers handed down to the generations that followed.

In March 1739 patrollers caught a man named Caesar running away to freedom in Saint Augustine. On the gallows he made what one Carolina correspondent described as a "very sensible Speech to those of his own Colour." The enslaved people who had gathered to see Caesar hang until dead heard him speak of honesty, virtue, and justice, and he implored all Christians to pray for him. With the noose around his neck, he led the crowd in the Lord's Prayer: "Thy kingdom come. Thy will be done in earth, as it is in heaven."[40] The freedom afforded by flight to Saint Augustine and the protection offered by the Christian faith had inspired him to run, but it had also given shape to the world as he imagined it, and the world of the spirits remained one with the world of the living. Catholic Florida offered both secular and sacred freedoms that slaves could not obtain in South Carolina, and this place that was so different from Carolina yet so close as well created a place of hope that for Caesar failed to deliver on its promise. But others would continue to try.

Freedom in Saint Augustine and Caesar's gallows prayer emboldened a handful of people to risk their lives in implementing the prophecies that had become a fundamental piece of the enslaved people's cosmology.

Although they shed the invaders' blood on 9 September 1739, a Sunday, the rebellion had actually begun on the preceding Saturday, the holiest day of the week for the BaKongo Catholics who had organized the rebellion. They and their ancestors had come into contact with Catholic missionaries through their contact with Portuguese traders long before. In 1491 the Bakongo king Nginga Nkuwu took the sacraments and then the name King João I which signaled to his subjects that the new faith of his kingdom would be theirs as well. As the Bakongo people adapted their indigenous ceremonial calendar to comport with the various feast and saint days of the Catholic one, Saturdays emerged as the days for prayer and remembrance of the dead. The white clothing that communicants wore and the drumming that marked the solemn yet joyous occasions enabled the people to call upon and interact with the spirits of their ancestors and the land that they both inhabited. The particular Saturday in which drummers called together the men who had chosen to fight the Carolinians was auspicious because it marked the nativity of the Virgin Mary, whom the BaKongo had seized upon as a feminine embodiment of the earth and the spiritual protection that came from honoring the land and its spirits.[41]

The twenty or so enslaved people who initiated the revolt knew Portuguese from having attended the Kongo kingdom's network of churches and schools and from the language's importance to trade in central Africa. Their familiarity with an Iberian tongue and their thorough attachment to the forms and practices of Catholicism made the men especially receptive to Spanish promises of freedom. They also knew the land. They gathered beside the Stono River, whose waters swirled with the chaotic power of life's force. Did it foretell the future? Did they feed it? After meeting, they moved on to Hutchinson's store, where they found guns, ammunition, and powder. When they left they deposited the shopkeepers' heads on the store's front steps. Was the gesture a play on the fact that their word for selling was the same as for trapping? Taking the main road to Saint Augustine, the party burned several homes and discriminated between some invaders they allowed to live and others they killed. As people flocked to the group's banner, drums sounded and underscored the men's shouts of "Liberty!" After a chance encounter with William Bull, the colony's lieutenant governor, the group, perhaps numbering fifty now, marched through the Pon Pon settlement south of Charles Town toward freedom in Saint Augustine. As the group enjoyed early success, their drum signals called others to their banner. After a while they huddled in a field near the Edisto River and began to dance, sing, and beat drums to prepare to cross the running water, to invoke the protective powers of the Virgin, and to gird themselves for the fighting that lay ahead.[42]

By late afternoon of the Sunday, the invaders had rallied and organized their own force. Those who had earlier flocked to the banner melted away from the battlefield, but those who remained fought as they had been trained to in Kongo. Avoiding the massed formations of European armies, Kongo musketeers tended to scatter and fight skirmishes in order to minimize casualties. Their style of withdrawing and counterpunching led to the kind of protracted battle that the Carolinians now faced. In the following weeks, settlers and first people tracked down the people who had fled, and, in the end, suppressed the rebellion. More than sixty people were killed, and the enslaved people's attempt to make use of their landscape of hope and power fundamentally changed not just their world but that of the invaders who owned them as well.[43]

The invaders who faced the aftermath of Stono quaked with every rumor that blew up the roads and rivers. One group of "insolent arm'd runaway Negroes" raised several alarms in the vicinity of St. Andrews, Stono, and Wadmelaw and kept alive the promise of insurrections.[44] In reply, the invaders set to recreating the world they inhabited by drafting a newer and tougher "Negro Act," by seeking to curtail imports of Africans to redress what slave owners took to be the colony's racial imbalance, by exploring ways to crush Saint Augustine, and by building an even more stark landscape of fear and control. It began with Stono. Like the Taensa chief's forebears, the men of Carolina marked their land with the severed heads of the men they had caught in their pursuit of the rebels through the fields and forests of the low country. The mileposts on the Saint Augustine highway each bore a bloody reminder of both the consequences of any challenge to the invaders' power and the need to arrive intact among the ancestors in the afterlife. But the creation of what historian Thomas Hatley described as a "terrain of fear" did not end with impaled heads spaced regularly along a road frequented by enslaved people. Under orders from the planters, crews of enslaved people attacked with axes the copses that afforded hiding places between low country plantations for "deserting slaves and wild beasts" as Governor Bull put it. They drained marshes that might offer refuge and claimed wetlands for rice cultivation. Workers heaped the heavy clay they excavated into large dikes that criss-crossed the new vacant landscape and raised travelers high upon the horizon where wary overseers and planters could monitor anyone's approach. Like the trustee's image of an orderly Savannah, a new blueprint for distress gave planters the illusion of control of the land.[45]

But they could not control the cosmology that explained it, and when the prophecy of the blood moon reached the Cherokees, worlds once again overlapped and merged. In 1751 a trader named Richard Smith reported to South Carolina officials that "some Negroes" had told Old Warrior of Keowee that there were far more enslaved people than free people in South Carolina. The logic of the situation, the men explained, was clear. "For the sake of liberty," they argued, the Cherokees should join them in plotting against the colony. The invaders caught one of the ringleaders, Phillip John, who had offered the Cherokees the role of the sword wielded by avenging angels. "The Indians," he informed his captors, "were to be concerned in the extermination of the white people from the face of this earth." The plot stunned the colony, especially when the invaders learned that the Cherokees planned to hold off until the maize was in before sending warriors to "assist in killing all the Buckraas."[46]

Eight years later Philip John, whom Charles Town's governors described as a "free Mulatto," made trouble again and was, Governor William Lyttelton wrote to his superiors in London, "tried whip'd & branded for endeavouring to stir up sedition among the Negroes." Like the Goose Creek man and Caesar before him, and like an English pastor who had raised such a scene in town only a few short months before with his warnings of doom, fire, and death, John preached that the end was nigh. His vision drew a kalunga line across Carolina and placed "the white people" under the ground where the dead dwelled. A sword he saw would slaughter the cannibals and shine "with their Blood." "There should be no more White Kings, Governors or great Men," he promised, "but the Negros shou'd live happily & have laws of their own." Even being whipped and burned did not stop John from spreading his gospel as his vision shot through the backstreets and the urban markets.[47]

The first people too saw themselves and their neighbors as people living under one power.[48] In 1751 the Raven of Toxaway, for example, spoke on behalf of a number of men and women when he explained to Governor James Glen that his memory recalled the earliest days of Carolina's friendship with the Cherokees, and King George's admission that "he and his people were the same as our People."[49] Some years later Ohatchie spoke on behalf of the Cherokee Middle and Lower Towns in a meeting at Fort Prince George as the leaves were turning. "The Ground we walk upon now was given you by us," he told the assembled Carolinians, "and it is yours, and ours."[50] Captain Raymond Demeré, who reported on Cherokee affairs to Governor Lyttelton, concurred. He remarked that the Cherokees saw "all the White People to be the same as themselves as they tred on the same ground."[51] "At the Creation of the World," Handsome Fellow, the speaker of the Creek town Oakfuskee, explained to the governor, "it was Ordered that the white and Red people should live together upon the same Land and in Friendship with one another" while Emisteseguo, the head warrior of Okchai, held out hope that "the Great King's White and Red Children, will daily increase & that as they grow up their hearts like the Tendrils of the Vine may be by time more Strongly United & Knit together."⁵² A Chickasaw headman Paya Mattaha explained to John Stuart and other British officials gathered at a congress in Mobile that, because of the "Benefits I have received from the white People," he admitted, "I almost look upon myself as one of them."⁵³ In a later meeting with the Creeks in May at Pensacola, the Mortar of Okchai seconded such sentiments. "I now look upon the Surrounding White Nations," he agreed, "as all United & Children of the same Family."⁵⁴

The invaders could become real and true. As one group of Cherokees explained to Governor William Lyttelton, they promised to keep their end of the path to Carolina clear and bright, and, in so doing, held out to the Carolinians the same possibility, so long as the "Sun & Moon rules the firmament."⁵⁵ Chulustamastabe, a Choctaw war leader, signaled that the deep relationship between his people and those who had come to Mobile to take it for their Crown was entirely new. "The old Fire which formerly warmed & cherished the People of this Nation," he regretted, "is now extinct." But the new fire that he hoped would burn brightly to warm him and his new kin tied the world of the 1760s to that of the 1650s or even the 750s, only now the sacred men who lighted it hailed not from the top of a mound but from even higher power, what one Choctaw leader described as "the Power of the Clouds."⁵⁶ And the clouds dropped a snow that Emisteseguo prophesied would cover the invaders and the walking people and their new fire, and make them all white.⁵⁷

The English were not uncomfortable with such notions of kin, fire, and whiteness, and the degree to which they accepted the indigenous vernacular of belonging and association exposed their inability to craft from whole cloth some kind of a New World that was in fact an Old World in the making. As Governor William Lyttelton explained to Hagler of the Catawbas, "For these many years past the Tree of Friendship that was planted by our Fathers and yours, has flourished." We live, the governor agreed, "under the shelter of [the tree] as one People." Lyttelton's choice of the tree was significant, for the standing people bespoke the passage of time, rootedness in the earth, the necessary mix of water and sun, and the finite reach of branches in an infinite space.⁵⁸ Other Crown officials likewise drew upon the vernacular of the landscape they had invaded to articulate its unity. James Glen had reveled in being elevated from the Cherokees' brother to their father, even if he did not necessarily understand that such a switch might in fact diminish his authority, while John Stuart learned that Sir Robert Filmer's patriarchalism had no place in the council grounds of the South. To the Choctaws who had assembled in Mobile he looked forward to a day when his Crown's "white subjects & you may be more nearly Connected, that you may Esteem one another like Brothers of the Same Mother."[59]

Brothers of the same mother was not just a pose by the able and intelligent Stuart. It was one of many instances of accommodation and acceptance between founding peoples. Other such instances can be seen not so much in their words and thoughts but on the land they inhabited and in the gardens that fed them. During his travels through the South in the 1770s, for example, English naturalist William Bartram read the creole landscape that had been born of the contact between the first nations, the settlers, and their gardens. Following an old road to Pensacola that had overgrown with weeds from disuse, he and his party journeyed four or five miles through old Spanish fields. Scattered fence posts marked long-forgotten boundaries, and fallen pillars signaled the sites of former homes. Behind the fences that once crawled across the land, however, he saw the remnants of small hills where the settlers had planted the maize they had gotten from the first people and the sweet potatoes that European trade networks had brought to the region from the Caribbean. Plowing had never taken hold in La Florida. The French old fields that he visited in the vicinity of Mobile showed similar signs of the early settlers living in the fashion of the country.[60]

Later invaders did much the same thing. In 1772 John Hutchins's father Anthony left South Carolina for better opportunities in Natchez. Just as French colonists had done less than a century before, the father sited his farm on top of where the old Natchez village White Apple had stood. Here in 1729 the Natchez had nearly destroyed the French outpost of Fort Rosalie, and here the elder Hutchins settled "with a view to bettering his situation." Others did what Hutchins had done, and like him, as they cleared their newly claimed but nonetheless old fields, they turned up pots, arrowheads, and other artifacts, reminders of the old order that they had come to usurp. Hutchins's spot had grown over with trees and canebrakes since the Natchez had fled, and his family set about clearing patches of land here and there along St. Catherine Creek. When John grew to maturity he cleared his own patch of land nearby with his slave Tim. The two planted maize and pounded it in a mortar to make the meal on which they subsisted during the lean years, and they harvested gourds, which were indigenous to both America and Africa, in which they stored the milk they pulled from their cows' teats.[61]

In other places it was the presence of first people, not just their artifacts, that tied the invaders and the enslaved to the region's long continuous history. John Nevitt, for example, owned a small plantation outside of Natchez in the 1820s, and he supplemented his slave labor force with first people who journeyed across the region in search of seasonal labor that would have afforded them the opportunity to return and work on land that had been cultivated by their forebears. In Nevitt's cotton fields, for example, first people worked alongside enslaved people. *Kishi* baskets that had formerly been used to contain the maize harvest now held cotton bolls, and mothers and daughters who would have walked the fields together now shared them with enslaved men and women. Payment came in many forms—blankets, cloth, manufactured items, or cash—a dollar for every hundred pounds they picked. How much and how often they picked is difficult to say, but on Nevitt's plantation, at least, on 23 December 1827 the "Indians" picked 240 pounds of the stuff. The following year his hired hands picked more than two tons of cotton before being discharged for the Christmas holidays.[62] What Nevitt's slaves might have thought of the hired laborers with whom they worked is difficult to tell, but from time to time he allowed them to pick cotton for their own profit too.[63]

What kinds of relationships were forged between first and enslaved people in plantation fields is difficult to say. Horace Fulkerson, a Mississippian who wrote down in his dotage what he remembered of the state's early days, argued that the first people who picked cotton "had a great repugnance to association with negroes."[64] But James Williams told a different story. Williams was a driver on a cotton plantation in Alabama who fled servitude in the 1830s. His escape to freedom began in the Creek nation where, he wrote, "The Indian women received me with a great deal of kindness." What made them kind? They fed him a "good supper of venison, corn-bread, and stewed pumpkin" before sending him on his way.[65] Williams's meal of ancient foods suggests an almost invisible world of social relations that might have come together wherever Choctaw or Creek women picked cotton alongside slaves; for these Creek women to share the produce of their gardens was no small matter. Remember Senauky. The women welcomed Williams into their homes with a meal that bespoke a relationship of reciprocity and perhaps even kinship. What his connection to them was is unknown, but the meal he enjoyed suggests the possibility of a prior relationship that may have been formed in the cotton fields that he supervised and where first and enslaved people worked side by side. And the meal he enjoyed gave life and purpose to a way of life that was resisting in its own way the annexation of their land by King Cotton. Thanks to those women he could follow, for a few days at least, the North Star.

The web of relationships that may have tied Williams to the Creek women who fed and sheltered him also extended to the plantation community he inhabited. While he and his parents may have been far removed from the forests and fields that had given rise to the African civilizations, they nonetheless lived in shadows cast by memories of their ancestral homes. Tales of Africa and another way of life may have been handed down from elders or reported once new imports mastered the language of their fellow slaves. But one could see the social history of removal, transport, and arrival in the gardens slaves cultivated to feed themselves and their families and to earn money or goods to enhance their lives as best they could. John Michael Vlach, a historian of plantation architecture, has argued that "the creation of a slaves' landscape was a reactive expression, a response to the plans enacted by white landowners."[66] But any invocation of the landscape of slavery that excludes the first people is only partial. The owner of a ten-year-old boy named Moses Gandy enacted his own plans for domination when he whipped the naked child because, Gandy remembered, he "could not learn his way of hilling corn."[67] The use of the lash in the example of Gandy stands out in support of Vlach's assertion, but the mound of dirt Gandy tried to pile around the base of the maize plant is important as well, for referents other than coercive action and resistant reaction were at work. Outside of the coercion of the plantation lay a broader social world that prompted actions and reactions every bit as much as the plantation, but in both cases creativity and mutuality, not reaction to brute force, animated both the people and the land they inhabited, for Moses was but one boy in a long line of youngsters in the region who, over a period of nine centuries, had had to learn how to hill maize.

Enslaved people etched their creative and creole imprints sharply on the region's fields and plantations. On Levin Covington's Adams County, Mississippi, plantation, people cultivated maize and cotton in an "old field," working soil that decades or centuries before would have been worked by native women. They also hilled maize in the "old sheep pasture," in the field behind "Jerry's house," and in a field named after Covington's slave Groce instead of the other two sisters, where it was intercropped with peas. Women also planted maize around the fruit trees that made up Covington's orchard, a planting style Soto had seen nearly three centuries earlier. On James Magruder's nearby plantation, Mount Ararat, he divided his land between commercial fields of cotton and plots he described as the "negroes ground" where the people he owned planted maize and other crops, but they sowed oats instead of maize among their peach trees. When rainy weather precluded outdoor work, the people Covington enslaved bided their time in ways that were little different from what the original inhabitants of the land they worked had done. While men either plaited corn shucks into mats and other objects or shelled the maize from the cobs, women pounded the kernels into meal in wooden mortars.[68]

Sociologist John Shelton Reed has argued, "The South should be defined by locating Southerners, not the other way around." Such points of mutual intelligibility as the gardens allow us to see and to name this place created by the founding peoples, and it is in the world of paths, maize, and place-making that we can see the first stirrings of a distinctly Southern people.[69] To be sure, each group could denigrate or dismiss the other as cowardly, mean, sinful, savage, or bestial, but in drawing such physical and moral boundaries between one another they extended as well an implicit promise of belonging and the need for the others to make sense of themselves. Real people needed false people to sustain their world, and "whites" needed "blacks." The Goose Creek man who prophesied a moon red with blood looked backward to create a future where he and others like him would be free as well as righteous. And while it is easy to place the invaders of Carolina under the ambit of the blood moon, the vision too captured the first people who were regular visitors to Charles Town and who interacted regularly with enslaved people on the paths and who would, in the end, wield the bloody sword. When Rev. Woodmason saw Carolina beset on all sides by enemies inside and out, he too recognized the degree to which the place he occupied was contingent upon the other people and the other places that constituted the colonial South.[70]

The man who sat down with Father Raphael in 1725 had a similar tale to tell, for he too juxtaposed separateness with belonging. He had heard long before the story of the creation of the place he inhabited, perhaps when he had been taken to water as a child. Changes demand new myths, and in this man's mind, like in the Goose Creek man's mind or in Philip John's, lived the knowledge of what had happened, how things had come to be, and how they ought to unfold. Long ago, he explained, there had been a cave that was home to a white man, a red man, and a black man. The white man left the cave first and found a good hunting ground. The red man left next, strayed off of the "good road" that the white man had followed, and claimed a less abundant territory while the black man "got entirely lost in a very bad country." What he taught the Capuchin was that the Taensas saw themselves as one constituent population of a broader colonial society that included different kinds of people with different kinds of colors and abilities that reflected their unique relationships to the land, to place, and to space. All three men, however, had crawled out of the same cave. They shared the same earth. And they shared the same mother. The line between who belonged to his colonial world and who did not, he explained, could not be drawn around a temple, a parcel of land, a particular plant, or even a skin color.[71]

First people had always recognized the need to have relationships with outsiders, and as they incorporated the invaders and enslaved people into their landscapes, they extended to them a certain kind of belonging. Yuchis, for example, explained the workings of the world in much the same way as the Taensa chief had. Good hunters who died, they believed, ascended to a white man who empowered them to catch game. Bad hunters, however, descended to a world of thickets, brambles, and brush where a mean-spirited black man made hunting all but impossible. And such histories were not limited to the colonial South. Nanticokes, Shawnees, and Delawares also remembered the origins of the world in the creation of red, black, and white brothers. As they found their places within the space of the colonial South, however, the first people's realness and trueness was no longer enough to express the position that they held in the colonial world. Their poetics of in-between had changed and mediated new conceptions of the colonial South as a place, as well as new perceptions of peoplehood and power. Names like Cherokee, Catawba, Creek, Natchez, and Chickasaw came to express more clearly their situation as people in-between the invaders and the enslaved than did notions of realness and truth. But not everything was lost. As ever, the sun and the earth remained in place to keep alive the stories and the memories of former times, beloved kinfolk, and lost places. Although white and black men might have come to hold powerful positions in the landscape, they did so in ways that kept alive the importance of hunting, of paths, and of mother earth.[72]

The ways in which the founding peoples understood the places of their pasts informed the intentions and outcomes of their thoughts and behaviors in the places they made together in the colonial South. Nevertheless, no matter how self-centered their views of the world were, each contained people, places, and things beyond their immediate grasp. In the interstices of their worlds, then, each group contested with the others the landscapes of the colonial society that evolved into the Old South. As long as the founding peoples had the ability to make places and landscapes that reflected their own meanings, they had power. Yet, at the same time, their efforts blended over time to yield landscapes and cosmologies to which they all belonged. But to accept divisions of skin color as the basis for telling their story against the unity of, for example, their gardens or their paths, is again to miss their creativity. Each founding people may have told the story of their land and their people differently, and, perhaps, in direct contradiction to one another, but what they shared was every bit as important as what they did not.

If there were "white," "black," and "red" worlds in the colonial South, there were also creole ones that could not exist without the conflict and collaboration of the founding peoples. And if, in the landscapes and cosmologies of the colonial South, one small corner of the Atlantic world, we can find the South's autobiography and recognize its multiple authors, then perhaps we can see that an ocean is not necessarily an ocean, the story of colonization does not have to be a story of conquest, and "white" men, "red" men, and "black" men can be brothers born of the same mother. The stories we tell, after all, make us who we are and the land what it is.

NOTES

Introduction

1. Father Raphael to Abbé Raguet, 15 May 1725, *Mississippi Provincial Archives: French Dominion*, 3 vols., trans. and ed. Dunbar Rowland and A. G. Sanders (Jackson: Mississippi Department of Archives and History, 1929), vol. 2: 486.
2. Minet, "Voyage Made from Canada Inland Going Southward during the year 1683," trans. Ann Linda Bell, annot. Patricia K. Galloway, *La Salle, the Mississippi, and the Gulf: Three Primary Documents*, ed. Robert S. Weddle (College Station: Texas A&M University Press, 1987), 60–61.
3. Edward S. Casey, "How to Get from Space to Place in a Fairly Short Stretch of Time: Phenomenological Prolegomena," *Senses of Place*, ed. Steven Feld and Keith H. Basso (Santa Fe: School of American Research Press, 1996), 27, emphasis in original.
4. Thomas King, *The Truth about Stories: A Native Narrative* (Toronto: House of Anansi Press, 2003), 2; Charles Wright, "All Landscape is Abstract, and Tends to Repeat Itself," *Appalachia* (New York: Farrar Straus Giroux, 1998), 19; and Casey, "How to Get from Space to Place," 26.
5. William Cronon, *Changes in the Land: Indians, Colonists, and the Ecology of New England* (New York: Hill and Wang, 1983); Jean M. O'Brien, *Dispossession by Degrees: Indian Land and Identity in Natick, Massachusetts, 1650–1790* (New York: Cambridge University Press, 1997); Tom Hatley, *The Dividing Paths: Cherokees and South Carolinians through the Era of Revolution* (New York: Oxford University Press, 1993); Matthew Dennis, *Cultivating a Landscape of Peace: Iroquois-European Encounters in Seventeenth-Century America* (Ithaca: Cornell University Press, 1993); Robbie Ethridge, *Creek Country: The Creek Indians and Their World* (Chapel Hill: University of North Carolina Press, 2004); April Lee Hatfield, *Atlantic Virginia: Intercolonial Relations in the Seventeenth Century* (Philadelphia: University of Pennsylvania Press, 2004); Philip P. Arnold, *Eating Landscape: Aztec and European Occupation of Tlalocan* (Boulder: University Press of Colorado, 1999); Wolfgang Natter and John Paul Jones III, "Signposts toward a Poststructuralist Geography," *Postmodern Contentions: Epochs, Politics, Space*, ed. John Paul Jones III, Wolfgang Natter, and Theodore R. Schatzki (New York: Guilford Press, 1993), 167; and Casey, "How to Get from Space to Place," 20.
6. Ethridge, *Creek Country*, 33–51.

7. William Cronon, "A Place for Stories: Nature, History, and Narrative," *Journal of American History* 78 (1992): 1350; Robert David Sack, *Homo Geographicus: A Framework for Action* (Baltimore: Johns Hopkins University Press, 1997), 4–18; James D. Proctor, "The Social Construction of Nature: Relativist Accusations, Pragmatist and Critical Realist Responses," *Annals of the Association of American Geographers* 88 (1998): 352–70; and Aletta Biersack, "From the 'New Ecology' to the 'New Ecologies,'" *American Anthropologist* 101 (1999): 7–8.
8. Fred R. Myers, *Pintupi Self: Sentiment, Place and Politics among Western Desert Aborigines* (Washington: Smithsonian Institute Press, 1986), 11; Joël Bonnemaison, *The Tree and the Canoe: History and Ethnogeography of Tanna*, trans. Josée Pénot-Demetry (Honolulu: University of Hawaii Press, 1994), 105; Carola Lentz and Hans-Jürgen Sturm, "Of Trees and Earth Shrines: An Interdisciplinary Approach to Settlement Histories in the West African Savanna," *History in Africa: A Journal of Method* 28 (2001): 145; and Barry Cunliffe, *Facing the Ocean: The Atlantic and Its People, 8000 BC–AD 1500* (Oxford: Oxford University Press, 2001), chap. 1.
9. Bernard Cohn, *An Anthropologist among the Historians and Other Essays* (Delhi: Oxford University Press, 1987), 43.
10. Patricia Seed, "Colonial and Postcolonial Discourse," *Latin American Research Review* 26 (1991): 200; Peter Hulme, "Postcolonial Theory and Early America: An Approach from the Caribbean," *Possible Pasts: Becoming Colonial in Early America*, ed. Robert Blair St. George (Ithaca: Cornell University Press, 2000), 35; Michel-Rolph Trouillot, "Anthropology and the Savage Slot: The Poetics and Politics of Otherness," *Recapturing Anthropology: Working in the Present*, ed. Richard G. Fox (Santa Fe, 1991), 23; Paul Rabinow, "Representation and Social Facts: Modernity and Post-Modernity in Anthropology," *Writing Culture: The Poetics and Politics of Ethnography*, ed. James Clifford and George E. Marcus (Berkeley: University of California Press, 1986), 234–61; Joel Kahn, "Culture: Demise or Resurrection," *Critique of Anthropology* 9 (1989); Lila Abu-Lughod, "Writing against Culture," *Recapturing Anthropology*, ed. Fox, 139–43; and Dipesh Chakrabarty, "Post Coloniality and the Artifice of History: Who Speaks for "Indian" Pasts?" *Representations* 37 (1992): 19.
11. Robert Brightman, "Forget Culture: Replacement, Transcendence, Relexification," *Cultural Anthropology* 10 (November 1995): 509–46; Irene Silverblatt, "Becoming Indian in the Central Andes of Seventeenth Century Peru," *After Colonialism: Imperial Histories and Postcolonial Displacements*, ed. Gyan Prakesh (Princeton: Princeton University Press, 1995), 291; Neil Whitehead, "Three Patamuna Trees: Landscape and History in the Guyana Highlands," *Histories and Historicities in Amazonia*, ed. Neil Whitehead (Lincoln: University of Nebraska Press, 2003), 59–60; Omer C. Stewart, "The Forgotten Side of Ethnogeography," *Method and Perspective in Anthropology: Papers in Honor of Wilson D. Wallis*, ed. Robert F. Spencer (Minneapolis: University of Minnesota Press, 1954), 221–22, 248; A. Endre Nyerges and Glen Martin Green, "The Ethnography of Landscape: GIS and Remote Sensing in the Study of Forest Change in West African Guinea Savanna," *American Anthropologist* 102 (2000): 275–76; and James Taylor Carson, "Ethnogeography and the Native American Past," *Ethnohistory* 49 (Fall 2002): 765–84.
12. Gaston Bachelard, *The Poetics of Space*, trans. Marie Jolas (New York: Orion Press, 1964); Edward W. Soja, "The Spatiality of Social Life: Towards a Transformative Retheorisation," *Social Relations and Spatial Structures*, ed. Derek

Gregory and John Urry (London: Macmillan, 1985), 90–92; and Kenneth R. Olwig, "Recovering the Substantive Nature of Landscape," *Annals of the Association of American Geographers* 86 (December 1996): 630–53.

13. Tina L. Thurston, *Landscapes of Power, Landscapes of Conflict: State Formation in the South Scandinavian Iron Age* (New York: Plenum, 2001), 37, 263, and Timothy Earle, *How Chiefs Come to Power: The Political Economy in Prehistory* (Stanford: Stanford University Press, 1997), 3, 12, 67–68, 143–44, 151–53.

14. Mark Haugaard, *The Constitution of Power: A Theoretical Analysis of Power, Knowledge and Structure* (Manchester: Manchester University Press, 1997), 7–116; and Andrew Sluyter, "Colonialism and Landscape in the Americas: Material/Conceptual Transformations and Continuing Consequences," *Annals of the Association of American Geographers* 91 (2001): 411–15.

15. Theda Perdue, *"Mixed Blood" Indians: Racial Construction in the Early South* (Athens: University of Georgia Press, 2003); Robert F. Berkhofer Jr., *The White Man's Indian: Images of the American Indian from Columbus to the Present* (New York: Vintage Books, 1979), 29, 125; Roland Barthes, *Mythologies*, trans. Annette Lavers (New York: Hill and Wang, 1972), 143; Neil L. Whitehead, "Introduction," *History and Historicities in Amazonia* (Lincoln: University of Nebraska Press, 2003), ix; Richard Slotkin, *Regeneration through Violence: The Mythology of the American Frontier, 1600–1860* (Middleton, Conn.: Wesleyan University Press, 1973), 3; and George B. Handley, "A New World Poetics of Oblivion," *Look Away: The U.S. South in New World Studies*, ed. Jon Smith and Deborah Cohn (Durham: Duke University Press, 2004), 28.

16. Whitehead, "Three Patamuna Trees," 60, and Édouard Glissant, *The Fourth Century*, trans. Betsy Wing (Lincoln: University of Nebraska Press, 2001), 39–40.

17. Édouard Glissant, *Caribbean Discourse: Selected Essays*, trans. and intro. J. Michael Dash (Charlottesville: University Press of Virginia, 1989), 66; E. Kamau Brathwaite, *Development of Creole Society in Jamaica, 1770–1820* (Oxford: Clarendon Press, 1971), 307. See also Jean Bernabé, Patrick Chamoiseau, and Raphaël Confiant, *Éloge de la créolité* (Paris: Gallimard, 1993); Raymond Relouzat, *Tradition orale et imaginaire créole* (Martinique: Ibis Rouge Editions, 1998); Ineke Phaf, ed., *Creole Presence in the Caribbean and Latin America* (Madrid: Iberoamericana, 1996); and Édouard Glissant, *Introduction á une poétique du divers* (Montréal: La Presse de la Université de Montréal, 1994).

18. Peter Wood, *Black Majority: Negroes in Colonial South Carolina from 1670 through the Stono Rebellion* (New York: W. W. Norton and Co., 1974); Judith A. Carney, *Black Rice: The African Origins of Rice Cultivation in the Americas* (Cambridge: Harvard University Press, 2001); Daniel H. Usner Jr., *Indians, Settlers, & Slaves in a Frontier Exchange Economy: The Lower Mississippi Valley before 1783* (Chapel Hill: University of North Carolina Press, 1992); and Woody Holton, *Forced Founders: Indians, Debtors, Slaves & the Making of the American Revolution in Virginia* (Chapel Hill: University of North Carolina Press, 1999).

19. Timothy Silver, *A New Face on the Countryside: Indians, Colonists, and Slaves in South Atlantic Forests, 1500–1800* (Cambridge: Cambridge University Press, 1990), 7–34, 140–41, and William J. Cooper Jr. and Thomas E. Terrill, *The American South: A History* (New York: McGraw-Hill, 1991), vol. 1: 1–6.

20. Francis Jennings, *The Invasion of America: Indians, Colonialism, and the Cant of Conquest* (New York: W.W. Norton & Co., 1976), 10–11; Tzvetan Todorov,

The Conquest of America: The Question of the Other, trans. Richard Howard (Norman: University of Oklahoma Press, 1984), 36–50; Marty J. Bowden, "The Invention of American Tradition," *Journal of Historical Geography* 18 (1992): 6–8, 16–20; William Cronon, "The Trouble with Wilderness: Or, Getting Back to the Wrong Nature," *Uncommon Ground: Toward Reinventing Nature*, ed. William Cronon (New York: W.W. Norton, 1995), 69–90; Thomas R. Vale, "Preface: The Pre-European Landscape of the United States: Pristine or Humanized," *Fire, Native Peoples, and the Natural Landscape*, ed. Thomas R. Vale (Washington: Island Press, 2002), xiii; Bernard Bailyn, *The Peopling of British North America: An Introduction* (New York: Alfred A. Knopf, 1986), 113; and Walter Mignolo, *The Darker Side of the Renaissance: Literacy, Territoriality, and Colonization* (Ann Arbor: University of Michigan Press, 1995), 259.
21. Handley, "New World Poetics of Oblivion," 43.

Chapter 1

1. Federico Garcia Lorca, *A Season in Granada: Uncollected Prose and Poems*, trans. and ed. Christopher Maurer (London: Anvil Press, 1998), 119.
2. Edward Kamau Brathwaite, "Calypso," *The Arrivants: A New World Trilogy* (Oxford: Oxford University Press, 1973), 48; Christopher Norris, *Language, Logic, and Epistemology: A model-Realist Approach* (Hampshire, N.Y.: Palgrave Macmillan, 2004), 4–9, 150, 181; Ivana Markova, *Dialogicality and Social Representation: The Dynamics of Mind* (Cambridge: Cambridge University Press, 2003), 82; and Lisa M. Dolling, "Dialogue as Praxis: Philosophical Hermeneutics, Historical Epistemology, and Truth," *Constructivism and Practice: Toward a Historical Epistemology*, ed. Carol C. Gould (New York: Rowman and Littlefield, 2003), 38–40.
3. David Armitage, "Three Concepts of Atlantic History," *The British Atlantic World, 1500–1800*, ed. David Armitage and Michael J. Braddick (New York: Palgrave, 2002), 21, 11–12; and David Armitage and Michael J. Braddick, "Introduction," *British Atlantic World*, 1.
4. Natter and Jones, "Signposts toward a Poststructuralist Geography," 167.
5. J. G. A. Pocock, "British History: A Plea for a New Subject," *Journal of Modern History* 47 (1975): 616; Édouard Glissant, *Introduction à une poétique du divers*; Relouzat, *Tradition orale et imaginaire créole*; Rex Nettleford, "The Caribbean: Crossroads of the Americas," *Crossroads of Empire: The Europe-Caribbean Connection 1492–1992*, ed. Alan Cobley (Cave Hill: Department of History, University of West Indies, 1994), 8; and Norris, *Language, Logic, and Epistemology*, 186.
6. Karen Ordahl Kupperman, "Foreword," *Envisioning an English Empire: Jamestown and the Making of the North Atlantic World*, ed. Robert Appelbaum and John Wood Sweet (Philadelphia: Pennsylvania University Press, 2005), xi.
7. Marvin T. Smith, *Coosa: The Rise and Fall of a Southeastern Mississippian Chiefdom* (Gainesville: University Press of Florida, 2000), 6; Jerald T. Milanich, *Archaeology of Precolumbian Florida* (Gainesville: University Press of Florida, 1994), 37–40; David G. Anderson, Jerald Ledbetter, Lisa O'Steen, Daniel T. Elliott, Dennis Blanton, Glen T. Hanson, and Frankie Snow, "Paleoindian and Early Archaic in the Lower Southeast: A View from Georgia," *Ocmulgee Archae-*

ology, 1936–1986, ed. David J. Halley (Athens: University of Georgia Press, 1994), 55–59; Stephen R. Potter, *Commoners, Tribute, and Chiefs: The Development of Algonquian Culture in the Potomac Valley* (Charlottesville: University Press of Virginia1993), 50; and Marilou Awiakta, "Daydreaming Primal Space," *The Poetics of Appalachian Space*, ed. Parks Lanier Jr. (Knoxville: University of Tennessee Press, 1991), 204.

8. James Axtell, *The Indians' New South: Cultural Change in the Colonial Southeast* (Baton Rouge: Louisiana State University Press, 1997), 1–3.
9. P. Allsworth-Jones, "The Earliest Human Settlement in West Africa and the Sahara," *Foundations of Civilization in Tropical Africa*, ed. Bassey W. Andah and A. Ikechukwu Okpoko (Ibadan: West African Journal of Archaeology, 1987), 99.
10. Joanne Rappaport, *The Politics of Memory: Native Historical Interpretation in the Columbian Andes* (Cambridge: Cambridge University Press, 1990), 1.
11. Milanich, *Archaeology of Precolumbian Florida*, 40–51; Anderson et al., "Paleoindian and Early Archaic in the Lower Southeast," 57–61; Potter, *Commoners, Tribute, and Chiefs*, 50; Fred B. Kniffen, Hiram F. Gregory, and George A. Stokes, *The Historic Indian Tribes of Louisiana from 1542 to the Present* (Baton Rouge: Louisiana State University Press, 1987), 28–30; and Tristram R. Kidder, "Making the City Inevitable: Native Americans and the Geography of New Orleans," *Transforming New Orleans and Its Environs: Centuries of Change*, ed. Craig E. Colten (Pittsburgh: University of Pittsburgh Press, 2000), 12–24.
12. Milanich, *Archaeology of Precolumbian Florida*, 63–67, and Kniffen et al., *The Historic Indian Tribes of Louisiana*, 29–31.
13. Milanich, *Archaeology of Precolumbian Florida*, 72–73.
14. Richard A. Yarnell, "The Importance of Native Crops during the Late Archaic and Woodland Periods," *Foraging and Farming in the Eastern Woodlands*, ed. Margaret Scarry (Gainesville: University Press of Florida, 1993), 13–14; Michael S. Nassaney, "The Late Woodland Southeast," *Late Woodland Societies: Tradition and Transformation across the Mid-Continent*, ed. Thomas E. Emerson, D. L. McElrath, and A. C. Fortier (Lincoln: University of Nebraska Press, 2000), 718; and Vernon James Knight, "Feasting and the Emergence of Platform Mound Ceremonialism in Eastern North America," *Feasts: Archaeological and Ethnographic Perspectives on Food, Politics, and Power*, ed. M. Dietler and B. Hayden (Washington, D.C.: Smithsonian Institution, 2001), 312.
15. Charles Hudson, *The Southeastern Indians* (Knoxville: University of Tennessee Press, 1976), 67–68, and Kniffen et al., *The Historic Indian Tribes of Louisiana*, 30–32.
16. Milanich, *Archaeology of Precolumbian Florida*, 86–89, and Anderson et al., "Paleoindian and Early Archaic in the Lower Southeast," 66–68.
17. John H. Blitz, *Ancient Chiefdoms of the Tombigbee* (Tuscaloosa: University of Alabama Press, 1993), 34–36; Nassaney, "Late Woodland Southeast," 719; Potter, *Commoners, Tribute, and Chiefs*, 72–75; Milanich, *Archaeology of Precolumbian Florida*, 144; Rebecca Saunders, "Swift Creek Design Assemblages from Two Sites on the Georgia Coast," *A World Engraved: Archaeology of the Swift Creek Culture*, ed. Mark Williams and Daniel T. Elliott (Tuscaloosa: University of Alabama Press, 1998), 161–77.
18. Yarnell, "Importance of Native Crops," 17; Sissel Johannessen, "Farms of the Late Woodland," *Foraging and Farming in the Eastern Woodlands*, ed. Scarry,

63; Nassaney, "Late Woodland Southeast," 718; Milanich, *Archaeology of Precolumbian Florida*, 144; and Thomas J. Pluckhahn, *Kolomoki: Settlement, Ceremony, and Status in the Deep South, A.D. 350 to 750* (Tuscaloosa: University of Alabama Press, 2003), 163–64.
19. Blitz, *Ancient Chiefdoms of the Tombigbee*, 33; Nassaney, "Late Woodland Southeast," 720; Potter, *Commoners, Tribute, and Chiefs*, 66.
20. Nassaney, "Late Woodland Southeast," 720; Milanich, *Archaeology of Precolumbian Florida*, 148; Pluckhahn, *Kolomoki*, 4, 8–9, 181–83; and Mark Williams and Daniel T. Elliot, "Swift Creek Research: History and Observations," *World Engraved*, ed. Williams and Elliott, 5.
21. Williams and Elliott, "Swift Creek Research," 1–5; and Frankie Snow, "Swift Creek Design Investigations: The Hartford Case," *World Engraved*, ed. Williams and Elliott, 63.
22. Snow, "Swift Creek Design Investigations," 76–78.
23. Frankie Snow and Keith Stephenson, "Swift Creek Designs: A Tool for Monitoring Interaction," *World Engraved*, ed. Williams and Elliott, 101–7; David G. Anderson, "Swift Creek in a Regional Perspective," *World Engraved*, ed. Williams and Elliott, 278–79; Mark Williams and Jennifer Freer Harris, "Shrines of the Prehistoric South: Patterning in Middle Woodland Mound Distribution," *World Engraved*, ed. Williams and Elliott, 38–46; Pluckhahn, *Kolomaki*, 34; Milanich, *Archaeology of Precolumbian Florida*, 144, 171; and Richard Jefferies, "The Swift Creek Site and Woodland Platform Mounds in the Southeastern United States," *Ocmulgee Archaeology, 1936–1986*, ed. Halley, 71
24. Knight, "Feasting and the Emergence of Platform Mound Ceremonialism," 312.
25. Knight, "Feasting and the Emergence of Platform Mound Ceremonialism," 323–27; Pluckhahn, *Kolomaki*, 181–83; Robert C. Mainfort Jr., "Middle Woodland Ceremonialism at Pinson Mounds, Tennessee," *American Antiquity* 53 (1988): 163; Mark Williams and Jennifer Freer Harris, "Shrines of the Prehistoric South: Patterning in Middle Woodland Mound Distribution," *World Engraved*, ed. Williams and Elliott, 46; Milanich, *Archaeology of Precolumbian Florida*, 178.
26. Pluckhahn, *Kolomoki*, 86–89, 183–96, and Mainfort, "Middle Woodland Ceremonialism," 158–68.
27. Jerald T. Milanich, Ann S. Cordell, Vernon Knight Jr., Timothy A. Kohler, and Brenda J. Sigler-Lavelle, *Archaeology of Northern Florida, A.D. 200–900* (Gainesville: University Press of Florida, 1997 [1984]), 41–42, 91–112, 176–77; and Patricia Galloway, *Choctaw Genesis, 1500–1700* (Lincoln: University of Nebraska Press, 1999), 276–79.
28. Karl T. Steinem, "Kolomoki and the Development of Sociopolitical Organization on the Gulf Coastal Plain," *World Engraved*, ed. Williams and Elliott, 188; Anderson, "Swift Creek in Regional Perspective," 296–97; Jefferies, "Swift Creek Site," 82; Knight, "Feasting and the Emergence of Platform Mound Ceremonialism," 311–21; and Bruce D. Smith, "Mississippian Patterns of Subsistence and Settlement," *Alabama and the Borderlands from Prehistory to Statehood*, ed. R. Reid Badger and Lawrence A. Cayton (Tuscaloosa: University of Alabama Press, 1985), 64–65.
29. Claudine Payne and John F. Scarry, "Town Structure at the Edge of the Mississippian World," *Mississippian Towns and Sacred Spaces: Searching for an Architectural Grammar*, ed. R. Barry Lewis and Charles Stout (Tuscaloosa: Univer-

sity of Alabama Press, 1998), 30–32; Blitz, *Ancient Chiefdoms of the Tombigbee*, 59–68; Randolph J. Widmer, "The Structure of Southeastern Chiefdoms," *The Forgotten Centuries: Indians and Europeans in the American South, 1521–1704*, ed. Charles Hudson and Carmen Chaves Tesser (Athens: University of Georgia Press, 1994), 125–55; Vernon James Knight Jr., "Symbolism of Mississippian Mounds," *Powhatan's Mantle: Indians in the Colonial Southeast*, ed. Peter H. Wood, Gregory A. Waselkov, and M. Thomas Hatley (Lincoln: University of Nebraska Press, 1989), 287–88; and Thomas J. Riley, "Ocmulgee and the Question of Mississippian Agronomic Practices," *Ocmulgee Archaeology, 1936–1986*, ed. Halley, 97–104.

30. Blitz, *Ancient Chiefdoms of the Tombigbee*, 45–49, and David H. Dye, "Feasting with the Enemy: Mississippian Warfare and Prestige-Goods Circulation," *Native American Interactions: Multiscalar Analyses and Interpretations in the Eastern Woodlands*, ed. Michael S. Nassaney and Kenneth E. Sassaman (Knoxville: University of Tennessee Press, 1995), 292–95.

31. Payne and Scarry, "Town Structure at the Edge of the Mississippian World," 30, 43–46, and Milanich, *Archaeology of Precolumbian Florida*, 355.

32. R. Barry Lewis, Charles Stout, and Cameron B. Wesson, "The Design of Mississippian Towns," *Mississippian Towns and Sacred Spaces*, ed. Lewis and Stout, 1–5.

33. Lewis, Stout, and Wesson, "Design of Mississippian Towns," 10–19; Cameron Wesson, "Mississippian Sacred Landscapes: The View from Alabama," *Mississippian Towns and Sacred Spaces*, ed. Lewis and Stout, 101; David J. Hally, "Archaeology and Settlement Plan of the King Site," *The King Site: Continuity and Contact in Sixteenth-Century Georgia*, ed. Robert L. Blakely (Athens: University of Georgia Press, 1988), 3–16; David J. Hally and Hypatia Kelly, "The Nature of Mississippian Towns in Georgia: The King Site Example," *Mississippian Towns and Sacred Spaces*, ed. Lewis and Stout, 49–58; Payne and Scary, "Town Structure at the Edge of the Mississippian World," 39–40; Gregory A. Waselkov, "Indian Maps of the Co-lonial Southeast," *Powhatan's Mantle*, ed. Wood, Waselkov, and Hatley, 292–342; Milanich, *Archaeology of Precolumbian Florida*, 369; David J. Hally and Mark Williams, "Macon Plateau Site Community Pattern," *Ocmulgee*, 87–91; and James B. Langford Jr. and Marvin T. Smith, "Recent Investigations in the Core of Coosa Province," *Lamar Archaeology: Mississippian Chiefdoms in the Deep South* (Tuscaloosa: University of Alabama, 1990), 106.

34. Milanich et al., *Archaeology of Northern Florida*, 43; John E. Worth, *Timucuan Chiefdoms of Spanish Florida*, 2 vols. (Gainesville: University Press of Florida, 1998), vol. 1: 13–21; Rebecca Saunders, "Guale Indian Pottery: A Georgia Legacy in Northeast Florida," *Florida Anthropologist* 45 (1992): 140–42; and Lynne P. Sullivan, "Mississippian Household and Community Organization in Eastern Tennessee," *Mississippian Communities and Households*, ed. J. Daniel Rogers and Bruce D. Smith (Tuscaloosa: University of Alabama Press, 1995), 102–3.

35. Potter, *Commoners, Tribute, and Chiefs*, 78–79, 83–85, 101, 142–43, 147, 155; and Martin D. Gallivan, *James River Chiefdoms: The Rise of Social Inequality in the Chesapeake* (Lincoln: University of Nebraska Press, 2003), 29–36, 44, 78, 84, 107–9, 124.

36. Fernand Braudel, *The Mediterranean and the Mediterranean World in the Age of Philip II*, 2 vols., trans. Siân Reynolds (New York: Harper & Row, 1972),

vol. 1: 276; Charles Hudson, "Introduction," *The Transformation of the Southeastern Indians, 1540–1760*, ed. Robbie Ethridge and Charles Hudson (Jackson: University Press of Mississippi, 2002), xxxix; Jack Goody, *Cooking, Cuisine and Class: A Study in Comparative Sociology* (Cambridge: Cambridge University Press, 1982), 37; and Larry McKee, "Food Supply and Plantation Social Order: An Archaeological Perspective," *"I, Too, Am American": Archaeological Studies of African-American Life*, ed. Theresa A. Singleton (Charlottesville: University Press of Virginia, 1999), 219.

37. Marija Gimbutas, *The Goddesses and Gods of Old Europe: Myths and Cult Images* (London: Thames & Hudson, Ltd., 1982), 91–112.
38. Catherine Delano Smith, "Cartography in the Prehistoric Period in the Old World: Europe, the Middle East, and North Africa," *History of Cartography: Volume 1: Cartography in Prehistoric, Ancient and Medieval Europe and the Mediterranean*, ed. J. B. Harley and David Woodward (Chicago: University of Chicago Press, 1987), 87–91; R. V. Tooley, *Maps and Map-Makers* (London: B. T. Batesford Ltd., 1987), 3; Karen Louise Jolly, *Popular Religion in Late Saxon England: Elf Charms in Context* (Chapel Hill: University of North Carolina Press, 1996), 27–28; and Alasdair Whittle, *Neolithic Europe: A Survey* (Cambridge: Cambridge University Press, 1985), 235.
39. J. B. Harley and David Woodward, "The Foundations of Theoretical Cartography in Archaic and Classical Greece," *History of Cartography*, ed. Harley and Woodward, 134.
40. Harley and Woodward, "Foundations of Theoretical Cartography," 134–44; Aristotle, "On the Heavens," *The Complete Works of Aristotle: The Revised Oxford Translation*, 2 vols., ed. Jonathan Barnes (Princeton: Princeton University Press, 1984), 1: 461–63, 473, 480; and Aristotle, "On the Universe," *Complete Works* 1: 628.
41. Aristotle, "Physics," *Complete Works* 1: 329, 349; Aristotle, "On the Universe," 628, 633–34; and Aristotle, "Meteorology," *Complete Works* 1: 329, 349; Frederick B. Artz, *The Mind of the Middle Ages: An Historical Survey, A.D. 200–1500*, 3rd ed. (Chicago: University of Chicago Press, 1980), 235–42; Galen, *On Antecedent Causes*, ed., trans., introd. R. J. Hankinson (Cambridge: Cambridge University Press, 1998), 29; John B. Friedman, *The Monstrous Races in Medieval Art and Thought* (Cambridge: Harvard University Press, 1981), 51.
42. Aristotle, "On the Universe," 639.
43. Aristotle, "On the Universe," 640.
44. Harley and Woodward, "Foundations of Theoretical Cartography," 136, 145; and Harley and Woodward, "Greek Cartography in the Early Roman World," *History of Cartography*, ed. Harley and Woodward, 168–69.
45. Pliny the Elder, *The Natural History of Pliny*, trans. John Bostock and H. T. Riley, 2 vols. (London: George Bell & Sons, 1893, 1890), 1: 13–14, 18–20.
46. Pliny the Elder, *Natural History* 1: 30–32, 92; and Galen, *On Antecedent Causes*, 11.
47. Pliny the Elder, *Natural History* 1: 110–11, from which the quote is taken, and vol. 2: 118.
48. Oliver Rackham, "The Medieval Countryside of England: Botany and Archaeology," *Inventing Medieval Landscapes: Senses of Place in Western Europe*, ed. John Howe and Michael Wolfe (Gainesville: University Press of Florida, 2002), 14; and Whittle, *Neolithic Europe*, 35, 52, 87–88.

49. Thomas F. Glick, *Islamic and Christian Spain in the Early Middle Ages* (Princeton: Princeton University Press, 1979), 31, 66, 84; Glick, "Tribal Landscapes of Islamic Spain: History and Archaeology," *Inventing Medieval Landscapes*, ed. Howe and Wolfe, 113–18; Andrew Watson, "Arab and European Agriculture in the Middle Ages: A Case of Restricted Diffusion," *Agriculture in the Middle Ages: Technology, Practice, and Representation*, ed. Del Sweeney (Philadelphia: University of Pennsylvania Press, 1995), 67; Bernard F. Reilly, *The Medieval Spains* (Cambridge: Cambridge University Press, 1993), 51–56; and Najla Akrawi, "Arabic Gardens in Spain," *Gardens and Culture: Eight Studies in History and Aesthetics*, ed. Hannah Disinger Demaray (Beirut: Eastern Press, 1969), 69–71.
50. George H. T. Kimble, *Geography in the Middle Ages* (New York: Russell & Russell, 1968 [1938]), 5, 12–18; O. A. W. Dilke, "The Culmination of Greek Cartography in Ptolemy," *History of Cartography*, ed. Harley and Woodward, 177; Tooley, *Maps and Map-Makers*, 9–10; David Buisseret, *The Mapmaker's Quest: Depicting New Worlds in Renaissance Europe* (Oxford: Oxford University Press, 2003), 16; Galen, *On Antecedent Causes*, 57; William Cohen, *The French Encounter with Africans: White Response to Blacks, 1530–1880* (Bloomington: Indiana University Press, 1980), 1–2; Bartholomew Anglicus, *Medieval Lore: An Epitome of the Science, Geography, Animal and Plant Folk-Lore and Myth of the Middle Ages*, ed. Robert Steele (London: Elliot Stock, 1893), 23–24; John Jones, *Galen's Book of Elementes* (London: William Jones, 1574); and Galen, *Certaine Workes of Galens, Called Methodus Medendi* (London: Thomas East, 1586).
51. Evelyn Edson, *Mapping Time and Space: How Medieval Mapmakers Viewed Their World* (London: British Library, 1999), 37–39, 53–54; and Kimble, *Geography in the Middle Ages*, 27.
52. Cosmas Indicopleustès, *Topographie chrétienne*, 2 vols., trans. Wanda Wolska-Conus (Paris: Les éditions du Cerf, 1968), vol. 1: 264, 310, 443, and 428.
53. John R. Stilgoe, *Common Landscapes of America, 1580–1845* (New Haven: Yale University Press, 1982), 13–19; Carlo Ginzburg, *The Cheese and the Worms: The Cosmos of a Sixteenth-Century Miller*, trans. John and Anne Tedeschi (Baltimore: Johns Hopkins University Press, 1980); Paul Edward Dutton, "Thunder and Hail over the Carolingian Countryside," *Agriculture in the Middle Ages*, ed. Sweeney, 111–20; Keith Thomas, *Religion and the Decline of Magic* (New York: Charles Scribner's Sons, 1971), 29–32, 648; Paul Meyvaert, "The Medieval Monastic Garden," *Medieval Gardens*, ed. Elizabeth MacDougall (Washington, D.C.: Dumbarton Oaks, 1986), 31; and, as quoted, Jolly, *Popular Religion in Late Saxon England*, 120–21.
54. Stilgoe, *Common Landscapes of America*, 127; and Thomas, *Religion and the Decline of Magic*, 48, 62–63.
55. Jolly, *Popular Religion in Late Saxon England*, 6–9.
56. Bruce M. S. Campbell, "Ecology versus Economics in Late Thirteenth- and Early Fourteenth-Century English Agriculture," *Agriculture in the Middle Ages*, ed. Sweeney, 81; Jean de Vigan with Phyllis Sutton, "The French Garden: Medieval to Modern," *Gardens and Culture*, ed. Hannah Disinger Demaray, 97; Emmanuel Le Roy Ladurie, *French Peasantry, 1450–1660*, trans. Alana Sheridan (Oxford: Scholar Press, 1987), 24, 60; James A. Yelling, *Common Fields and Enclosure in England, 1450–1850* (London: Macmillan Press, Ltd., 1977), 147–48; Robin Briggs, *Early Modern France, 1560–1715*, 2nd ed. (Oxford: Oxford University Press, 1998), 34–50; Georges Duby, *Rural Economy and Country Life in the Medieval West*, trans. Cynthis Postan (Columbia: University of South Carolina Press,

1968), 5–10, 16, 22, 67–76, 116; Robert Bartlett, *England under the Norman and Angevin Kings, 1075–1225* (Oxford: Clarendon Press, 2000), 294–306; Adriaan Verhulst, *The Carolingian Econ-omy* (Cambridge: Cambridge University Press, 2002), 11, 32–43, 61; Eric Kerridge, *The Common Fields of England* (Manchester: Manchester University Press, 1992), 1–34; Marjorie Chibnall, *Anglo-Norman England, 1066–1166* (Oxford: Basil Blackwell, 1986), 139–41; Arthur Lovejoy, *The Great Chain of Being: A Study of the History of an Idea* (Cambridge: Harvard University Press, 1936), 42–76; Gustav Jahoda, *Images of Savages: Ancient Roots of Modern Prejudice in Western Culture* (London: Routledge, 1999), 32; and Aristotle, "On the Heavens," 480.
57. Lovejoy, *Great Chain of Being*, 42–76.
58. Cosmas Indicopleustès, *Topographie chrétienne* 1: 480; Carolly Erickson, *The Medieval Vision: Essays in History and Perception* (New York: Oxford University Press, 1976), 12–20; Harald Kleinschmidt, *Understanding the Middle Ages: The Transformation of Ideas and Attitudes in the Middle Ages* (Woodbridge, U.K.: Boydell Press, 2000), 94, 120–33; Lovejoy, *Great Chain of Being*, as quoted, 72; Colin S. MacLachlan, *Spain's Empire in the New World: The Role of Ideas in Institutional and Social Change* (Berkeley: University of California Press, 1988), 3; Keith Thomas, *Man and the Natural World: Changing Attitudes in England, 1500–1800* (New York: Pantheon Books, 1983), 124; and Artz, *Mind of the Middle Ages*, 235, 290–91.
59. Friedman, *Monstrous Races in Medieval Art and Thought*, 7; Seymour Phillips, "The Outer World of the European Middle Ages," *Implicit Understandings: Observing, Reporting, and Reflecting on the Encounters between Europeans and Other Peoples in the Early Modern Era*, ed. Stuart B. Schwartz (Cambridge: Cambridge University Press, 1994), 46; Julius Solinus, *The Excellent and Pleasant Worke of Julius Solinus Polyhistor* (London: Charlewood, 1587), chaps. 42, 43; Cohen, *French Encounter with Africans*, 5; Cosmas Indicopleustès, *Topographie chrétienne* 1: 284; Jahoda, *Images of Savages*, 30; Anglicus, *Medieval Lore*, 75
60. Friedman, *Monstrous Races in Medieval Art and Thought*, 31; Phillips, "Outer World of the European Middle Ages," 47; and Thomas, *Man and the Natural World*, 41.
61. Phillips, "Outer World of the European Middle Ages," 28–29, 44–45; Isidore de Séville, *Étymologies* 9, ed. and trans. Marc Reydellet (Paris: Societé d'éditions, 1984), 42; Cosmas Indicopleustès, *Topographie chrétienne* 1: 328–30; Jahoda, *Images of Savages*, 26–29; Cohen, *French Encounter with Africans*, 9; Anglicus, *Medieval Lore*, 75.
62. David Woodward, "Medieval Mappaemundi," *History of Cartography*, ed. Harley and Woodward, 286–90, 334–41, and David Woodward, "Reality, Symbolism, Time and Space in Medieval World Maps," *Annals of the Association of American Geographers* 75 (1985): 511.
63. Edson, *Mapping Time and Space*, 4–17; Rhonda Lemke Sanford, *Maps and Memory in Early Modern England* (New York: Palgrave, 2002), 5–6; Norman Joseph William Thrower, *Maps & Civilization: Cartography in Culture and Society* (Chicago: University of Chicago Press, 1996), 42; John Hale, *The Civilization of Europe in the Renaissance* (London: Fontana Press, 1993), 15; Frank Lestringant, *Mapping the Renaissance World: The Geographical Imagination in the Age of Discovery*, trans. David Fausett (Cambridge: Polity Press, 1994), 23; Thomas, *Man and the Natural World*, 17–22; Anthony Pagden, *European Encounters with the New World: From Renaissance to Romanticism* (New Haven: Yale University Press, 1993), 6; and Genesis 9: 5, *King James Bible*.

64. Woodward, "Reality, Symbolism, Time and Space," 510–15; Joyce E. Chaplin, "Race," *British Atlantic World, 1500–1800*, ed. Armitage and Braddick, 158; Woodward, "Medieval Mappaemundi," 340–41; Dilke, "Culmination of Greek Cartography," 177; Tooley, *Maps and Map-Makers*, 10–15; and Tony Campbell, "Portolan Charts from the Late Thirteenth Century to 1500," *History of Cartography*, ed. Harley and Woodward, 371–75 and, as quoted, 372.
65. J. D. Fage with William Torduff, *A History of Africa*, 4th ed. (New York: Routledge, 2002), 215–21; Ivor Wilks, *Forests of Gold: Essays on the Akan and the Kingdom of Asante* (Athens, Ohio: Ohio University Press, 1993), 3; Lestringant, *Mapping the Renaissance World*, 2; and Woodward, "Medieval Mappaemundi," 292.
66. Fage, *History of Africa*, 218–36; Thomas Astley, "The First Voyages of the Portugueze to the East Indies," *A New General Collection of Voyages and Travels Consisting of the Most Esteemed Relations Which Have Been Hitherto Published in Any Language*, 4 vols. (London: Frank Cass and Company Limited, 1968), vol. 1: 10–12; E. Savage, "Berbers and Blacks: Ibadi Slave Traffic in Eighth Century North Africa," *Journal of African History* 33 (1992): 351–53; A. Ryder, *Benin and the Europeans, 1485–1897* (New York: Humanities Press, 1969), 24; Jerry Brotton, *Trading Territories: Mapping in the Early Modern World* (Ithaca: Cornell University Press, 1998), 58–63; and Ivor Wilks, "Wangara, Akan, and Portuguese in the Fifteenth and Sixteenth Centuries. I. The Matter of Bitu," *Journal of African History* 23 (1982): 335.
67. Astley, "First Voyage of the Portugueze," 16–17, and Ryder, *Benin and the Europeans*, 26.
68. Elizabeth Ishichei, *A History of the Igbo People* (London: Macmillan, 1976), 2–9; Tadeusz Lewicki, *West African Food in the Middle Ages According to Arabic Sources* (Cambridge: Cambridge University Press, 1974), 19–24, 51; William R. Bascom, "Yoruba Food," *Africa* 21 (1951): 41–44; Thurston Shaw, *Igbo-Ukwu: An Account of Archaeological Discoveries in Eastern Nigeria*, 2 vols. (London: Faber and Faber Ltd., 1970), vol. 1: 284; K. Williamson, "Linguistic Evidence for the Use of Some Tree and Tuber Food Plants in Southern Nigeria," *The Archaeology of Africa: Food, Metals and Towns*, ed. Thurston Shaw, Paul Sinclair, Bassey Andah, and Alex Okpoko (New York: Routledge, 1993), 152; V. E. Chikwendu and C. E. A. Okezie, "Factors Responsible for the Ennoblement of African Yams: Inferences for Experiments in Yam Domestication," *Foraging and Farming: The Evolution of Plant Exploitation*, ed. David R. Harris and Gordon C. Hillman (London: Unwin Hyman, 1989), 345; and Bassey W. Andah, "Agricultural Beginnings and Early Farming Communities in West and Central Africa," *Foundations of Civilization in Tropical Africa*, ed. Andah and Okpoko, 179–80.
69. Jan Vansina, *Paths in the Rain Forest: Toward a History of Political Tradition in Equatorial Africa* (Madison: University of Wisconsin Press, 1990), 49–65; Christopher Ehret, "Bantu Expansions: Re-Envisioning a Central Problem of Early African History," *International Journal of African Historical Studies* 34 (2001): 6–7, 29–32; A. Norman Klein, "Toward a New Understanding of Akan Origins," *Africa* 66 (1996): 249–55; Andah, "Agricultural Beginnings and Early Farming Communities," 171–72; Frank B. Livingstone, "Anthropological Implications of Sickle Cell Gene Distribution in West Africa," *American Anthropologist* 60 (1958): 551–53.
70. K. Onwuka Dike, *Trade and Politics in the Niger Delta 1830–1885* (Oxford: Clarendon Press, 1965), 4.

71. Bassey W. Andah and A. Ikechukwu Okpoko, "Introduction to Foundations of Civilization in Tropical Africa," *Foundations of Civilization in Tropical Africa*, ed. Andah and Okpoko, vii; K. Onwuka Dike, "Introduction to the Ibadan History Series," J. D. Omer-Cooper, *The Zulu Aftermath: A Nineteenth-Century Revolution in Bantu Africa* (Evanston: Northwestern University Press, 1969), xiii; David P. Henige, *The Chronology of Oral Tradition: Quest for a Chimera* (Oxford: Clarendon Press, 1974), 190–91; Arnold Temu and Bonaventure Swai, *Historians and Africanist History: A Critique* (London: Zed Press, 1981), 61, 113, 160; P. E. H. Hair, 'The Task Ahead: The Editing of Early European Language Texts on Black Africa' in "European Sources for Sub-Saharan Africa before 1900: Use and Abuse," ed. Adam Jones and Beatrix Heintze, *Paideuma: Mitteilungen zur Kulturkunden* 33 (Stuttgart: Franz Steinen Verlag, 1987), 30; David Henige, 'The Race Is Not Always to the Swift: Thoughts on the Use of Written Sources for the Study of Early African History' in "European Sources for Sub-Saharan Africa before 1900: Use and Abuse," 57–60; and Robin Law, 'Problems of Plagiarism, Harmonization and Misunderstanding in Contemporary European Sources: Early (Pre-1680s) Sources for the 'Slave Coast' of West Africa' in "European Sources for Sub-Saharan Africa before 1900: Use and Abuse," 337–42; A. Hampaté Bâ, "The Living Tradition," *General History of Africa, I: Methodology and African Prehistory* (London: UNESCO, 1981), 168; Lilian Prevost and Bernabé Laye, *Guide de la Sagesse Africaine* (Montréal: L'Harmattan, 1999), 7; Elizabeth Tonkin, *Narrating Our Pasts: The Social Construction of Oral History* (Cambridge: Cambridge University Press, 1992); and Bethwell A. Ogot, "The Construction of Luo Identity and History," *African Words, African Voices: Critical Practices in Oral History*, ed. Luise White, Stephan F. Miescher, and David William Cohen (Bloomington: Indiana University Press, 2001), 31–32.
72. Bernth Lindfors and Oyekan Owomoyels, *Yoruba Proverbs: Translations and Annotation*, Papers in International Studies: African Series No. 17 (Athens: Ohio University Center for International Studies, 1973), 9.
73. Ivie Betty Erhahon, "Proverbs and Praise-Poetry: Forms of Communication among the Edo of Southern Nigeria," unpublished paper presented at the Intercultural Narrative, Lancaster University, England, December 2003, as quoted, 6; and Uyilawa Usuanlele, "Perception of Europeans in the Proverbs of the Edo People of Benin Kingdom, Nigeria," unpublished paper presented at the conference "Africa and Europe: Myth, Masses, and Masquerades," University of Wittswatersrand, Johannesburg, South Africa, April 2001.
74. Emmanuel Ikponmwosa Aigbe, *1040 Edo Proverbs with Their English Translations* (Ibadan, 1960), 23; and Camilla Townsend, "Burying the White Gods: New Perspectives on the Conquest of Mexico," *American Historical Review* 108 (June 2003): 660.
75. Wilks, "Wangara, Akan, and Portuguese in the Fifteenth and Sixteenth Centuries," 333–38; Robin Law, "Trade and Politics behind the Slave Coast: The Lagoon Traffic and the Rise of Lagos, 1500–1800," *Journal of African History* 24 (1983): 321; David E. Skinner, "Mande Settlement and the Development of Islamic Institutions in Sierra Leone," *International Journal of African Historical Studies* 11 (1978): 34–35; and Michael Brett, "Islam and Trade in the Bilad al-Sudan, Tenth–Eleventh Century A.D.," *Journal of African History* 24 (1983): 435–37.
76. Temu and Swai, *Historians and Africanist History*, 21; José da Silva Horta, "La Perception du Mande et de l'Identité Mandingue dans les Textes Européens,

1453–1508," *History in Africa: A Journal of Method* 23 (1996): 75–80; Lamont DeHaven King, "State and Ethnicity in Precolonial Northern Nigeria," *Conceptualizing/Re-Conceptualizing Africa: The Construction of African Historical Identity*, ed. Maghan Keita (Leiden: Brill, 2002), 9–30; and Donald R. Wright, "'What Do You Mean there Were No Tribes in Africa?': Thoughts on Boundaries—and Related Matters—in Precolonial Africa," *History in Africa: A Journal of Method* 26 (1999): 420.

77. Vansina, *Paths in the Rain Forest*, xi, 20; Gwendolyn Midlo Hall, *Slavery and African Ethnicities in the Americas: Restoring the Links* (Chapel Hill: University of North Carolina Press, 2005), 22–54; L. B. Breitborde, "City, Countryside and Kru Ethnicity," *Africa* 61 (1991): 186–90; D. Kiyaga-Mulindwa, "The Akan Problem," *Current Anthropology* 21 (1980): 503–6; Robin Law, "Ethnicity and the Slave Trade: 'Lucumi' and 'Nago' as Ethnonyms in West Africa," *History in Africa: A Journal of Method* 24 (1997): 205–6; Robert Baum, *Shrines of the Slave Trade: Diola Religion and Society in Precolonial Senegambia* (Oxford: Oxford University Press, 1999), 62; and, as quoted, D. Kiyaga-Mulindwa, "Social and Demographic Change in the Birim Valley, Southern Ghana, c. 1450 to c. 1800," *Journal of African History* 23 (1982): 69–70.

78. John Thornton, *Africa and Africans in the Making of the Atlantic World, 1400–1680*, 2nd ed. (Cambridge: Cambridge University Press, 1998), 191; Eugene D. Genovese, *Roll, Jordan, Roll: The World the Slaves Made* (New York: Vintage Books, 1976), 394–97; Mechal Sobel, *The World They Made Together: Black and White Values in Eighteenth Century Virginia* (Princeton: Princeton University Press, 1987), 18; Charles Joyner, *Down by the Riverside: A South Carolina Slave Community* (Urbana: University of Illinois Press, 1984), xxii, 15, 37; James Sidbury, *Ploughshares into Swords: Race, Rebellion, and Identity in Gabriel's Virginia, 1730–1810* (Cambridge: Cambridge University Press, 1997), 83–84; Merrick Posnansky, "West Africanist Reflections on African-American Archaeology," "*I, Too, Am America*," ed. Singleton, 22; Adam Kuper and Pierre van Leynseele, "Social Anthropology and the 'Bantu Expansion,'" *Africa* 48 (1978): 335; Robin Horton, "On the Rationality of Conversion," *Africa* 45 (1975): 219–35, 373–99; Humphrey J. Fisher, "The Juggernaut's Apologia: Conversion to Islam in Black Africa," *Africa* 55 (1985): 154; and Anthony D. Buckley, "The God of Smallpox: Aspects of Yoruba Religious Knowledge," *Africa* 55 (1985): 187.

79. Michael Mullin, *Africa in America: Slave Acculturation and Resistance in the American South and the British Caribbean, 1736–1831* (Urbana: University of Illinois Press, 1992), 24–26; Daniel C. Littlefield, *Rice and Slaves: Ethnicity and the Slave Trade in Colonial South Carolina* (Baton Rouge: Louisiana State University Press, 1981), 8, 13, 31; Betty Wood, *Slavery in Colonial Georgia, 1730–1775* (Athens: University of Georgia Press, 1984), 103; and Philip D. Morgan, *Slave Counterpoint: Black Culture in the Eighteenth-Century Chesapeake and Lowcountry* (Chapel Hill: University of North Carolina Press, 1998), 63–66.

80. Christopher R. DeCorse, "Oceans Apart: Africanist Perspectives on Diaspora Archaeology," "*I, Too, Am America*," ed. Singleton, 132–55; Merrick Posnansky, "West Africanist Reflections on African-American Archaeology," "*I, Too, Am America*," ed. Singleton, 21–38; and Michael A. Gomez, *Exchanging Our Country Marks: The Transformation of African Identities in the Colonial and Antebellum South* (Chapel Hill: University of North Carolina Press, 1998), 7.

81. Lindfors and Owomoyels, *Yoruba Proverbs*, 71.

82. Jospeh Thérèse Agbassiere, *Women in Igbo Life and Thought* (London: Routledge, 2000), 39–63; Geoffrey Parrinder, *West African Religions: A Study of the Beliefs and Practices of Akwan, Ewe, Yoruba, Ibo, and Kindred Peoples* (London: Epworth Press, 1949), 37–39; Anthony D. Buckley, "The Secret—An Idea in Yoruba Medicinal Thought," *Social Anthropology and Medicine*, ed. J. B. Loudon (New York: Academic Press, 1976), 399–403; Buckley, "God of Smallpox," 190; Wauthier de Mahieu, "Cosmologie et structuration de l'éspace chez les Komo," part 2, *Africa* 45 (1975): 236–37; I. Chukwukere, "Akan Theory of Conception: Are the Fante Really Aberrant?" *Africa* 48 (1978): 137; Harry Sawyerr, *God, Ancestor or Creator?: Aspects of Traditional Belief in Ghana, Nigeria and Sierra Leone* (London: Longman, 1970), 71–72; Alma Gottlieb, "Sex, Fertility and Menstruation among the Beng of the Ivory Coast: A Symbolic Analysis," *Africa* 52 (1982): 35–41; Gomez, *Exchanging Our Country Marks*, 49; and Thomas Astley, "Of the Marriages, Diversions, Diseases and Funerals of the Natives," *New General Collection* 3: 19.
83. Elisha P. Renne, *Cloth that Does Not Die: The Meaning of Cloth in Bùnú Social Life* (Seattle: University of Washington Press, 1995), 3–11, 23–25, 38, 42–43, 69; Philip D. Curtin, "The Lure of Bambuk Gold," *Journal of African History* 13 (1972): 624; Thomas Astley, "The Kingdoms of Koto and Popo," *New General Collection* 3: 6; John K. Thornton, *The Kongolese Saint Anthony: Dona Beatriz Kimpa Vita and the Antonian Movement, 1684–1706* (Cambridge: Cambridge University Press, 1998), 161; Law, "Problems of Plagiarism," 347–48; Anne Hilton, *The Kingdom of Kongo* (Oxford: Clarendon Press, 1985), 10; as quoted, Thomas Astley, "The Third Voyage of the Sieur Brüe up the Sanaga, Made in the Year 1715," *New General Collection* 2: 129; and Thomas Astley, "An Account of the Jalofs," *New General Collection* 2: 255–60.
84. Renne, *Cloth that Does Not Die*, 86, 98; Thomas Astley, "Voyage and Travels along the Western Coast of Africa, from Cape Blance to Sierra Leona," New General Collection 2: 47–48, 94, 126; 'Andreas Josua Ulsheimer's Voyage of 1603–4,' "German Sources for West African History 1599–1669," ed. Adam Jones, *Studien zur Kulturkunde* 66 (Wiesbaden: Franz Steiner Verlag, 1983), 38; Thomas Astley, "A Voyage to Ardrah, and Travels to the Capital Assem, in 1669 and 1670," *New General Collection* 3: 67; Thornton, *Kongolese Saint Anthony*, 83–84; and Rosalind Shaw, *Memories of the Slave Trade: Ritual and the Historical Imagination in Sierra Leone* (Chicago: University of Chicago Press, 2002), 48, 61.
85. Thomas Astley, "Voyages and Travels to Guinea and Benin," *New General Collection* 3: 3.
86. Thomas Astley, "The Religion of the Whidah Blacks," *New General Collection* 3: 26–27; Peter Mark, "The Evolution of 'Portuguese' Identity: Luso-Africans on the Upper Guinea Coast from the Sixteenth to the Early Nineteenth Century, " *Journal of African History* 40 (1999): 176–77; M. C. Jedrej, "An Analytical Note on the Land and Spirits of the Sewa Mende," *Africa* 44 (1974): 42–43; John C. McCall, "Rethinking Ancestors in Africa," *Africa* 65 (1995): 257–65; Jane Parish, "The Dynamics of Witchcraft and Indigenous Shrines among the Akan," *Africa* 69 (1999): 426; Robin Horton, "100 Years of Change in Kalabari Religion," *Black Africa: Its People and Their Culture Today*, ed. John Middleton (London: Macmillan Co., 1971), 194; Baum, *Shrines of the Slave Trade*, 36, 41, 48; and Aigbe, *1040 Edo Proverbs*, 43.

87. Jean Barbot, *Barbot on Guinea: The Writings of Jean Barbot on West Africa, 1678–1712*, 2 vols., ed. P. E. H. Hair, Adam Jones, and Robin Law, Works Issued by the Hakluyt Society, 2nd ser., no. 175 (London: Hakluyt Society, 1992), vol. 2: 579.
88. 'Michael Hemmersam's Description of the Gold Coast, 1639–1645,' "German Sources for West African History," ed. Jones, 117.
89. Barbot, *Barbot on Guinea* 1: 222, 2: 579; Thornton, *Kongolese Saint Anthony*, 12–13; and Hilton, *Kingdom of Kongo*, 24.
90. Helaine K. Minkus, "The Concept of Spirit in Akwapian Akan Philosophy," *Africa* 50 (1980): 182; Sobel, *World They Made Together*, 18, 71; Barbot, *Barbot on Guinea* 1: 125–26; Vansina, *Paths in the Rain Forest*, 95–98; Robin Horton, *Patterns of Thought in Africa and the West: Essays on Magic, Religion and Science* (Cambridge: Cambridge University Press, 1993), 217–19; Olaudah Equiano, *The Life of Olaudah Equiano, or Gustavus Vassa the African Written by Himself*, ed. Paul Edwards (Essex: Longman, 1988), 5, 11; Kenneth Little, "The Mende in Sierra Leone," *African Worlds: Studies in the Cosmological Ideas and Social Values of African Peoples*, ed. Daryll Forde (London: Oxford University Press, 1954) 115–16; Ishichei, *History of the Igbo People*, 25; and "Michael Hemmersam's Description of the Gold Coast," 122.
91. Nick Gabrilopoulos, Charles Mather, and Caesar Roland Apentiik, "Lineage Organisation of the Tallensi Compound: The Social Logic of Domestic Space in Northern Ghana," *Africa* 72 (2002): 225; Susan D. Gillespie, "Rethinking Ancient Maya Social Organization: Replacing 'Lineage' with 'House,'" *American Anthropologist* 102 (2000): 467–84; Anne Hilton, "Family and Kinship among the Kongo South of the Zaïre River from the Sixteenth to the Nineteenth Centuries," *Journal of African History* 24 (1983): 189–94; Hilton, *Kingdom of Kongo*, 37; and Thornton, *Kongolese Saint Anthony*, 16.
92. Dunja Hersak, "There Are Many Kongo Worlds: Particularities of Magico-Religious Beliefs among the Vili and Yomba of Congo-Brazzaville," *Africa* 71 (2001): 622–24; Wyatt MacGaffey, "The Cultural Roots of Kongo Prophetism," *History of Religion* 17 (1977): 184–85; Hilton, *Kingdom of Kongo*, 10–16; and Thornton, *Kongolese Saint Anthony*, 54.
93. Aigbe, *1040 Edo Proverbs*, 25, 46; Baum, *Shrines of the Slave Trade*, 44; James Albert Ukawsaw Guonniosaw, "A Narrative of the Most Remarkable Particulars in the Life of James Albert Ukawsaw Guonniosaw, An African Prince, As Related by Himself," *Slave Narratives*, ed. William L. Andrews and Henry Lewis Gates Jr. (New York: Library of America, 2000), 6; Pieter de Marees, *Description and Historical Account of the Gold Kingdom of Guinea (1602)*, ed. and trans. Adam Jones and Albert van Dantzig (Oxford: Oxford University Press, 1987), 69; Thornton, *Kongolese Saint Anthony*, 157–58; Barbot, *Barbot on Guinea* 2: 578–79; and Gabrilopoulos, Mather, and Apentiik, "Lineage Organisation of the Tallensi Compound," 228–29.
94. Barbot, *Barbot on Guinea* 1: 319; and Thomas Astley, "The Sieur Brüe's Voyage to the Isles of Bissao and Bissagos with His Negotiations in These Parts, in the Year 1700," *New General Collection* 2: 94.
95. Astley, "Sieur Brüe's Voyage to the Isles of Bissao and Bissagos with His Negotiations in These Parts," 95; and McCall, "Rethinking Ancestors in Africa," 260.
96. James Sanders, "Village Settlement among the Fante: A Study of the Anomabo Paramountcy," *Africa* 55 (1985): 179–80.

97. Thomas Astley, "A General Description of the River Gambra, or Gambia," *New General Collection* 2: 163–65.
98. Thomas Astley, "The Sieur Brüe's Journey from Albreda, on the River Gambra, to Kachao, by Land, in the Year 1700," *New General Collection* 2: 86.
99. Thomas Astley, "The Customs and Rights Common to the Inhabitants of This Part of Africa, Particularly the Jalofs, Fûli, and Mandingoes," *New General Collection* 2: 301.
100. Thomas Astley, "Differences between the English and French about the Trade of the River Gambra," *New General Collection* 2: 83.
101. Mahieu, "Cosmologie et structuration de l'éspace chez les Komos," part 1, 134–35.
102. B. W. Hodder and U. I. Ukwu, *Markets in West Africa: Studies of Markets and Trade among the Yoruba and Ibo* (Ibadan: Ibadan University Press, 1969), 128; Gomez, *Exchanging Our Country Marks*, 148–49; Sterling Stuckey, *Slave Culture: Nationalist Theory and the Foundations of Black America* (New York: Oxford University Press, 1987), 11–14; Barbot, *Barbot on Guinea* 2: 494; and Marees, *Description and Historical Account of the Gold Kingdom of Guinea*, 89.
103. Aigbe, *1040 Edo Proverbs*, 55; Vansina, *Paths in the Rain Forest*, 94, 103; Thomas Astley, "The Kingdom of Whidah," *New General Collection* 3: 7–14; Law, "Common People," 205; Isichei, *History*, 32; Hodder and Ukwu, *Markets in West Africa*, 24–31, 127; Barbot, *Barbot on Guinea* 2: 547; and Marees, *Description and Historical Account of the Gold Kingdom of Guinea*, 64.
104. Fage, *History of Africa*, 244–50; and Thornton, *Africa and Africans*, 43–66.
105. P. Mercier, "The Fon of Dahomey," *African Worlds*, ed. Forde, 210–12; Astley, "Religion of the Whidah Blacks," 26, 28–29; Law, "Common People," 202, 209, 213n72; and Astley, "The Kingdom of Whidah," 1, 7–8.
106. Robin Law, "'The Common People Were Divided': Monarchy, Aristocracy, and Political Factionalism in the Kingdom of Whydah, 1671–1727," *International Journal of African Historical Studies* 23 (1990): 201–10, 228; Thomas Astley, "The Kingdom of Ardrah," *New General Collection* 3: 87; William Snelgrave, *A New Account of Some Parts of Guinea and the Slave-Trade* (1734, rpt. London: Frank Cass & Co. Ltd., 1971), 10–11; Stuckey, *Slave Culture*, 15; Robin Law, "A Neglected Account of the Dahomean Conquest of Whydah (1727): The 'Relation de la guerre de Juda' of the Sieur Ringard of Nantes," *History in Africa: A Journal of Method* 15 (1988): 323–24, quotation on 321; J. D. Fage, "Slaves and Society in Western Africa, c. 1445–c. 1700," *Journal of African History* 21 (1980): 302; and Thornton, *Africa and Africans*, 73, 99.
107. Francis Moore, "Travels into the Inland Parts of Africa," Astley, *New General Collection* 2: 217; Kiyaga-Mulindwa, "Social and Demographic Change in the Birim Valley, 70–77; Klein, "Towards a New Understanding of Akan Origins," 257–62; Gabrilopoulos, Mather, and Apentiik, "Lineage Organisation of the Tallensi Compound," 222; Wilks, *Forests of Gold*, 96–100; Shaw, *Memories of the Slave Trade*, 14, 67; and Baum, *Shrines of the Slave Trade*.
108. Shaw, *Memories of the Slave Trade*, 227; and "Andreas Josua Ulsheimer's Voyage," 31.
109. "Michael Hemmersam's Description of the Gold Coast," 104.
110. Astley, "Voyage to Ardrah, and Travels to the Capital Assem," 71.
111. MacGaffey, "Cultural Roots of Kongo Prophetism," 183–87; and Thornton, *Kongolese Saint Anthony*, 26–27, 110–11.

112. Gomez, *Exchanging Our Country Marks*, 135–47.
113. Barbot, *Barbot on Guinea* 2: 639; Ottobah Cuguono, "Thoughts and Sentiments of the Evil and Wicked Traffic of the Slavery and Commerce of the Human Species," *Three Black Writers in Eighteenth Century England*, ed. Francis D. Adams and Barry Sanders (Belmont, Calif.: Wadsworth Publishing Company, Inc., 1971), 50; Equiano, *Life of Olaudah Equiano*, 22; Thomas Astley, "The Sieur Brüe's Second Voyage up the Sanagra to the Kingdom of Galam, in 1698," *New General Collection* 2: 68.

Chapter 2

1. Derek W. Lomax, *The Reconquest of Spain* (London: Longman, 1978), 28, 44, 58, 102, 163, 177.
2. Mary W. Helms, "Long-Distance Contacts, Elite Aspirations, and the Age of Discovery in Cosmological Context," *Resources, Power, and Interregional Interaction*, ed. Edward M. Schortman and Patricia A. Urban (New York: Plenum Press, 1992), 167–69.
3. Christopher Columbus, *The Diario of Christopher Columbus's First Voyage to America, 1492–1493*, trans. Oliver Dunn and James E. Kelley Jr. (Norman: University of Oklahoma Press, 1989), 19; David J. Weber, *The Spanish Frontier in North America* (New Haven: Yale University Press, 1992), 20; Anne McLintock, *Imperial Leather: Race, Gender and Sexuality in the Colonial Conquest* (New York: Routledge, 1995). 21–22; and Margarita Zamora, *Reading Columbus* (Berkeley: University of California Press, 1993), 143–44, 174.
4. Robert Finley, *The Accidental Indies* (Montréal: McGill-Queen's University Press, 2000), 60–61; Phillips, "Outer World of the European Middle Ages," 25.
5. Columbus, *Diario*, 69, 91–93, 145, and, as quoted, 133; Ashis Nandy, Zia Sardar, and Merryl Wyn Davies, *Barbaric Others: A Manifesto on Western Racism* (Boulder: Pluto Press, 1993), 53; Pagden, *European Encounters with the New World*, 47–48; and Peter Mason, *Deconstructing America: Representations of the Other* (London: Routledge, 1990), 18.
6. Alfred W. Crosby, *The Columbian Exchange: Biological and Cultural Consequences of 1492* (Westport, Conn.: Greenwood Publishing Co., 1972), 9; Miguel Angel Ledero Quesada, "Spain, circa 1492: Social Values and Structures," *Implicit Understandings*, ed. Schwartz, 98–100; McLintock, *Imperial Leather*, 24; Zamora, *Reading Columbus*, 176; and Columbus, *Diario*, 111, 157.
7. Columbus, *Diario*, 235; McLintock, *Imperial Leather*, 28; Jamaica Kincaid, *My Garden (Book)* (New York: Farrar Strauss Giroux, 1999), 155; and Mason, *Deconstructing America*, 17.
8. Berkhofer, *White Man's Indian*, 3; Ter Ellington, *The Myth of the Noble Savage* (Berkeley: University of California Press, 2001), 12; and Johannes Fabian, *Time and the Other: How Anthropology Makes Its Object* (New York, 1983).
9. Columbus, *Diario*, 235–37.
10. McLintock, *Imperial Leather*, 1–3; Zamora, *Reading Columbus*, 143–48; Helms, "Long-Distance Contacts," 171–72; and Awiakta, "Daydreaming Primal Space," 194.
11. Mason, *Deconstructing America*, 18.
12. Hernán Cortés, *Letters from Mexico*, trans. and ed. Anthony Pagden (New Haven: Yale University Press, 2001), 63, 67, 106, 212; Paul E. Hoffman, *A New Andalucia*

and a Way to the Orient: The American Southeast during the Sixteenth Century* (Baton Rouge: Louisiana State University, 1990), 21; and Alvar Nuñez Cabeza de Vaca, *Castaways*, ed. and introd. Enrique Pupo-Walker, trans. Frances M. López-Morillas (Berkeley: University of California Press, 1993), 22, 25–26.
13. Paul E. Hoffman, "Hernando de Soto: A Brief Biography," *The De Soto Chronicles: The Expedition of Hernando de Soto to North America in 1539–1543*, 2 vols., ed. Lawrence A. Clayton, Vernon James Knight Jr., and Edward C. Moore (Tuscaloosa: University of Alabama Press, 1993), vol. 1: 421–60; Rodrigo Rangel, "Account of the Northern Conquest and Discovery of Hernando de Soto," *De Soto Chronicles*, ed. Clayton, Knight, and Moore, vol. 1: 251; "Account by a Gentleman of Elvas," *De Soto Chronicles*, ed. Clayton, Knight, and Moore, vol. 1: 47, 57, 61, 64, 68, 70, 77, 87, 89; Lomax, *Reconquest of Spain*, 109; Weber, *Spanish Frontier*, 22 Luys Hernández de Biedma, "Relation of the Island of Florida," *De Soto Chronicles*, ed. Clayton, Knight, and Moore, vol. 1: 232
14. "Account by a Gentleman of Elvas," 65.
15. "Account by a Gentleman of Elvas," 77.
16. "Account by a Gentleman of Elvas," 77.
17. Rangel, "Account of the Northern Conquest," 290.
18. Biedma, "Relation of the Island of Florida," 1: as quoted, 232; Rangel, "Account of the Northern Conquest," 290–91; "Account by a Gentleman of Elvas," 96; and David S. Mathews, "The Massacre: The Discovery of De Soto in Georgia," *King Site*, ed. Blakely, 103–6.
19. Biedma, "Relation of the Island of Florida," 234–36; Rangel, "Account of the Northern Conquest," 292–93; "Account by a Gentleman of Elvas," 98–104; and Patricia Galloway, "Colonial Period Transformation in the Mississippi Valley: Dis-integration, Alliance, Confederation, Playoff," *Transformation of the Southeastern Indians*, ed. Ethridge and Hudson, 236.
20. Worth, *Timucuan Chiefdoms of Spanish Florida* 1: 21–25; Ellington, *Myth of the Noble Savage*, 25; Berkhofer, *White Man's Indian*, 13; Colin M. Coates, *The Metamorphoses of Landscape and Community in Early Quebec* (Montreal: McGill-Queen's University Press, 2000), 10; Donald W. Meinig, *The Shaping of America: A Geographical Perspective on 500 Years of History*, 2 vols. (New Haven: Yale University Press, 1986), as quoted, vol. 1: 25; and Olive Dickason, *The Myth of the Savage and the Beginning of French Colonialism in the America* (Edmonton: University of Alberta, 1984), 33–34, and, as quoted, 30.
21. Hoffman, *New Andalucia*, 206–9; and Sarah Lawson, comp. and ed., *A Foothold in Florida: The Eye-Witness Account of Four Voyages Made by the French to that Region and Their Attempt at Colonization, 1562–1568* (Somerset, England: Antique Atlas Publications, 1992), 17–19, 35–39, 60, 93.
22. Lawson, ed., *Foothold in Florida*, 8, 50; Meinig, *Shaping of America* 1: 27; Patricia Seed, *Ceremonies of Possession in Europe's Conquest of the New World, 1492–1640* (Cambridge: Cambridge University Press, 1995), 56, 64–65; as quoted, Letter to Charles IX, King of France, 1564, box 6, Miscellaneous Manuscript Collection, Special Collections, University of Florida, Gainesville; and "The Narrative of Jacques Le Moyne de Morgues," *The New World: The First Pictures of America*, ed. Stefan Lorant (New York: Duell, Sloan, & Pearce, 1946), 40.
23. Letter to Charles IX, King of France, 1564; Lawson, ed., *Foothold in Florida*, 62, 68, 73, 76, 92, 104–8, quotation on 106; Jerald T. Milanich, *Laboring in the Fields of the Lord: Spanish Missions and Southeastern Indians* (Washington:

Smithsonian Institution Press, 1999), 48; and David B. Quinn, *North America from Earliest Discovery to First Settlements: The Norse Voyages to 1612* (New York: Harper and Row, 1977), 247.
24. Hoffman, *New Andalucia*, 222–23; Weber, *Spanish Frontier*, 60; Kathleen Deagan, "St. Augustine and the Mission Frontier," *Spanish Missions of La Florida*, ed. Bonnie McEwan (Gainesville: University Press of Florida, 1993), 93.
25. Amy Turner Bushnell, "Ruling 'the Republic of Indians' in Seventeenth-Century Florida," *Powhatan's Mantle*, ed. Wood, Waselkov, and Hatley, 134–37; Amy Turner Bushnell, *Situado and Sabana: Spain's Support System for the Presidio and Mission Provinces of Florida*, American Museum of Natural History Anthropological Papers, no. 74 (New York: American Museum of Natural History, 1994), 104–5; Jerald T. Milanich, *Florida Indians and the Invasion from Europe* (Gainesville: University Press of Florida, 1995), 158; Milanich, *Laboring in the Fields of the Lord*, 91.
26. Bushnell, *Situado and Sabana*, 111; and Milanich, *Laboring in the Fields of the Lord*, 35.
27. Stilgoe, *Common Landscapes of America*, 34–35; Worth, *Timucuan Chiefdoms of Spanish Florida* 1: 128; David Hurst Thomas, "Saints and Soldiers at Santa Catalina: Hispanic Designs for Colonial America," *The Recovery of Meaning: Historical Archaeology in the Eastern United States*, ed. Mark P. Leone and Parker B. Potter Jr. (Washington D.C.: Smithsonian Institution Press, 1988), 104; Stanley South, "Santa Elena: Threshold of Conquest," *Recovery of Meaning*, ed. Leone and Potter, 28–39; Thomas, "Saints and Soldiers at Santa Catalina," 76, 96–97; John E. Worth, *The Struggle for the Georgia Coast: An Eighteenth-Century Spanish Retrospective on Guale and Mocama*, American Museum of Natural History, Anthropological Papers, no. 75 (1995): 15, 24; General *Auto* of the Visitation of Guale, 1685, *Struggle for the Georgia Coast*, 109–10; and Visitation of San Phelipe, 25 December 1685, *Struggle for the Georgia Coast*, 116–17.
28. Worth, *Timucuan Chiefdoms of Spanish Florida* 1: 128–34; and Thomas, "Saints and Soldiers at Santa Catalina," 98.
29. Bushnell, "Ruling 'the Republic of Indians,'" 137; and, as quoted, Bushnell, *Situado and Sabana*, 71.
30. Potter, *Commoners, Tribute, and Chiefs*, 161–62; and Carville Earle, *The American Way: A Geographical History of Crisis and Recovery* (New York: Rowan & Littlefield Publishers, Inc., 2003), 212.
31. "Arthur Barlowe's Narrative of the 1584 Voyage," *Virginia Voyages from Hakluyt*, ed. David B. Quinn and Alison M. Quinn (New York: Oxford University Press, 1973), 4–5.
32. "Arthur Barlowe's Narrative," 4–5.
33. "Arthur Barlowe's Narrative," 8.
34. Michael Leroy Oberg, *Dominion and Civility: English Imperialism and Native America, 1585–1685* (Ithaca: Cornell University Press, 1999), 45.
35. Martin D. Gallivan, *James River Chiefdoms: The Rise of Social Inequality in the Chesapeake* (Lincoln: University of Nebraska Press, 2003), 11; Frederick W. Gleach, *Powhatan's World and Colonial Virginia: A Conflict of Culture* (Lincoln: University of Nebraska Press, 1997), 23; and Potter, *Commoners, Tribute, and Chiefs*, 14, 24–29, 33–40, 75, 94, 153.
36. Gallivan, *James River Chiefdoms*, as quoted, 24; and John Smith, "A Map of Virginia, with a Description of the Countrey, the Commodities, People,

Government and Religion (1612)," *Complete Works of Captain John Smith*, ed. Philip L. Barbour, 3 vols. (Chapel Hill: University of North Carolina Press, 1986): 1: 171–72.

37. Seed, *Ceremonies of Possession*, 18–20, 26–28, 32–34; Oath of Supremacye, 1607, *Records of the Virginia Company of London*, ed. Susan Myra Kingsbury, 4 vols. (Washington: Government Printing Office, 1906–1935), vol. 3: 4, hereafter cited as *RVC*; A Justification for planting in Virginia, pre-1609, *RVC* 3: 2; John Smith, "A True Relation (1608)," *Complete Works* 1: 27–29; Smith, "A Map of Virginia," *Complete Works* 1: 146; George Percy, "Discourse (1608?)," *Jamestown Voyages under the First Charter, 1606–1609*, ed. Philip L. Barbour, Works Issued by the Hakluyt Society, 2nd ser., nos. 136 and 137 (Cambridge: Cambridge University Press, 1969), vol. 1: 135–42; and Earle, *American Way*, 215–18.
38. Smith, "True Relation," 29–33; "A relatyon . . . written . . . by a gent. Of ye Colony (1607)," *Travels and Works of Captain John Smith*, 2 vols., ed. Edward Arber (New York: Burt Franklin, 1967), vol. 1: xliv–xlvii; and Percy, "Discourse," 145.
39. Smith, "Map of Virginia," 144, 160; John Smith, "The Generall Historie of Virginia, New-England, and the Summer Isles (1624)," *Complete Works* 2: 172; and Smith, "True Relation," 33–35.
40. Smith, "Generall Historie," 172–78; and Gallivan, *James River Chiefdoms*, xi.
41. Smith, "True Relation," 59; Smith, "Generall Historie," 149–50; Gleach, *Powhatan's World*, 109–21; and Waselkov, "Indian Maps of the Colonial Southeast," 209–10.
42. Smith, "Generall Historie," 147; Smith, "True Relation," 47; Joyce E. Chaplin, *Subject Matter: Technology, the Body, and Science on the Anglo-American Frontier, 1500–1676* (Cambridge: Harvard University Press, 2001), 120–24; and Lestringant, *Mapping the Renaissance World*, 21.
43. Smith, "Generall Historie," 147, as quoted, 214; Gallivan, *James River Chiefdoms*, 18; and Carville Earle, "Environment, Disease and Mortality in Early Virginia," *Journal of Historical Geography* 5 (1979): 374–75.
44. James Horn, *Adapting to a New World: English Society in the Seventeenth-Century Chesapeake* (Chapel Hill: University of North Carolina Press, 1994), 132; Hatfield, *Atlantic Virginia*, 8–16; Smith, "True Relation," 35–39, 49, 53, 67; and Gallivan, *James River Chiefdoms*, xii, 24–25, 53.
45. Gordon M. Sayre, *Les Sauvages Américains: Representations of Native Americans in French and English Colonial Literature* (Chapel Hill: University of North Carolina Press, 1997), 65–66; Smith, "True Relation," 57; and Smith, "Generall Historie," 183–84, 197.
46. Smith, "Generall Historie," 186, 191, 213–14, 232–33.
47. Instructions to Gov. Thomas Gates, May 1609, *RVC* 3: 14–15, 18.
48. Instructions to Gov. Thomas Gates, May 1609, *RVC* 3: 15–19; Smith, "Generall Historie," 178, 246; and Sobel, *World They Made Together*, 90, 94.
49. John Norris, "Profitable Advice for Rich and Poor (London 1712)," *Selling a New World: Two Colonial South Carolina Promotional Pamphlets*, ed. Jack Greene (Columbia: University of South Carolina Press, 1989), 84; Samuel Wilson, "An Account of the Provinces of Carolina (1682)," *Narratives of Early Carolina, 1650–1708*, ed. Alexander S. Salley Jr. (New York: Charles Scribner's Sons, 1911), 173; and John Archdale, "A New Description of that Fertile and Pleasant Province of Carolina (1707)," *Narratives of Early Carolina*, ed. Salley, 285.

50. Bushnell, *Situado and Sabana*, 135–36, 146, 161; Steven C. Hahn, "The Mother of Necessity: Carolina, Its Creek Indians, and the Making of a New Order in the American Southeast," *Transformation of the Southeastern Indians*, ed. Ethridge and Hudson, 85; Robert Johnson, "Governor's Questionnaire, 1719/20, "*The Colonial South Carolina Scene: Contemporary Views, 1697–1774*, ed. H. Ray Merrens (Columbia: University of South Carolina Press, 1977), 58; and Steven J. Oatis, *A Colonial Complex: South Carolina's Frontiers in the Era of the Yamassee War, 1680–1730* (Lincoln: University of Nebraska Press, 2004), 23–27, 37–38, 52, 58, 70.

51. William Craven and Ashley Colleton to Thomas Smith, 29 November 1693, *Records in the British Public Records Office Relating to South Carolina*, vol. 3 (Atlanta: Historical Commission of South Carolina, 1931), 109.

52. "An Interview with James Freeman (1712)," *Colonial South Carolina Scene*, ed. Merrens, 42–45; and Mark Catesby, "An Account of Carolina, and the Bahama Islands," *The Natural History of Carolina, Florida and the Bahama Islands*, 2 vols. (London: Benjamin White, 1731), vol. 2: ii, xvi, xviii, emphasis in original, and xii.

53. Francis Le Jau to the Secretary, 12 April 1711, *The Carolina Chronicle of Dr. Francis Le Jau*, ed. Frank J. Klingberg, University of California Publications in History, vol. 53 (Berkeley: University of California Press, 1956), 89.

54. Charles Woodmason, *The Carolina Backcountry on the Eve of the Revolution: The Journal and Other Writings of Charles Woodmason, Anglican Itinerant*, ed. Richard J. Hooker (Chapel Hill: University of North Carolina Press, 1953), 13, 17, 19.

55. Kenneth E. Lewis, "Economic Development in the South Carolina Backcountry," *Southern Colonial Backcountry*, ed. David Colin Crass, Steven D. Smith, Martha A. Zierden, and Richard D. Brooks (Knoxville: University of Tennessee Press, 1998), 92.

56. As quoted, Wood, *Slavery in Colonial Georgia*, 5–7; and Sir Robert Montgomery, "A Discourse Concerning the Design'd Establishment of a New Colony to the South of Carolina in the most Delightful Country of the Universe (1717)," *The Most Delightful Country of the Universe: Promotional Literature of the Colony of Georgia, 1717–1734*, ed. Trevor R. Reese (Savannah: Beehive Press, 1972), 5–8. Emphasis in original.

57. James Oglethorpe, "A New and Accurate Account of the Province of South Carolina and Georgia (1732)," *Most Delightful Country*, ed. Reese, 124.

58. Montgomery, "Discourse Concerning the Design'd Establishment of a New Colony," 15.

59. Oglethorpe, "New and Accurate Account," 124; Thomas Nairne, "A Letter from South Carolina (London, 1710)," *Selling a New World*, ed. Greene, 37; Benjamin Martyn, "Reasons for Establishing the Colony of Georgia (1733)," *Most Delightful Country*, ed. Reese, 165–66; and Edward Bland, "The Discovery of New Brittaine (1650)," *Narratives of Early Carolina*, ed. Salley, 9–12.

60. Claudio Saunt, *A New Order of Things: Property, Power, and the Transformation of the Creek Indians, 1733–1816* (Cambridge: Cambridge University Press, 1999), 14–17.

61. Pierre Le Moyne d'Iberville, *Iberville's Gulf Journals*, trans. and ed. Richebourg Gaillard McWilliams, introd. Tennant S. McWillians (Tuscaloosa: University of Alabama Press, 1981), 169.

62. M. Nellis Crouse, *Lemoyne d'Iberville: Soldier of New France* (New York: Vail-Ballou Press, Inc., 1954), 3–4; Charles B. Reed, *The First Great Canadian: The Story of Pierre Le Moyne Sieur d'Iberville* (Cambridge: University Press, 1910), 39; André Pénicaut, *Fleur de Lys and Calumet: Being the Pénicaut Narrative of French Adventure in Louisiana*, trans. and ed. Richebourg Gaillard McWilliams (Tuscaloosa: University of Alabama Press, 1953), 4, 9–13; Coates, *Metamorphoses of Landscape*, 13–14; Lawson, ed., *Foothold in Florida*, 19–21; and Iberville, *Journals*, 1–4, 46.
63. Vernon J. Knight Jr. and Sheree L. Adams, "A Voyage to the Mobile and Tomeh in 1700, with Notes on the Interior of Alabama," *Ethnohistory* 28 (1981): 182, 187; Ian W. Brown, "Certain Aspects of French-Indian Interaction in Lower Louisiane," *Calumet & Fleur-de-Lys: Archaeology of Indian and French Contact in the Midcontinent*, ed. John A. Walthall and Thomas E. Emerson (Washington: Smithsonian Institution Press, 1992), 17, 23; Marcel Giraud, *A History of French Louisiana*, vol. 1, trans. Joseph C. Lambert (Baton Rouge: Louisiana State University Press, 1974), 190–94; Antoine Simon Le Page du Pratz, *The History of Louisiana* (2 vols., London, 1763), vol. 1: 304; and Usner, *Indians, Settlers, & Slaves in a Frontier Exchange Economy*, 192–97, and, as quoted, 194.
64. Iberville, *Gulf Journals*, 125; Dumont du Montigny, *Memoires historiques sur la Louisiane*, 2 vols. (Paris: C. J. B. Bauche, 1753), vol. 1: 139; and Jean-Baptiste Bénard de la Harpe, *Journal historique du l'établissement des Français á la Louisiane* (New Orleans: A. L. Boimare, 1831), 28.
65. Pierre-François-Xavier de Charlevoix, *Journal d'un voyage fait par ordre du roi dans l'Amerique Septentrionale*, 2 vols. (Montréal: Les Presses de l'Université de Montréal, 1994), vol. 2: 800–815; Antoine Simon Le Page du Pratz, *Histoire de la Louisiane* (3 vols., Paris: DeBure, 1758), vol. 3: 15–18; Montigny, *Memoires historiques*, 159–60; and Harpe, *Journal historique*, 29.
66. Kidder, "Making the City Inevitable," 12–17; Christopher Morris, "Impenetrable but Easy: The French Transformation of the Lower Mississippi Valley and the Founding of New Orleans," *Transforming New Orleans*, ed. Colton, 25–31; and Le Page du Pratz, *History of Louisiana* 1: 222.
67. Hoffman, *New Andalucia*, 3–14.
68. James Merrell, "The Racial Education of the Catawba Indians," *Journal of Southern History* 50 (August 1984): 369; Hoffman, *New Andalucia*, 74–80; Theda Perdue, *Slavery and the Evolution of Cherokee Society, 1540–1866* (Knoxville: University of Tennessee Press, 1979), 36; and Gomez, *Exchanging Our Country Marks*, as quoted, 159.
69. "Voyage of the Hannibal, 1693–1694," *Documents Illustrative of the History of the Slave Trade to America*, 4 vols., ed. Elizabeth Donnan (Washington: Carnegie Institution of Washington, 1930), vol. 1: 403–6; Snelgrave, *New Account of Some Parts of Guinea and the Slave-Trade*, 184; and W. Pierce, "White Cannibals, Black Martyrs: Fear, Depression, and Religious Faith as Causes of Suicide among Slaves," *Journal of Negro History* 62 (1977): 147–59.
70. Marie Jenkins Schwartz, *Born in Bondage: Growing Up Enslaved in the Antebellum South* (Cambridge: Harvard University Press, 2000), 37, 124; Laurie A. Wilkie and Paul Farnsworth, *Sampling Many Pots: An Archaeology of Memory and Tradition at a Bahamian Plantation* (Gainesville: University Press of Florida, 2005), 6; John Michael Vlach, "Arrival and Survival: The Maintenance of an Afro-American Tradition in Folk Art and Craft," *Perspectives on American Folk*

Art, ed. Ian M. G. Quimby and Scott T. Swank (New York: W. W. Norton and Company, 1980), 181–86; Levin Covington Diary, Mississippi Department of Archives and History, Jackson; James Trueman Magruder Journal, Mississippi Department of Archives and History; Anonymous Plantation Diary, Mississippi Department of Archives and History; Morgan, *Slave Counterpoint*, 28, 153, 442; Bascom, "Yoruba Food," 47; Catesby, "Account of Carolina," xvii–xviii; Catesby, *Natural History* 2: 60; Usner, *Indians, Settlers, & Slaves in a Frontier Exchange Economy*, 158–64; and Mark Wagner, "The Introduction and Early Use of African Plants in the New World," *Tennessee Anthropologist* 6 (1981): 113–16.

71. Theresa A. Singleton, "An Archaeological Framework for Slavery and Emancipation," *Recovery of Meaning*, ed. Leone and Potter, 351; Leland G. Ferguson, *Uncommon Ground: Archaeology and Early African America, 1650–1800* (Washington, D.C.: Smithsonian Institution Press, 1992), xxi–xxiii, 37, 68; and Morgan, *Slave Counterpoint*, 102.

72. Morgan, *Slave Counterpoint*, 201; Guonniosaw, "Narrative of the Most Remarkable Particulars," 17; Schwartz, *Born in Bondage*, 61; Ferguson, *Uncommon Ground*, 10–16, 26, 110–12; Leland Ferguson, "'The Cross Is a Magic Sign': Marks on Eighteenth-Century Bowls from South Carolina," *"I, Too, Am American,"* ed. Singleton, 118–19; Patricia Samford, "The Archaeology of African-American Slavery and Material Culture," *William and Mary Quarterly*, 3rd ser. 53 (1996): 102–5; Monica L. Beck, "'A Fer Ways off from the Big House': The Changing Nature of Slavery in the South Carolina Backcountry," *Southern Colonial Backcountry*, ed. Crass, Smith, Zierden, and Brooks 118–19.

73. Terry G. Jordan, *North American Cattle Ranching Frontiers: Origins, Diffusion, and Differentiation* (Albuquerque: University of New Mexico Press, 1993), 55–64, 82–83, 110–17; Wood, *Black Majority*, 28–34; and Usner, *Indians, Settlers, & Slaves in a Frontier Exchange Economy*, 181–90.

74. Carney, *Black Rice*, 5–6, 28–31, 46–47, 64, 85–86, 118; and Wood, *Black Majority*, 55–62.

75. Francis Le Jau to the Secretary, 20 October 1709, *Carolina Chronicle of Dr. Francis Le Jau*, 61.

76. Francis Le Jau to the Secretary, 9 February 1711, *Carolina Chronicle of Dr. Francis Le Jau*, 86; and 4 March 1712, Instructions of the Clergy of South Carolina, *Carolina Chronicle: The Papers of Commissary Gideon Johnston, 1707–1716*, ed. Frank J. Klingberg, University of California Publications in History, vol. 35 (Berkeley: University of California Press, 1946), 123.

77. *South Carolina Gazette*, 19–26 March 1737; President, Assistants and Councilmen to Benjamin Martin, 10 January 1749, *Colonial Records of the State of Georgia*, comp. Allen D. Candler, vol. 25 (New York: AMS Press, 1970), 349; and "An Extract of the Journals of Mr. Commissary Von Reck and the Reverend Mr. Bolzius (1733–1734)," *Our First Visit in America: Early Reports from the Colony of Georgia, 1732–1740*, introd. Trevor R. Reese (Savannah: 1974), 45.

78. Usner, *Indians, Settlers, & Slaves in a Frontier Exchange Economy*, 200–218; and *South Carolina Gazette*, 21–28 October 1732.

79. *South Carolina Gazette*, 23–30 March 1734; and Hilary Beckles, "An Economic Life of Their Own: Slaves as Commodity Producers and Distributors in Barbados," *Caribbean Slavery in the Atlantic World*, ed. Verene Shepherd and Hilary Beckles (Princeton: Marcus Wiener Publisher, 2000), 733–34.

80. Gerald W. Mullin, *Flight and Rebellion: Slave Resistance in Eighteenth-Century Virginia* (Oxford: Oxford University Press, 1972), 70–71; *South Carolina Gazette*, 11 June 1744 and 13 July 1745.
81. *South Carolina Gazette*, 23–30 March 1734.
82. *A Compilation of the Patrol Laws of the State of Georgia, in Conformity with a Resolution of the General Assembly* (Milledgeville, Ga.: S. & F. Garland, 1818), 7.
83. Wood, *Slavery in Colonial Georgia*, 170–80; and Wood, *Black Majority*, 240–41, 242–47; Mullin, *Flight and Rebellion*, 35–47; John W. Blassingame, *The Slave Community: Plantation Life in the Antebellum South*, rev. ed. (Oxford: Oxford University Press, 1979), 192–202; Thornton, *Africa and Africans*, 279; and Morgan, *Slave Counterpoint*, 553.
84. Schwartz, *Born in Bondage*, 168; *South Carolina Gazette*, 11 April 1771 and 28 June 1770; *Georgia Gazette* 23 March 1774; *South Carolina Gazette*, 26 May–2 June 1759 and 20–27 March 1749.

Chapter 3

1. James Edward Oglethorpe, "An Appeal for the Georgia Colony (1732)," *The Publications of James Edward Oglethorpe*, ed. Rodney M. Baine (Athens: University of Georgia Press, 1994), 164, emphasis in original; Oglethorpe, "A New and Accurate Account of the Provinces of South Carolina and Georgia (1732)," *Publications of James Edward Oglethorpe*, 220; and Numan V. Bartly, *The Creation of Modern Georgia* (Athens: University of Georgia Press, 1983), 1–3.
2. Oglethorpe, "Appeal for the Georgia Colony," *Publications of James Edward Oglethorpe*, 165; Ann Laura Stoler, "Developing Historical Negatives: Race and the (Modernist) Visions of a Colonial State," *From the Margins: Historical Anthropology and Its Futures*, ed. Brian Keith Axel (Durham: Duke University Press, 2002), 157; and Wood, *Slavery in Colonial Georgia*, 15–16.
3. Green, "Mary Musgrove: Creating a New World," *Sifters: Native American Women's Lives*, ed. Theda Perdue (Oxford: Oxford University Press, 2001), 31; Bushnell, *Situado and Sabana*, 166; and Jordan, *North American Cattle-Ranching Frontiers*, 55–59, 68–69, 112.
4. Joel W. Martin, *Sacred Revolt: The Muskogees' Struggle for a New World* (Boston: Beacon Press, 1991), 92–93; James H. Merrell, "'The Customes of Our Countrey': Indians and Colonists in Early America," *Strangers within the Realm: Cultural Margins of the First British Empire*, ed. Bernard Bailyn and Philip D. Morgan (Chapel Hill: University of North Carolina Press, 1991), 118, 125; Andrew R. L. Cayton and Fredrika Teute, "Introduction: On the Connection of Frontiers," *Contact Points: American Frontiers from the Mohawk Valley to the Mississippi, 1750–1830*, ed. Andrew R. L. Cayton and Fredrika Teute (Chapel Hill: University of North Carolina Press, 1998), 2; Daniel K. Richter, *Facing East from Indian Country: A Native History of Early America* (Cambridge: Harvard University Press, 2001); and Smadar Lavie and Ted Swedenburg, "Displacement, Diaspora, and Geographies of Identity," *Displacement, Diaspora, and Geographies of Identity*, ed. Smadar Lavie and Ted Swedenburg (Durham: Duke University Press, 1996), 14.
5. Claudio Saunt, "'The English Has Now a Mind to Make Slaves of Them All': Creeks, Seminoles, and the Problem of Slavery," *Confounding the Color Line: The Indian-Black Experiences in North America*, ed. James F. Brooks (Lincoln: University of Nebraska Press, 2002), 49–50; Casey, "How to Get from Space to

Place in a Fairly Short Stretch of Time," 36; Henri LeFebvre, *La production de l'éspace* (Paris: Édition Anthropos, 1974), 138; and Whitehead, "Introduction," *History and Historicities in Amazonia*, x.
6. John Smith, "The Generall Historie of Virginia, New-England, and the Summer Isles (1624)," *Complete Works of Captain John Smith* 2: 236–39, 247; [?] Hamor, *A True Discourse of the Present State of Virginia* (Richmond: Virginia State Library, 1957 [1615]), 17, 26; and Minutes, Great and General Quarter Court, 17 November 1619, *RVC* 1: 267; Records of the Virginia Assembly 2 August 1619, *RVC* 3: 166; Minutes, Quarter Court, 17 May 1620, *RVC* 1: 350.
7. Smith, "Generall Historie," 241–42.
8. Instructions for Governor Thomas Gates, May 1609, *RVC* 3: 20.
9. Smith, "Generall Historie," 244–45.
10. Hamor, *True Discourse*, 12–14; and Smith, "Generall Historie," 262.
11. Hatley, *Dividing Paths*, xiv, 6, 17, 20.
12. Hahn, "Mother of Necessity," 89, 92–93; and John E. Worth, "Spanish Missions and the Persistence of Chiefly Power," *Transformation of the Southeastern Indians*, ed. Ethridge and Hudson, 57.
13. Green, "Mary Musgrove," 29–32; Steven C. Hahn, *Invention of the Creek Nation, 1670–1763* (Lincoln: University of Nebraska Press, 2004), 29–39, 152–55; and Oglethorpe, "A Description of the Indians in Georgia (1733)," *Publications of James Edward Oglethorpe*, 243.
14. As quoted, "A Voyage to Georgia, Begun the 15th of October, 1735," Francis Moore Papers, 73–76, 212–13, Special Collections, William R. Perkins Library, Duke University, Durham, N.C.; Amelia Rector Bell, "Separate People: Speaking of Creek Men and Women," *American Anthropologist* 92 (1992): 332–45; and John R. Swanton, *Creek Religion and Medicine* (Lincoln: University of Nebraska Press, 2000 [1928]), 517.
15. "Voyage to Georgia," Moore Papers, 73–76.
16. Étienne Perier to Jean-Fréderic Phélypeaux, Comte de Maurepas, 18 March 1730, *Mississippi Provincial Archives: French Dominion* 1: 72; and Richard White, "Red Shoes: Warrior and Diplomat," *Struggle and Survival in Colonial America*, ed. David G. Sweet and Gary B. Nash (Berkeley: University of California Press, 1981), 54–55.
17. Étienne Perier to Jean-Fréderic Phélypeaux, Comte de Maurepas, 18 March 1730, *Mississippi Provincial Archives: French Dominion* 1: 72, and White, "Red Shoes," 54–55.
18. Tobias Fitch's Journal, 1726, Howard Sharp Papers, box 9, Miscellaneous Manuscript Collection, Special Collections, University of Florida, Gainesville.
19. Le Page du Pratz, *History of Louisiana* 1: 74.
20. Talk of the Cherokee Indians to Governor Glen, 14 November 1751, *Colonial Records of South Carolina: Documents Relating to Indian Affairs, May 21 1750–August 7, 1754*, ed. William L. McDowell, Jr., (Columbia: South Carolina Archives Department, 1958), vol. 1: 175; and James Glen, fragmentary notes, 1746, Letterbook, 1746–1752, *British Records Relating to America in Microform*, ed. Walter Minchinton, Joseph Stauffer Library, Queen's University, Kingston, Ontario, Canada.
21. Mobile Congress, 27 March 1765, *Mississippi Provincial Archives, 1763–1766: English Dominion*, ed. and comp. Dunbar Rowland (Nashville: Brandon Printing Co., 1911), 227.

22. Samuel Argall, Proclamations, 18 May 1618, *RVC* 3: 93; and Records of the Virginia Assembly, 4 August 1619, *RVC* 3: 170–71.
23. Instructions to George Yeardley, 18 November 1618, *RVC* 3: 104.
24. "A Valuation of the Commodities Growing and to the Had in Virginia," 1620, *RVC* 3: 328; Minutes, Quarter Court, 17 May 1620, *RVC* 1: 351; Records of the Virginia Assembly, 31 July 1619, *RVC* 3: 276; George Yeardley to Edwin Sandys, 1619, *RVC* 3: 128; and Proceedings of the Virginia Assembly, 2 August 1619, *RVC* 3: 165.
25. Captain Butler, "The Unmasked Face of our Colony in Virginia as it were in the Winter of the yeare 1622," 23 April 1623, *RVC* 2: 375; Court, 30 April 1623, *RVC* 2: 381; "Notes for an Answer to the Propositions made by Lord Chichester," August or September 1623, *RVC* 4: 259; and Gleach, *Powhatan's World*, 4, 53.
26. "Notes for an Answer to the Propositions made by Lord Chichester," August or September 1623, *RVC* 4: 259; Captain Butler, "The Unmasked Face of our Colony in Virginia as it were in the Winter of the yeare 1622," 23 April 1623, *RVC* 2: 375–76; Council of Virginia to Virginia Company, April 1622, *RVC* 3: 614; William Hobart to his father, 12 April 1623, *RVC* 4: 229; Governor Francis Wyatt, Proclamation, 1623, *RVC* 4: 167; Smith, "Generall Historie," 293–94; and Gleach, *Powhatan's World*, 157.
27. Council in Virginia to Virginia Company, 20 January 1623, *RVC* 4: 9; John Martin, "The Manner of Howe to Bringe the Indians into Subjection," 15 December 1622, *RVC* 3: 204; Council in Virginia to Virginia Company, April 1622, *RVC* 3: 614; Governor Francis Wyatt, Commission to Captain Maddison, 17 June 1622, *RVC* 3: 654; John Martin, "How Virginia May Be Made A Royal Plantation," 15 December 1622, *RVC* 3: 707–9; Edward Waterhouse, "A Declaration of the State of the Colony," 1622, *RVC* 3: 550–51, 556–58; and Virginia Company to the Governor and Council, 7 October 1622, *RVC* 3: 683.
28. Council and Assembly, Laws and Orders, 5 March 1623/4, *RVC* 4: 581, 583.
29. John Rolfe to Edwin Sandys, January 1619/20, *RVC* 3: 243; and Letter to Virginia Company of London, 1621/22, *RVC* 3: 584.
30. Edward Waterhouse, "Declaration of the State of the Colony," 1622, *RVC* 3: 542; and Letter to Virginia Company of London, 1621–1622, *RVC* 3: 584.
31. Le Page Pratz, *Histoire de la Louisiane* 3: 51; and Montigny, *Memoires historiques* 1: 220, 222, 232.
32. James Adair, *Adair's History of the American Indians*, ed. Samuel Cole Williams (Nashville: National Society of the Colonial Dames of America, Nashville, Tenn., 1953 [1930]), 310.
33. Adair, *Adair's History*, 35, emphasis in original; and Robbie Ethridge, "Shatter Zone: Early Colonial Slave Raiding and Its Consequences for the Natives of the Eastern Woodland," paper presented at the annual meeting of the American Society for Ethnohistory, November 7–12, 2003, Riverside, Calif.
34. Alan Gallay, *The Indian Slave Trade: The Rise of the English Empire in the American South, 1670–1717* (New Haven: Yale University Press, 2002), 299, 314. The figures exclude Virginia.
35. Milanich, *Laboring in the Fields of the Lord*, 184–87.
36. Journal, Jerome Courtonne, box 1, William Henry Lyttelton Papers, William L. Clements Library, University of Michigan, Ann Arbor, Mich.

37. Headmen and Warriors of the Chickasaw Nation to the King of Carolina and His Beloved Men, 5 April 1756, box 1, Lyttelton Papers.
38. Richard Coytmore to William Lytellton, 11 November 1759, box 13, Lyttelton Papers.
39. Saunt, "'The English Has Now a Mind,'" 49–50, 53; Journal of Thomas Bosomworth, July 1752, *Colonial Records of South Carolina* 1: 278; Kathryn E. Holland Braund, "The Creek Indians, Blacks, and Slavery," *Journal of Southern History* 57 (November 1991): 608; Perdue, *Slavery and the Evolution of Cherokee Society*, 50–69; James Germany to John Rae and Barksdale, 10 June 1756, enclosed in White Outerbridge to William Lyttelton, 17 July 1756, box 2, Lyttelton Papers; and Memorandum of a Talk by Col. Polley of South Carolina to Catawba Indians, 14 December 1756, box 4, Lyttelton Papers.
40. Morgan, *Slave Counterpoint*, 56, 257, 339–40, 367–68; Francis Le Jau to the Secretary, 22 March 1709, *Carolina Chronicle of Dr. Francis Le Jau*, 54; James Glen to Board of Trade, March 1751, box 1, Lyttelton Papers; Vlach, "Arrival and Survival," 194; *South Carolina Gazette*, 5 November 1744; and Betty Wood, *Women's Work, Men's Work: The Informal Slave Economies of Low Country Georgia* (Athens: University of Georgia Press, 1995), 81–82.
41. "A Report of the Governor and Council, 1708," *Colonial South Carolina Scene*, 32; Morgan, *Slave Counterpoint*, 481; *South Carolina Gazette*, 10–17 June 1732, 28 October–4 November 1732, 27 August–3 September 1750, 20–27 November 1749, 4 June 1753, 16 July–23 July 1748; *Georgia Gazette*, 26 May 1763 and 8 February 1769; *South Carolina Gazette* 7–14 June 1740 and 29 September 1746.
42. Richard Coytmore to William Lyttelton, 7 February 1760, box 14, Lyttelton Papers; as quoted, Merrell, "Racial Education of the Catawba Indians," 363; White Outerbridge to William Lyttelton, 10 October 1756, box 2, Lyttelton Papers; and Minutes of a Conference between Edmund Atkin and the Savannah Chickasaws, enclosed in Edmund Atkin to William Lyttelton, 24 November 1758, box 9, Lyttelton Papers.
43. Usner, *Indians, Settlers, & Slaves in a Frontier Exchange Economy*, 72–73; Merrell, "Racial Education of the Catawba Indians," 371; Perdue, *Slavery and the Evolution of Cherokee Society*, 41; *Georgia Gazette*, 10 August 1768; *South Carolina Gazette*, 15 August 1743; and *Georgia Gazette*, 29 June 1768 and 13 July 1768.
44. Saunt, *New Order of Things*, 11–14; Braund, "Creek Indians," 611–12; Merrell, "Racial Education of the Catawba Indians," 371; Perdue, *Slavery and the Evolution of Cherokee Society*, 37–38; Articles of Friendship and Commerce Proposed by the Lords Commissioners for Trade & Plantations to the Deputies of the Cherokee Nation in S.C., 7 September 1730, box 1, Lyttelton Papers; and Gov. George Johnstone's Talk to the Choctaws and Chickasaws, 26 March 1765, *Mississippi Provincial Archives, 1763–1766: English Dominion*, 223.
45. As quoted, Hatley, *Dividing Paths*, 74.
46. As quoted, Braund, "Creek Indians," 613.
47. Gregory A. Waselkov, "The Macon Trading House and Early European-Indian Contact in the Colonial Southeast," *Ocmulgee Archaeology, 1936–1986*, ed. Halley, 193–94; and Hahn, "Mother of Necessity," 100.
48. Francis Le Jau to Secretary, 21 May 1715, *Carolina Chronicle of Dr. Francis Le Jau*, 158; Joel Martin, "Southeastern Indians and the English Trade in Skins

and Slaves," *Forgotten Centuries*, ed. Hudson and Tesser, 313; Gallay, *Indian Slave Trade*, 327–28; Oatis, *Colonial Complex*, 124–26.
49. Le Page Pratz, *Histoire de la Louisiane* 3: 230.
50. Le Page Pratz, *Histoire de la Louisiane* 3: 238, 240.
51. Old Hop and Attakullakulla to Raymond Demeré, 30 August 1757, enclosed in Paul Demeré to William Lyttleton, 31 August 1757, box 5, Lyttleton Papers; Hatley, *Dividing Paths*, 14, 47, 92; Ethridge, *Creek Country*, 82; Daniel H. Thomas, *Fort Toulouse: The French Outpost at the Alabamas on the Coosa*, intro. Gregory A. Waselkov (Tuscaloosa: University of Alabama Press, 1989), 3, 7, 10–11; Paul Demeré to William Lyttleton, 28 August 1759, box 11, Lyttleton Papers; and, as quoted, Perdue, *Cherokee Slavery*, 8.
52. Robert Johnson, Thomas Broughton, and Paul Jenys to the King, 9 April 1734, Thomas Coster Papers, Special Collections, William R. Perkins Library, Duke University, Durham, N.C.
53. James Glen to Lords Commissioners for Trade and Plantations, January 1749, Letterbook.
54. James Glen to Lords Commissioners of Trade and Plantations, July 1750, Letterbook; and Hatley, *Dividing Paths*, 78, 92, 94, 98.
55. Richard Coytmore to William Lyttleton, 23 July 1753, box 11, Lyttelton Papers; and Richard Coytmore to William Lyttleton, 11 November 1759, box 13, Lyttelton Papers.
56. Paul Demeré to William Lyttleton, 11 October 1757, box 6, Lyttelton Papers.
57. James Glen to Old Hop, 1758, box 9, Lyttelton Papers.
58. Tistoe and the Wolf to William Lyttleton, 12 July, 1758, enclosed in Lachlan McIntosh to William Lyttleton, 21 July 1758, box 8, Lyttelton Papers.
59. Robert Davies et al. to Samuel Wyly, 16 April 1759, enclosed in Samuel Wyly to William Lyttleton, 26 April 1759, box 10, Lyttelton Papers.
60. Samuel Francis to William Lyttleton, 29 August 1759, box 11, Lyttelton Papers; and Hatley, *Dividing Paths*, 76.
61. William Lyttleton to Head Men and Warriors of the Lower Towns of the Cherokee Nation, March 1758, box 7, Lyttelton Papers; Lachlan McGillivray to William Lyttleton, 17 October 1758, box 8, Lyttelton Papers; John Rae to William Lyttleton, 11 December 1759, enclosed in White Outerbridge to William Lyttleton, 19 December 1759, box 13, Lyttelton Papers; Declaration of War against the Cherokees, 1759, box 13, Lyttelton Papers; Christopher Howe to William Lyttleton, 8 February 1760, box 14, Lyttelton Papers; and Henry Gallman to William Lyttleton, 17 February 1760, box 14, Lyttelton Papers.
62. Richard Coytmore to William Lyttleton, 23 August 1759, box 11, Lyttelton Papers; William Lyttleton to King Hagler, 11 January 1759, box 10, Lyttelton Papers; and William Lyttleton to Samuel Wyly, 16 February 1759, box 10, Lyttelton Papers.
63. Peter Henley to Arthur Dobbs, 27 June 1757, enclosed in Arthur Dobbs to William Lyttleton, 19 July 1757, box 5, Lyttelton Papers.
64. Abstract minutes of a council, 29 October 1757, enclosed in Henry Ellis to William Lyttleton, 3 November 1757, box 6, Lyttelton Papers; and Saunt, *New Order of Things*, 39–40.
65. Peter Sahlins, *Boundaries: The Making of France and Spain in the Pyrenees* (Berkeley: University of California Press, 1989), 26.

Chapter 4

1. Father Raphael to Abbé Raguet, 15 May 1725, *Mississippi Provincial Archives: French Dominion* 2: 486.
2. Chaplin, "Race," 154; and Walter Mignolo, "Colonial and Postcolonial Discourse: Cultural Critique or Academic Colonialism," *Latin American Research Review* 28 (1993): 129.
3. Handley, "New World Poetics of Oblivion," 43; Germaine Warkentin and Carolyn Podruchny, eds., *Decentreing the Renaissance: Canada and Europe in Multidisciplinary Perspective, 1500–1700* (Toronto: University of Toronto Press, 2001); Saunt, *New Order of Things*; Chaplin, *Subject Matter*, 9; and Amy Turner Bushnell and Jack P. Greene, "Peripheries, Centers, and the Construction of Early Modern American Empires," *Negotiated Empires: Centers and Peripheries in the Americas, 1500–1820*, ed. Christine Daniels and Michael V. Kennedy (New York: Routledge, 2002), 3–6.
4. Gary B. Nash, "The Hidden History of Mestizo America," *Journal of American History* 82 (December 1995): 941–64; Jeremy Adelman and Stephen Aron, "From Borderlands to Borders: Empires, Nation-States, and the Peoples in Between in North American History," *American Historical Review* 104 (June 1999): 814–41; D. A. Brading, *The First America: The Spanish Monarchy, Creole Patriots, and the Liberal State, 1492–1867* (New York: Cambridge University Press, 1991); Jorge Cañizares-Esguerra, *How to Write the History of the New World: Histories, Epistemologies, and Identities in the Eighteenth-Century Atlantic World* (Stanford: Stanford University Press, 2001), 205–6; Latin American Subaltern Studies Group, "Founding Statement," *Dispositio/n* 19 (1994): 3; and Gustavo Verdisio, "Colonialism Now and Then: Colonial Latin American Studies in the Light of Latin Americanism," *Colonialism Past and Present: Reading and Writing about Colonial Latin America Today*, ed. Alvaro Félix Bolaños and Gustavo Verdisio (Albany, 2002), 10.
5. Marvyn Bacigalupo, *A Changing Perspective: Attitudes toward Creole Society in New Spain (1521–1610)* (London: Tamesis, 1981), 13; Relouzat, *Tradition orale et imaginaire créole*, 15; Veronica Marie Gregg, *Jean Rhys's Historical Imagination: Reading and Writing the Creole* (Chapel Hill: University of North Carolina Press, 1995), 73; and Glissant, *Introduction à une poétique du divers*, 45.
6. Brathwaite, *Development of Creole Society in Jamaica*, 296, 307.
7. Brathwaite, *Development of Creole Society in Jamaica*, 307; and Mignolo, "Colonial and Postcolonial Discourse," 129.
8. Glissant, *Introduction á une poétique du divers*; Bernabé, Chamoiseau, and Confiant, *Éloge de la Creolité*; Daniel H. Usner Jr., "'The Facility Offered by the Country': The Creolization of Agriculture in the Lower Mississippi Valley," *Creolization in the Americas*, ed. David Buisseret and Steven G. Reinhardt (College Station: University of Texas A&M Press, 2000), 35–62; Hulme, "Postcolonial Theory and Early America," 44; Lavie and Swedenburg, "Displacement, Diaspora, and Geographies of Identity," 8; and Handley, "New World Poetics of Oblivion," 45.
9. Minet, "Voyage Made from Canada Inland Going Southward," 60–61; and Richard White, *The Roots of Dependency: Subsistence, Environment, and Social Change among the Choctaws, Pawnees, and Navajos* (Lincoln: University of Nebraska Press, 1983), 7.

10. Minet, "Voyage Made from Canada Inland Going Southward," 60–61.
11. Minet, "Voyage Made from Canada Inland Going Southward," 60–61; *Iberville's Gulf Journals*, 129–31; and Richebourg Gaillard McWilliams, trans. and ed., *Fleur de Lys and Calumet: Being the Pénicaut Narrative of French Adventure in Louisiana* (Tuscaloosa: University of Alabama Press, 1953), 29.
12. Minet, "Voyage Made from Canada Inland Going Southward," 60–61; James Merrell, *The Indians' New World: Catawbas and Their Neighbors from European Contact through the Era of Removal* (Chapel Hill: University of North Carolina Press, 1989); and Neal Salisbury, "The Indians' Old World: Native Americans and the Coming of Europeans," *William and Mary Quarterly*, 3rd series, vol. 53 (1996): 435–58.
13. Marvin T. Smith, "Aboriginal Population Movements in the Early Historic Period Interior Southeast," *Powhatan's Mantle*, ed. Wood, Waselkov, and Hatley, 21–34; Marvin T. Smith, "Aboriginal Depopulation in the Postcontact Southeast," *Forgotten Centuries*, ed. Hudson and Tesser, 257–75; James H. Merrell, *Indians' New World: Catawbas and Their Neighbors from European Contact through the Era of Removal* (New York: W.W. Norton & Co., 1991), 18–27; and Galloway, *Choctaw Genesis*, 346–52.
14. Mason, *Deconstructing America*, 25; and Edmundo O'Gorman, *Invention of America: An Inquiry into the Historical Invention of the New World and the Meaning of Its History* (Bloomington: University of Indiana Press, 1961), 61, 139.
15. As quoted, Crosby, *Columbian Exchange*, 9; Catesby, "Account of Carolina," vii; and Pagden, *European Encounters with the New World*, 89.
16. Francis Le Jau to the Secretary, 22 March 1709, *Carolina Chronicle of Dr. Francis Le Jau*, 55.
17. Mr. Stephens to the Trustees, 31 December 1741, *Colonial Records of the State of Georgia*, comp. Candler, vol. 23: 190.
18. Richard Coytmore to William Lyttelton, 23 August 1759, box 11, Lyttelton Papers.
19. As quoted, Bushnell, *Situado and Sabana*, 62; John R. Swanton, "An Early Account of the Choctaw Indians," *Memoirs of the American Anthropological Association*, vol. 5, no. 2 (Lancaster, Pa.: American Anthropological Association, 1918), 67; and Saunt, *New Order of Things*, 112.
20. Lower Creek Conference, 3 February 1760, box 14, Lyttelton Papers; and Journal and Field Notes of Levin Wailes, 1809, p. 26, folder 16, box 2, John F. H. Claiborne Papers, Southern Historical Collection, Manuscript Division, Wilson Library, University of North Carolina, Chapel Hill.
21. Mobile Congress, 1 April 1765, *Mississippi Provincial Archives, 1763–1766: English Dominion*, 241.
22. Paul Demeré to William Lyttelton, 26 January 1760, box 14, Lyttelton Papers; Deposition of Isaac Atwood, 31 January 1760, enclosed in White Outerbridge to William Lyttelton, 2 February 1760, box 14, Lyttelton Papers; and Hatley, *Dividing Paths*, 12.
23. John Stuart to William Lyttelton, 2 September 1759, box 12, Lyttelton Papers.
24. Chaplin, *Subject Matter*, 115; and Neil L. Whitehead, *Dark Shamans: Kanaimà and the Poetics of Violent Death* (Durham: Duke University Press, 2002), 42–43.
25. King Hagler to Little Carpenter, 26 May 1757, enclosed in Raymond Demeré to William Lyttleton, 4 July 1757, box 5, Lyttelton Papers.
26. Lachlan McIntosh to William Lyttelton, 4 March 1759, box 10, Lyttelton Papers.

27. Gwendolyn Midlo Hall, *Africans in Colonial Louisiana: The Development of Afro-Creole Culture in the Eighteenth Century* (Baton Rouge: Louisiana University Press, 1992), 100–103; Usner, *Indians, Settlers, & Slaves in a Frontier Exchange Economy*, 72.
28. Hall, *Africans in Colonial Louisiana*, 100–104, and, as quoted, 103; and Usner, *Indians, Settlers, & Slaves in a Frontier Exchange Economy*, 74.
29. Oatis, *Colonial Complex*, 145–46, 169–70.
30. George Chicken, "A Letter from Carolina in 1715 and Journal of the March of the Carolinians into the Cherokee Mountains in the Yemassee Indian War," *Year Book, 1894, City of Charleston, South Carolina*, ed. Langdon Cheves (Charleston: Walker, Evans & Cogswell Co., 1894), 344.
31. Chaplin, *Subject Matter*, 114.
32. James Glen to Board of Trade, March 1751, box 1, Lyttelton Papers.
33. Minutes of a conference between Edmund Atkin and Savannah Chickasaws, 14 November 1758, enclosed in Edmund Atkin to William Lyttelton, 24 November 1758, box 9, Lyttelton Papers; and Henry Ellis to William Lyttelton, 25 November 1759, box 13, Lyttelton Papers.
34. Woodmason, *Carolina Backcountry*, 93–94.
35. Jeffrey Robert Young, *Domesticating Slavery: The Master Class in Georgia and South Carolina, 1670–1837* (Chapel Hill: University of North Carolina Press, 1999), as quoted, 21; Thomas Jenys to the Trustees, 24 April 1738, *Colonial Records of the State of Georgia*, comp. Candler, vol. 22, part 2: 136–37; and John Gerald to Harman Verelst, 17 May 1739, *Colonial Records of the State of Georgia*, comp. Cadler, vol. 22, part 2: 134.
36. Account of the Negroe Insurrection in South Carolina, *Colonial Records of the State of Georgia*, comp. Candler, vol. 22, part 2: 232; and Wood, *Black Majority*, 309–10.
37. Morgan, *Slave Counterpoint*, 420.
38. Francis Le Jau to the Secretary, 14 July 1710, *Carolina Chronicle of Dr. Francis Le Jau*, 81; and as quoted, Francis Le Jau to Philip Stubbs, 15 April 1707, *Carolina Chronicle of Dr. Francis Le Jau*, 24.
39. Morgan, *Slave Counterpoint*, 456; and Francis Le Jau to the Secretary, 1 February 1710, *Carolina Chronicle of Dr. Francis Le Jau*, 70
40. Morgan, *Slave Counterpoint*, 450; *South Carolina Gazette*, 5–12 April 1739; Matthew 6: 9, *King James Bible*.
41. Mark M. Smith, "Remembering Mary, Shaping Revolt: Reconsidering the Stono Rebellion," *Journal of Southern History* 67 (2001): 522–29.
42. John K. Thornton, "African Dimensions of the Stono Rebellion," *American Historical Review* 96 (1991): 1101–13; Account of the Negroe Insurrection in South Carolina, *Colonial Records of the State of Georgia*, comp. Candler, vol. 22, part 2: 232; and Wood, *Black Majority*, 314–16.
43. Wood, *Black Majority*, 316–20; and Thornton, "African Dimensions of the Stono Rebellion," 1112–13.
44. Peter Timothy to William Lyttelton, 3 November 1759, box 13, Lyttelton Papers.
45. Wood, *Black Majority*, 317–26; and Hatley, *Dividing Paths*, 72–74, as quoted, 73.
46. Deposition of Richard Smith, 12 July 1751, *Colonial Records of South Carolina* 1: 103, and, as quoted, Hatley, *Dividing Paths*, 111–12.
47. William Lyttelton to the Board of Trade, 1 September 1759, box 10, William Lyttelton Papers.

48. Kathleen M. Brown, *Good Wives, Nasty Wenches, and Anxious Patriarchs: Gender, Race, and Power in Colonial Virginia* (Chapel Hill: University of North Carolina Press, 1996), 112.
49. Talk of the Cherokee Indians to Governor Glen, 14 November 1751, *Colonial Records of South Carolina* 1: 177.
50. Talk of the Fourteen Towns of the Middle and Lower Cherokees, 16 October 1758, enclosed in Lachlan McIntosh to William Lyttelton, 21 October 1758, box 8, Lyttelton Papers.
51. Talk of Headmen of Lower Cherokees to Raymond Demeré, 18 September 1756, box 2, Lyttelton Papers.
52. Minutes of a Congress at Pensacola, 27 May 1765, *Mississippi Provincial Archives, 1763–1766: English Dominion*, 198.
53. Mobile Congress, 2 April 1765, *Mississippi Provincial Archives, 1763–1766: English Dominion*, 245.
54. Pensacola Congress, 27 May 1765, *Mississippi Provincial Archives, 1763–1766: English Dominion*, 199.
55. Cherokee Headmen to William Lyttelton, 16 May 1759, enclosed in Richard Coytmore to William Lyttelton, 23 May 1759, box 10, Lyttelton Papers.
56. Mobile Congress, 2 April 1765, *Mississippi Provincial Archives, 1763–1766: English Dominion*, 244; and Mobile Congress, 1 April 1765, *Mississippi Provincial Archives, 1763–1766: English Dominion*, 237.
57. Pensacola Congress, 28 May 1765, *Mississippi Provincial Archives, 1763–1766: English Dominion*, 201.
58. William Lyttelton to King Hagler, 12 April 1759, box 10, Lyttelton Papers; and Whitehead, "Three Patamuna Trees," 61.
59. James Glen to the Duke of Newcastle, fragmentary notes, 1746, Letterbook; and Mobile Congress, 27 March 1765, *Mississippi Provincial Archives, 1763–1766: English Dominion*, 226.
60. Gregory A. Waselkov and Kathryn E. Holland Braund, eds., *William Bartram on the Southeastern Indians* (Lincoln: University of Nebraska Press, 1995), 61, 95, 236; and Bushnell, *Situado and Sabana*, 140.
61. Le Page du Pratz, *History of Louisiana* 1: 45; Anthony Hutchins manuscript, c. 1800, 1, 24, 59–60, Mississippi Department of Archives and History, Jackson, MS; Andrew Ellicott, *The Journal of Andrew Ellicott* (Chicago: Quadrangle Books 1962 [1803]), 134; and Jim Barnett, *The Natchez Indians* (Jackson: Mississippi Department of Archives and History, 1998), 5.
62. John Nevitt Diary, 97, 105, 170, Southern Historical Collection, University of North Carolina, Chapel Hill; Francis DuBose Richardson Memoirs, 27, 33, Southern Historical Collection; Horace Smith Fulkerson, *Random Recollections of Early Days in Mississippi* (Vicksburg: Vicksburg Printing and Publishing, 1885), 12; Mary J. Welsh, "Recollections of Pioneer Life in Mississippi," *Publications of the Mississippi Historical Society* 4 (1906): 350; H. G. Hawkins, "History of Port Gibson," *Publications of the Mississippi Historical Society* 10 (1909): 283; and James R. Creecy, *Scenes in the South and Other Miscellaneous Pieces* (Washington: Thomas McGill, 1860), 121.
63. Nevitt Diary, 87, 248.
64. Fulkerson, *Random Recollections of Early Days in Mississippi*, 12.

65. James Williams, *Narrative of James Williams, an American Slave, Who Was for Several Years a Driver on a Cotton Plantation in Alabama* (American Anti-Slavery Society, 1838), 87–88.
66. John Michael Vlach, *Back of the Big House: The Architecture of Plantation Slavery* (Chapel Hill: University of North Carolina Press, 1993), 1.
67. Walter Johnson, *Soul by Soul: Life Inside the Antebellum Slave Market* (Cambridge: Harvard University Press, 1999), 21.
68. Covington Diary.
69. John Shelton Reed, *One South: An Ethnic Approach to Regional Culture* (Baton Rouge: Louisiana State University Press, 1982), 6.
70. Charles Hudson, "William Gilmore Simms and the Portrayal of the American Indian: An Ethnohistorical View," *An Early and Strong Sympathy: The Indian Writing of William Gilmore Simms*, ed. John Caldwell Guilds and Charles Hudson (Columbia: University of South Carolina Press, 2003), xxxiv–xxxv; and Whitehead, "Three Patamuna Trees," 72–73.
71. Father Raphael to Abbé Raguet, 15 May 1725, *Mississippi Provincial Archives: French Dominion* 2: 486.
72. Braund, "The Creek Indians," 608; Gregory Evans Dowd, *War under Heaven: Pontiac, the Indian Nations & the British Empire* (Baltimore: Johns Hopkins University Press, 2002), 40; and Nancy Shoemaker, "How Indians Got to Be Red," *American Historical Review* 102 (1997): 625–44.

Index

Abelard, Pierre, 23–25
Achese town, 49
Adair, James, 88
Africanus, Leo, 25
Ais people, 53
Akan people, 31
Alibamon Mingo, 108
Alphonse de St. Onge, 24
Altamaha, 64
Andalusia (al-Andalus), xii, 19–20, 23, 25, 45, 48, 49, 65, 68, 69
Anaximander, 17
Anglicus, Barthlomew, 20, 24–25, 60
Apalachee mission, 88
Apalachee people, 53–54, 93
Arágon, kingdom of, 45, 47
Argall, Samuel, 80, 84
Aristotle, 17–19, 20–21, 23, 26, 45–47, 58, 60, 77
Atlantic world, x, xiii, xix, 1–2, 98, 100, 101, 105, 112, 122
Avilés, Pedro Menéndez de, 53, 55
Ayllón, Luca Vásquez, 48, 70

Babylon, 16
BaKongo people, 32, 36, 40, 43, 113
Bantu people, 28–29, 32, 40
Bartram, William, 117
Bayagoula people, 67
beads, 13, 53, 56, 59, 61, 62, 67, 86, 87, 91, 95. *See also* prestige goods
beans, 12, 15, 29, 49, 52, 54, 56, 57, 65, 68, 69, 85, 86, 99, 103. *See also* gardens; horticulture
Benin, kingdom of, 30, 34
Bermudas settlement, 80, 85
Biloxi colony, 67–68
Biloxi people, 67
Bissaõ kingdom, 34, 37–38
Brims, 81–82
Brown, John, 94–95, 109
Bull, William, 92, 113, 114

Calusa people, 53
Canadian people, 67–68, 95, 104
Cançо, Gonzalo Méndez de, 54
Castile, kingdom of, 45, 47–48
Castilian people, xiv, 50, 51, 53, 54, 77, 78, 103
Catawba people, 65–66, 84, 89, 91, 95–97, 104, 107–8, 116, 121
Catesby, Mark, 65, 105
cattle, xiii, 1, 55, 65, 66, 72, 78, 82, 86, 96, 97, 111
Charles City, 85, 86
Charles Town, 64, 65, 71–74, 81, 83, 88–91, 93–94, 96, 106, 111, 113, 115, 120
Charlesfort, 51, 54
Cheraw settlement, 65
Cherokee people, xiii, xviii, xx, 4, 65, 89–92, 94–97, 106–10, 114–16, 121

Chickahominy people, 62, 81
Chickasaw people, xx, 83–84, 88–89, 91–92, 94, 106, 109–10, 121
chickens. *See* poultry
Choctaw people, 83, 88, 92, 94, 104, 106, 108, 116–18
Chota town, 1, 74, 94
Christianity, 20–26, 45, 47–51, 53–54, 56, 61, 63, 66–67, 73, 111–12
Chulustamastabe, 116
cloth, 6, 28, 33–34, 39–41, 47, 52, 54, 81, 84, 88, 89, 90, 97, 109, 113, 116, 118
Columbus, Christopher, 4, 45–48, 56, 70, 75, 105
Coosa town, xiii, 14
Coosaponakeesa, 81–82
copper, 6, 8, 10–15, 56–58, 61–62, 67, 86–87, 91, 95. *See also* prestige goods
Cortés, Hernán, 48
cosmology, 14, 16–18, 20–26, 32–33, 39–40, 43, 60–61, 68–69, 71–72, 83, 99–100, 112–14
cotton, 118–19. *See also* horticulture; plantations
Covington, Levin, 119
Coytmore, Richard, 95
Craven, Charles, 93, 109
Creek people, xiii, xx, 64, 66, 81, 88–92, 97, 98, 105–7, 110, 116, 118, 121
creole, (creolization), xvii, xix, 2, 75, 100–103, 107, 117, 119, 121

Dahomé, kingdom of, 41–42
Dale, Thomas, 63, 80
Demeré, Raymond, 95, 115
d'Iberville, Pierre Le Moyne, 67–69
disease, xii, xv, 24, 29, 41–42, 50, 53, 61, 64, 67, 87–88, 104

earth (deity), 9, 12, 14, 16–18, 32–33, 35, 57, 60, 68–69, 104, 120–22
Emisteseguo, 115–16
England, kingdom of, 1, 21–23

Filmer, Sir Robert, 116
fire, xi, 5–6, 8, 9, 10, 12, 14, 17, 22, 32, 33, 40, 50, 60, 61, 62, 65, 69, 78, 82, 87, 91, 93, 103, 104, 109, 112, 115, 116
firearms, 28, 42, 53, 64, 79, 81, 84, 80, 88, 91, 97, 99, 103, 108, 113
Florida, la, 48–49, 50–55, 64, 67, 72, 81, 88, 93, 111–12
Fort Loudon, 91, 94
Fort Maurepas, 68
Fort Prince George, 115
Fort Rosalie, 94, 117
Fort Toulouse, 94
France, kingdom of, 22–23
Franciscans, 53

Gandy, Moses,
gardens, xii, 7, 9, 10, 22, 28, 34, 57, 65, 67, 68, 71, 73, 77, 90, 104, 117–21. *See also* beans; gourds; horticulture; maize; okra; sorghum; squashes; sweet potatoes; yams
Gates, Thomas, 63, 80
Georgia colony, xii, 64, 66, 71, 73, 775, 77, 82, 90–91, 96, 105, 110–11
Glen, James, 84, 89, 91, 95, 110, 115, 116
Gold Coast, xviii, 31–32, 35, 37–39
Gordillo, Francisco, 69
gourds, 7, 29, 57, 59, 117. *See also* gardens; horticulture
Granganimeo, 55–56
Great Chain of Being, 23–25
Great Sun, 68–69, 87–88, 92–93
Greece, 16–18
Guale people, 53–55, 64, 106
Guinea, 28, 30, 42

Hagler, 84, 96, 107, 116
Handsome Fellow, 115
Hausa people, 31
Henrico town, 85–86
Hilton, William, 64
Hobe people, 53
Hopewell people, 8, 10, 12, 15
horses, 5, 86, 88, 90, 96, 106

INDEX 159

horticulture, 19, 29, 59, 65–66, 117, 119. *See also* beans; cotton; gourds; maize; okra; rice; sorghum; squashes; sweet potatoes; tobacco; yams
hunters, 8, 10, 13, 15, 29, 36, 38, 40, 42, 88, 92, 99, 121
Hutchins, John, 117

idea of Europeans, aboriginal, 47, 106–7
idea of Indians, European, 4–5, 47, 51, 56
Igbo people, 31–32, 40
Indicopleustés, Cosmas, 21, 23–25
Isidore of Seville, 20, 60
Islam, 19–20, 30–31, 34

Jamestown, Va., 3, 58–59, 60–64, 79–81, 85
Jau, Francis le, 65, 73, 89, 105, 111–12
Jesuits, 53
John, Phillip, 115
Johnstone, George, 92

Kasihta people, 66, 82, 106
Kecoughtan, 58–59, 61, 79, 85
Kelley, John, 106
Keowee, 89
kinship, 14, 36, 39, 40, 43, 52, 55, 60, 62, 74, 75, 80, 82, 84, 88, 91, 96, 106, 107, 116–18, 121, 122
Kolomaki site, 8, 11
Kongo, kingdom of, 28, 33, 35, 37, 43, 113–14
Koto, kingdom of, 34

Laudonnière, René de la, 51–52
Little Carpenter, 107
Lords Proprietors, 64, 81
Louisiane, la, 67–69, 71–72, 83–84, 93–96, 108–9
Lyttelton, William, 89, 92, 95, 96, 115, 116

maize, xi, xii, xvii, 12, 15–16, 48–49, 52–54, 56–57, 60–66, 68–69, 71, 74, 75, 80, 85–86, 94, 96–97, 99, 103, 115, 117–20. *See also* gardens; horticulture
Mali, kingdom of, 31
Mande people, 31
Mandingo people, 31
manhood, 15, 58
Mankiller, 94
mappaemundi, 26–27, 47
markets, xii, 19, 27, 40–41, 70, 73–74, 89–90, 111–12, 116
Martin, John, 86
Mauvila town, 50
McKeithen site, 10
menstruation, 32, 57, 112
Middle Passage, 70
Mingo Chito, 83
Mississippian tradition, 12–15, 39, 53
Mobile, 73, 83–84, 88, 92, 106, 116, 117
Mobilien people, 67–68
Montgomery, Sir Robert, 66
moon (deity), 18, 20, 21, 32, 33, 39–40, 116
Moore, James, 88
Mortar of Okchai, 116
mounds, 7, 10–12, 14–15, 94
Musgrove, John, 82

Nairne, Thomas, 93
Nansemond people, 62
Natchez colony, 73, 117–18
Natchez people, 68, 84, 87–88, 93–94, 121
Natchez war, 93–94, 108–9, 117
Nevitt, John, 117–18
New France, 104
New Orleans, xi, xii, 68, 69, 71–73, 88, 95, 106
New Spain, 55, 70, 104
New World, xix, 48, 104
Newport, Christopher, 59, 62
Nkuwu, Nginga, 113

Ocute town, 49
Oglethorpe, James, 66, 77–78, 82–83, 98

Ohatchie, 115
Okfuskee town, 84
okra, 71. *See also* gardens; horticulture
Old Hop, 94–95, 109
Old Warrior of Keowee, 45, 115
Opechancanough, 60–62, 80, 85–87, 92
Outina, 51–53

palm wine, 34–35, 38, 40
Pamunkey town, 60–62
Pardo, Juan, 70
Pascagoula people, 67
Paspihe town, 58–59, 61
Paya Mattaha, 116
Pettigrew, John, Jr., 91
Piamallaha, 89, 92
pigs, xiii, 55, 65, 97
plantations, xviii, 1, 63, 71–72, 75, 78, 80, 82, 85, 89–91, 93, 101–2, 114, 117–19
Plato, 23, 77
Pliny the Elder, 18–21, 24–25, 46–47, 60
Pocahontas, 80
Pocataligo town, 93
portolan maps, 27, 46
Portugal, kingdom of, 27–28, 37
pottery, 6, 8–11, 14–16, 40, 72
poultry, 35, 40, 86, 90, 106
Poverty Point site, 7
Powhatan, 59–63, 79–81
Powhatan war, 86
Powhatan's confederacy, 59–63, 80
prestige goods, 13, 62. *See also* beads; copper
Ptolemy, 20–21, 26–27, 45, 46, 48, 58, 105

Quejo, Pedro de, 69
Quinipissa people, 69

race, xvi, 25–26, 87, 99–100, 115, 120–21
Raleigh, Sir Walter, 55
Rappahanock people, 60
Raven of Hiawassee, 84
Raven of Toxaway, 115

Red Shoe, 83
Ribault, Jean, 51–52, 67
rice, xvii, 71–73. *See also* horticulture; plantations
Roanoke colony, 56
Rolfe, John, 80
Rome, 18–19
Roullet, Régis du, 83
rum, 88, 97, 106

Saint Augustine, 23–25, 53
Saint Augustine town, 53–54, 78, 90, 92, 110–14
Santa Elena mission, 54, 64
Saturnia, 51–53
Savannah town, 77–79, 82, 90–91, 97–98, 114
Savannah people, 64, 81, 92
Senauky, 82–83, 98, 118
Serpent Woman, 88, 93
shrines, 34–35, 42, 57
sky (deity). *See* sun
slavery, 27, 30–31, 37, 42–44, 69–75, 82, 87, 88–91; aboriginal perceptions of, 87–89, 94; enslaved people's perception of, 112–15; European perception of, 105; flight from, 75, 90–92
Smith, John, 58–60, 68, 79
Smith, Thomas, 64
snakes, xi, xii, 1, 8, 9, 12, 16, 44, 71, 95, 100, 107
Solinus, 20, 24
sorghum, 71
Soto, Hernando de, 48–50, 53, 67–68, 70, 103, 104, 119
South Carolina, colony of, xii, xvii, 32, 48, 64, 71–75, 84, 88–92, 95, 106–7, 110–12, 115, 117
Spain, kingdom of, 45–50
squashes, 7, 54, 57, 68, 69, 99, 103. *See also* gardens; horticulture
Stuart, John, 84, 116–17
Stono rebellion, 113–14
Stung Serpent, 84
sun (deity), 9, 11, 12, 14, 16–18, 32–33, 49, 50, 52, 57, 68–69, 83, 104

sweet potatoes, 71, 117. *See also* gardens; horticulture
Swift Creek tradition, 8–12, 14–15

Taensa people, xviii, xi–xii, xix, xx, 99–100, 103–4, 114, 120–21
Tascaluza town, 50–51, 68, 105
Tattooed Serpent, 87–88, 93
Terrapin Chief, 88
Thevet, André, 51, 105
Timucua people, 53, 54
Tistoe, 95
T/O maps, 26, 46
tobacco, 57–59, 67, 83–84, 87–88, 93. *See also* horticulture; plantations
Tomochichi, 82, 98
trade, 8, 10, 13, 15, 27–28, 30, 33, 40–42, 54, 62, 80–81
Treaty of London (1730), 92
trees, 37–39
tribute, 10, 23, 38, 41, 53–55, 57, 63–64, 80, 92, 96–97
Tsenacommacah, 56–64, 86–87
Tuareg people, 19, 27, 30
Tuska Mobby, 89, 92

Vaca, Alvar Núñez Cabeza de, 48
Virginia Company, 58, 60, 63–64, 79–80, 85
Visigoths, 19

Ware, Lord de la, 79
warriors, 13, 15, 40, 41, 50, 58, 60, 62, 65, 80, 81, 86, 88, 89, 91–93, 95, 96, 103, 106–9, 115
Waxhaw settlement, 96
Weeden Island tradition, 11–12
Werawocomocco, 62
werowance, 58, 62–63, 79
Westo people, 64, 81, 92
White Apple town, 94, 117
Whydah kingdom, 34, 40–42
Williams, James, 118
Wingina, 55–56
women, 40, 56, 60, 89, 118
Woodmason, Charles, 65, 110, 120
Wyatt, Francis, 86

Yamacraw Bluff, 77, 82
Yamacraw town, 82
Yamassee people, 64, 92, 109–10
Yamassee war, 93–94, 109
yams, 28–29, 32, 40, 71. *See also* gardens; horticulture
Yeardley, George, 84, 85
Yoruba people, 30, 31, 40
Yuchi people, 82, 121

Zeus, 17–18

Making an Atlantic World was designed and typeset on a Macintosh OS 10.4 computer system using InDesign software. The body text is set in 10/13 Janson Text and display type is set in Trajan Pro. This book was designed and typeset by Stephanie Thompson.

www.ingramcontent.com/pod-product-compliance
Lightning Source LLC
Chambersburg PA
CBHW030323080526
44584CB00012B/685